DATE DUE

MAY 2 4 1996	
June 7	
OCT - 2 1996	
Oct 17	
29	
Nov. 23	
Dec. 6	
OCT - 2 1997	
SEP 2 9 1998	

BRODART.   Cat. No. 23-221

NEUROBEHAVIORAL ANATOMY

NEUROBEHAVIORAL ANATOMY

CHRISTOPHER M. FILLEY, M.D.
Associate Professor of Neurology and Psychiatry
University of Colorado School of Medicine
Denver Veteran Affairs Medical Center

Foreword by Michael P. Alexander, M.D.

Illustrations by Mel Drisko

UNIVERSITY PRESS OF COLORADO

© 1995 by the University Press of Colorado
Published by the University Press of Colorado
P. O. Box 849
Niwot, Colorado 80544

The University Press of Colorado is a cooperative publishing enterprise supported, in part, by Adams State College, Colorado State University, Fort Lewis
College, Mesa State College, Metropolitan State College of Denver, University of
Colorado, University of Northern Colorado, University of Southern Colorado,
and Western State College of Colorado.

Library of Congress Cataloging-in-Publication Data

Filley, Christopher M., 1951–
     Neurobehavioral anatomy / Christopher M. Filley; foreword by
  Micheael P. Alexander; illustrations by Mel Drisko.
       p.   cm.
     Includes bibliographical references and index.
     ISBN 0-087081-404-4 (alk. paper)
     1. Neurobehavioral disorders.   2. Clinical neuropsychology.
  3. Neuroanatomy.   4. Neuropsychiatry.   I. Title.
     [DNLM: 1. Brain—anatomy & histology.   2. Behavior—physiology.
  3. Cognition Disorders.   4. Brain Diseases—psychology.   5. Brain
  Injuries—psychology.   WL 300 F485n 1995]
  RC386.F55   1995
  616.8—dc20
  DNLM/DLC
  for Library of Congress   95-811
                                                                          CIP

This book was set in Adobe Garamond and Adobe AG Oldface.

The paper used in this publication meets the minimum requirements of the
American National Standard for Information Sciences—Permanence of Paper
for Printed Library Materials. ANSI Z39.48–1948
∞

10   9   8   7   6   5   4   3   2   1

To my father, Giles Franklin Filley, whose scholarship remains an inspiration

Contents

Foreword

There was a time—an amazingly recent time—when physicians who cared for patients with brain disease could use phenomenological descriptions derived from the methods of clinical medicine to characterize mental functions, and those characterizations would have been remarkably close to the deepest concurrent scientific understanding of these mental functions.

Clinical medicine identified signs of impairment (chorea, poor long-term memory, impaired comprehension, and so forth) and grouped them into syndromes, constellations of signs that had empirical specificity for particular diseases (e.g., Huntington's disease) or for damage to particular brain regions (e.g., limbic system or left superior temporal gyrus). These syndromes had, and still have, great utility in clinical diagnosis.

As with all other fields of medicine, however, the scientific distance between these ultimately pragmatic, clinical descriptions and detailed knowledge of the underlying biological processes has enlarged enormously. It grows ever more difficult to maintain clinical competence and develop scientific skills simultaneously—thus the divergence between clinicians (physicians) and investigators (increasingly—probably inevitably —Ph.D.'s). For the clinician-investigator (there are still some) the divergence between basic clinical skills and the critical scientific issues presents another problem: how to introduce clinical material, based on sound anatomical, physiological, and pathological knowledge—and for behavioral neurology, psychological principles—in a manner that can provide practical clinical tools while opening the vista of exciting scientific study. In behavioral neurology there have been very few sources that might serve as the front door into the house where clinical observation and scientific study still live together, albeit (to push this metaphor to the limit) perhaps on separate floors.

This book will serve that purpose. The student, whether actually a student or a neurologist, psychiatrist, neurosurgeon, or psychologist trying to gain a foothold to begin a clinical or scientific career, should start here. As Dr. Filley will tell you in the Preface, this is an introduction to the field, but it is an introduction that will give the reader the essential historical, clinical, and anatomical background necessary to understand modern behavioral neurology.

Michael P. Alexander, M.D.
Braintree Rehabilitation Hospital
Boston University School of Medicine

Preface

The complexities of human behavior have challenged physicians, scientists, philosophers, and other observers since antiquity. There is, perhaps, no more essential field of study. A better understanding of the human mind offers not only the satisfaction of enhanced self-knowledge, but also the prospect of improving individual health and the collective well-being of the human species.

Although the vast repertoire of human behavior may appear formidably difficult to explain in scientific terms, many notable gains have been made in this direction. Recent advances in the clinical and basic neurosciences have produced a compelling portrayal of the brain as the organ of the mind. It is now increasingly feasible to understand the mind by investigating the brain, and all that is being learned supports the notion that the brain is solely responsible for the extraordinary range of behaviors that are considered distinctly human.

This book evolved from a series of neurobehavior seminars given to neurology residents, students, and fellows at the University of Colorado School of Medicine for the past several years. The gratifying response to these seminars has been a major impetus to the preparation of this volume. I have endeavored to produce a practical summary of current knowledge regarding how clinically recognizable mental functions are represented in the adult human brain—in essence, a clinical anatomy book devoted to the unique behaviors of *Homo sapiens*. As it is written from the perspective of behavioral neurology, the primary source of information is the clinical literature describing deficits in behavior that result from demonstrable brain disease or injury. This approach, taking particular advantage of focal brain lesions, allows a stepwise delineation of the contributions brain structures make to mental functions, and ultimately a tentative reconstruction of the relationship of brain and behavior. Insights from neuropsychology, cognitive science, and neurophysiology also contribute to this synthesis; the assumption is that a complete depiction of brain-behavior interaction will require the integration of analytic levels ranging from the molecular to the organismic.

The organization of the book emphasizes the evaluation of disturbed behavior that may occur in individuals with acquired brain disease or injury. First, an introductory chapter serves to review some philosophical antecedents of this endeavor and demonstrate how an analysis of the brain can illuminate some heretofore intractable problems. Then follows a detailed description of the clinical mental status evaluation, the sine qua non of behavioral neurology. The remainder of the book deals with specific neurobehavioral syndromes that are clinically important and serve to illustrate principles of brain-behavior relationships. Disease states are discussed as they pertain to these principles, but details of etiology, treatment, and prognosis are left to standard textbooks in neurology, psychiatry, and medicine.

Given the prodigious and expanding body of knowledge to be reviewed, the intent of a book this size must be more introductory than comprehensive. I hope, however, that this relatively compact volume will prove useful to those who care for individuals afflicted with brain disorders disrupting normal behavior, to investigators whose interests lie in the many relevant areas of research, and to anyone intrigued with the neuroanatomic basis of singularly human capacities. More generally stated, my goal is to synthesize and condense a large amount of clinical and neuroanatomic information in an effort to understand what is surely the most fascinating and impressive biological structure known in the universe.

Acknowledgments

Many individuals have contributed to this book by listening to my ideas, correcting and expanding them, and helping to clarify my thinking. Mick Alexander has long been a trusted mentor and a source of continual insight and information. Jim Kelly offered valuable advice and frequent encouragement. Karl Gross provided thoughtful comments and criticisms. Thanks are also due to Al Anderson and Elizabeth Gerard, who read the manuscript at an early stage and made many helpful suggestions. My gratitude is extended as well to Stuart A. Schneck, Steven P. Ringel, James H. Austin, Bette Kleinschmidt-DeMasters, Richard C. Simons, Munro Cullum, Robert Heaton, Bruce Price, M.-Marsel Mesulam, Antonio Damasio, Neill Graff-Radford, Jonathan Woodcock, Bruce Pennington, Angelika Voelkel, Norbert Voelkel, Kenneth L. Tyler, H. Richard Tyler, and Aaron Paul. Finally, this book would not have been possible without the outstanding secretarial skills of Linda Baldwin and Jane Brzuchalski.

NEUROBEHAVIORAL ANATOMY

All the evidence goes to show that what we regard as our mental life is bound up with brain structure and organized bodily energy.

Bertrand Russell
What I Believe, 1925

CHAPTER 1

Behavior and the Brain

Human behavior has an enduring appeal. Who among us has not reflected from time to time on how it is that a memory is formed, a sentence produced, or an emotion experienced? What is the origin of the thoughts and feelings that seem so distinctively to characterize the human species? Despite the enormous interest of this subject, however, our knowledge of human behavior is remarkably limited. Many scientific investigators are deterred by the extraordinary complexity of the topic and select a more restricted area of inquiry in which meaningful advances—and research grants—are assumed to be more easily attainable. Much of the formal study of behavior is descriptive, and even at this level there are formidable difficulties in the reliable characterization of the observed phenomena. This state of relative ignorance is particularly regrettable since an understanding of behavior would provide limitless benefits both in the enhancement of human achievement and in the reduction of human destructiveness. It is not unreasonable to suppose that a more enlightened view of behavior would have important implications for every realm of human activity.

By way of introduction to the main body of this book, it will be useful first to consider some philosophical and historical background that continues to influence the study of behavior. Then follows a discussion of selected features of brain anatomy that pertain to neurobehavioral function in general. A brief digression into the discredited area of phrenology is presented as an illustration of the perils of simplistic thinking. Finally, behavioral neurology and its particular viewpoint are considered, in the hope of demonstrating how knowledge of the brain's structure and function is critical to a comprehensive understanding of human behavior.

The Mind-Brain Problem

Traditionally, philosophers have taken a primary role in considering the phenomena of human behavior. The introspective method of thinking about one's own thoughts and feelings was the sole available technique throughout most of human history. Scientific investigation of how and why people act as they do has a rather short history. Only in recent times has there been the development of a systematic empirical approach to the study of behavior, first with the rise of psychology in the nineteenth century (James, 1890), and then the explosive growth of neuroscience in the twentieth (Corsi, 1991). These two traditions can be seen as "top down" and "bottom up" to signify their different approaches, and both have made major contributions to our understanding of behavior. Yet it hardly need be stated that these empirical endeavors have not laid to rest ancient philosophical issues. Science has by no means provided answers to all questions about the nature of the mind, and some would maintain that it never can (Horgan, 1994). Biology can, however, provide provocative information with which to explore these issues. Although it may seem imprudent for a clinical neuroscientist to indulge in the discussion that follows, there is good reason to suppose that old philosophical problems can be more clearly addressed in the light of new biological knowledge (Young, 1987).

One of the oldest and most difficult questions in philosophy is that of the relation of mind to body, commonly known as the mind-body problem. It is reasonable for human beings to believe, by virtue of daily conscious experience, that there exists an entity commonly referred to as the mind, and, because of even more evident physical realities, that there is another entity known as the body. It is also apparent that the brain is the part of the body that very likely has the most to do with the mind, and the issue is therefore more precisely called the mind-brain problem. The difficulty arises when one realizes that mental states are clearly subjective, whereas the brain is manifestly an objective reality. Consciousness—to most people an obvious, albeit puzzling, human characteristic—does not readily appear to spring from the physical object that we recognize as the brain. Many question whether a collection of nerve cells and chemicals can explain the ineffable phenomenon of consciousness, which is often equated with or regarded as akin to such concepts as soul or spirit. As the philosopher John Searle bluntly poses the mind-brain problem: "How could this gray and white gook inside my skull be conscious?" (Searle, 1984). Consciousness does indeed appear to be the most mysterious feature of the human mind, and establishing it as a property of the brain is by no means straightforward.

Two fundamental solutions have dominated philosophical inquiry into this dilemma. For the sake of simplicity, these may be termed dualism and materialism. Dualism, most notably propounded by René Descartes in the seventeenth century, holds that mind and brain are independent; the famous "Cogito ergo sum" (I think, therefore I am) embodies the view that the mind is entirely separate from the body and that mental activities are quite divorced from physical events (Descartes, 1637). Descartes did imagine that there was a point of intersection between the mind and the body, and he suggested the unpaired pineal gland as the site where the mind receives sensory traffic and acts upon the brain. But his steadfast separation of the immaterial mind from the material brain has exerted enormous influence for more than three centuries.

Materialism, advanced in various ways by thinkers as diverse as John Locke, Bertrand Russell, and Francis Crick, contends in general that mind and body are inseparable; as a result, mental events are nothing more than the expression of the brain's physical activities (Dennett, 1991). Advocates of this "identity theory" argue that the Cartesian division between mental and physical substances is no more than an assertion, in the trenchant phrase of Gilbert Ryle, that there is a "ghost in the machine" (Ryle, 1949). An extreme variant of materialism is B.F. Skinner's behaviorism, an influential movement in twentieth century American psychology emphasizing the manipulation of behavior by environmental conditions (Skinner, 1971), and, in effect, holding the concept of mind to be irrelevant to the scientific study of behavior.

The mind-brain problem continues to be pursued with vigor. Among modern philosophers who have continued the debate are Karl Popper (Popper and Eccles, 1977), an advocate of dualist interactionism, and the materialists John Searle (1984), Patricia Churchland (1986), and Daniel Dennett (1991). In particular, Churchland and Dennett have embraced neuroscience to such an extent that they employ the term "mind-brain" to express complete acceptance of the identity of mind and brain (Churchland, 1986; Dennett, 1991).

At first glance, the dualist position may seem untenable in view of modern conceptions of neuroscience, but difficult problems remain nonetheless. Prominent among them is the question of free will. Do people act "freely" or under strictly determined laws of physics and chemistry? This dilemma can be more precisely posed as follows: If the mind and brain are in fact identical, and the brain is an organ whose actions can eventually be understood and entirely predicted, then where is an escape from the determinist trap into which materialism must fall? Will not all behavior be governed by physical forces and therefore free will be impossible? Here are questions to which science has not as yet offered an answer. Considerations such as these continue to pose for some a significant obstacle to an enthusiastic acceptance of the materialist position.

Notwithstanding the lingering uncertainties raised by the dualist tradition, it is difficult to deny that there is considerable practical utility in the materialist viewpoint. Advances in science are no less impressive if they pertain to the neural basis of behavior than if, for instance, they lead to the discovery of penicillin for the treatment of bacterial pneumonia. It is indisputable thus far that the brain mediates every aspect of human behavior that has been amenable to investigation. In the clinical arena, experience with stroke or traumatic brain injury patients leaves little doubt that activities of the mind are reliably and often dramatically affected by physical alterations in the brain. Although occasional neuroscientists who adhere to a dualist position can be found (Penfield, 1975; Popper and Eccles, 1977), the great majority hold that physical events are providing increasingly complete and satisfying explanations for the activities of the mind. As a heuristic principle, the notion that brain events underlie and are directly correlated with mental events has been enormously productive to date. Without necessarily presuming to answer the thorny philosophical questions introduced above, neuroscience has nevertheless built up an impressive body of data indicating that the mind's activities are an unequivocal result of the brain's structure and function. In this sense, scientific advances shed light on old problems that, while not solved, at least seem less imposing.

The position taken in these pages is unreservedly materialistic, embracing without hesitation the assumptions and methods of neuroscience. Although it is true, of course, that a nonphysical reality is not excluded by a pragmatic materialism, there seems little to gain by postulating a spiritual or mystical essence that cannot be reduced to the level of scientific analysis, especially when such complex human functions as memory, language, and emotion are already yielding to this kind of inquiry. Until such time as neuroscientific study is stymied in pursuing the neural basis of mental activities—if indeed that obstacle should ever appear—there is every reason to assume that the explication of the brain's operations will also unravel the secrets of the mind.

General Aspects of Brain Anatomy

Neuroanatomy is a vast and growing field that continues to provide many insights into the neural organization of human behavior. This book is concerned with the anatomy of higher functions, and clinically relevant regions of the brain will be covered in the chapters that follow. As an introduction, however, it will be helpful to begin with some general anatomic features of the brain as they bear upon neurobehavioral concepts; complete accounts of neuroanatomy can be found elsewhere (Nauta and Fiertag, 1986; Nolte, 1993).

The human brain is a soft, gelatinous collection of gray and white matter weighing about 1,400 grams (roughly three pounds) in the adult. Estimates vary, but there may be 100 billion or more neurons in the brain, and at least ten times this number of glial cells (Kandel et al., 1991). As an indicator of the astonishing degree of connectivity between cerebral neurons, each neuron makes contact with as many as 10,000 others. Most of the brain's neurons, in excess of 99%, are classified as interneurons, so that the great majority of the brain's neuronal activity is concerned with the processing of information that occurs between sensory input and motor output. In other words, there is a large quantity of nervous tissue standing interposed between the sensory and motor systems to intervene in exceedingly complex ways to elaborate behavior.

The brain is made up of the cerebrum, the brain stem, and the cerebellum (Figures 1.1 and 1.2). Most important for the higher functions is the cerebrum, which is composed of the paired cerebral hemispheres and the diencephalon (thalamus and hypothalamus). The hemispheres are folded into ridges called gyri, and the grooves between these are known as sulci or fissures. These gross anatomical features form the basis for the division of the hemispheres into their four lobes—frontal, temporal, parietal, and occipital.

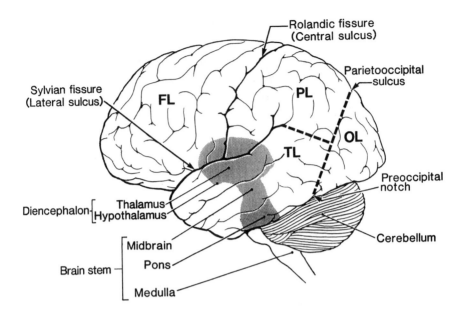

Figure 1.1 Lateral view of the brain depicting lobes and major fissures. FL—frontal lobe; TL—temporal lobe; PL—parietal lobe; OL—occipital lobe.

The parcellation of the hemispheres into four lobes is somewhat arbitrary, but it serves to produce convenient neuroanatomical landmarks that have important functional affiliations. Table 1.1 gives a brief outline of some prominent brain-behavior relationships, which will be developed in greater detail throughout this book. The frontal lobes, largest and most

Table 1.1 Regional functions of the human brain

Frontal lobes	Parietal lobes
Voluntary movement	Tactile sensation
Language production (left)	Visuospatial function (right)
Motor prosody (right)	Reading (left)
Comportment	Calculation (left)
Executive function	**Occipital lobes**
Motivation	Vision
Temporal lobes	Visual perception
Audition	
Language comprehension (left)	
Sensory prosody (right)	
Memory	
Emotion	

Neurobehavioral Anatomy

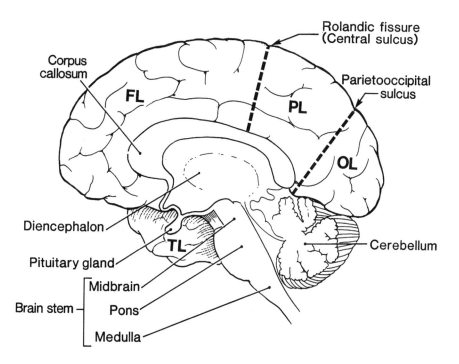

Figure 1.2 Medial view of the brain depicting the four lobes, diencephalon, brain stem, and cerebellum. FL—frontal lobe; TL—temporal lobe; PL—parietal lobe; OL—occipital lobe.

anterior, provide for voluntary movement via the corticospinal tracts, mediate the production of language and prosody, and organize the integrative capacities of comportment, executive function, and motivation. The temporal lobes receive primary auditory input, mediate comprehension of language and prosody, and, in concert with the closely connected limbic system, subserve important aspects of memory and emotion. The parietal lobes receive tactile input, mediate visuospatial competence, and subserve reading and calculation skills. The occipital lobes, smallest and most posterior, receive primary visual input and mediate perception of visual material before further processing occurs in more anterior regions.

The hemispheres are connected to each other primarily by the corpus callosum, a massive white matter tract containing some 300 million axons (Figure 1.2). This structure permits the continuous interhemispheric exchange of information and joins many distant cerebral areas into functionally unified networks. The diencephalon is found deep in the brain and has a major role in sensory, motor, arousal, and limbic activities. Within the diencephalon, the egg-shaped thalamus serves as a central relay station for all sensory systems with the exception of olfaction and has a critical role in wakefulness. The tiny hypothalamus exerts an extensive influence through its control of the autonomic nervous system, with its sympathetic and parasympathetic divisions, and through its connections with the pituitary gland mediating the neural regulation of the endocrine system. In posterior and inferior regions of the brain lie the brain stem and the cerebellum. The brain stem, made up of the midbrain, pons, and medulla, plays an essential role in motor and sensory function, and the caudal brain stem contains centers for the control of respiration and cardiac function. The cerebellum acts in combination with gray matter nuclei in the hemispheres and the brain stem known as the basal ganglia (caudate, putamen, globus pallidus, and substantia nigra) to enable fine motor coordination and postural control. At the base of the brain, the medulla exits the skull through the foramen magnum, where it merges with the spinal cord, the most caudal portion of the central nervous system (CNS).

The brain is housed within and protected by the skull, and between the brain and the skull are three membranes: the dura mater, the arachnoid, and the pia mater. Within the subarachnoid space, cerebrospinal fluid (CSF) envelops the entire CNS and provides a buoyancy that adds further protection. The CSF is continually produced within the four ventricles of the brain—the paired lateral ventricles in the hemispheres, the third ventricle situated between the two thalami, and the fourth ventricle between the cerebellum and the brain stem—and enters the subarachnoid space through apertures in the fourth ventricle. Eventually the CSF circulates to the vertex of the brain and is absorbed into the venous system through the arachnoid villi. The ventricular system and the CSF are important for the structural support of the brain and probably for its metabolic activity as well.

The arterial blood supply of the brain varies somewhat but usually originates with two pairs of large vessels in the neck: the internal carotid and the vertebral arteries. The internal carotid arteries then bifurcate into middle and anterior cerebral arteries, which irrigate, respectively, the lateral hemispheric surfaces and the medial aspects of the frontal and parietal lobes. The vertebral arteries join at the junction of the medulla and pons to form the basilar artery, which then also bifurcates at the midbrain level to form the two posterior cerebral arteries. These vessels supply the medial and inferior surfaces of the temporal and occipital lobes as well as the caudal diencephalon. Interruption of the blood supply from any of these arteries, as occurs in a stroke, leads to a wide spectrum of important neurobehavioral syndromes.

The process of evolution has produced an impressive expansion of the human brain, relative to body weight, in comparison with other animals. There are some species, however—among them some small primates and dolphins—that have proportionately larger brains (Nolte, 1993). The size of the brain, therefore, is only one factor accounting for singularly human capacities. In humans, the large percentage of the brain devoted exclusively to higher functions is undoubtedly important, as is its abundant intraneuronal connectivity (Nolte, 1993).

The surface of the brain is called the cortex, from the Latin for "bark," and its regional cytoarchitectonic variations have provided the rationale for attempts to divide it into discrete areas. The most enduring of these cortical maps was devised by the German anatomist Korbinian Brodmann (1909). Figure 1.3 depicts Brodmann's cortical areas, which number 47 in this illustration. It will be noted on close inspection that areas 13 through 16 are not shown; these areas represent a region called the insula, or island of Reil, which is not visible on the outer surface of the brain (Gorman and Unützer, 1993). The insula is a small cortical zone buried deep in the Sylvian fissure that is overlain by parts of the frontal, parietal, and temporal lobes known as opercula (*operculum* is Latin for "lid"). Apart from having a role in taste perception, the function of the insula is obscure. Many of the surface parcellations of Brodmann, however, have well-established functional affiliations, and frequent reference to Brodmann's schema will be made in this book. More detailed divisions of cortical zones based on structural complexity have been presented (Mesulam, 1985), but for our purposes the areas of Brodmann (Figure 1.3) will serve as convenient landmarks.

A detailed account of the cerebral cortex is unnecessary for this book, but selected aspects of cortical structure are relevant. The cortex is a convoluted sheet of gray matter on the outer surface of the brain, much of which is hidden from view in the depths of sulci and fissures. Its thickness

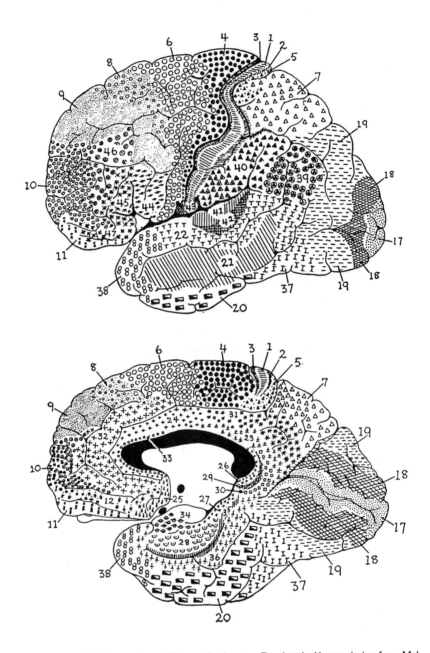

Figure 1.3 Brodmann areas of the cerebral cortex. Reprinted with permission from Malcolm B. Carpenter, M.D., *Human Neuroanatomy.* Baltimore: Williams and Wilkins, 1976.

Neurobehavioral Anatomy

ranges between one and one-half and four and one-half millimeters, with an average of three millimeters. More than 90% is made up of neocortex, the phylogenetically recent six-layered cortex that contains about 10 billion of the 100 billion neurons in the brain (Popper and Eccles, 1977). Other cortical areas, notably the hippocampus and certain olfactory regions linked with the limbic system, have three layers and are known as allocortex.

The neocortex has classically been divided into motor, sensory, and association areas. The last of these is so named because of a philosophical tradition dating back to the British empiricist philosopher John Locke, which holds that mentation is the result of the association between mental events (Duffy, 1984). Association areas occupy the majority of the neocortical surface and have been regarded as regions where the higher functions take place, although a certain imprecision in the understanding of the operations of these regions has persisted.

Recent neurophysiologic studies of the neocortex have indicated that the fundamental unit of cortical function is a vertically oriented column, perpendicular to the cortical surface, that contains as few as 100 neurons and that is extensively connected with others like it throughout the neocortex (Mountcastle, 1978). The most convincing evidence for these columns comes from studies of the primate visual cortex, where it is possible to show with microelectrode insertion that all cells within a column respond similarly to a given external stimulus (Hubel and Wiesel, 1977). It is likely that this arrangement is widespread throughout the neocortex (Mountcastle, 1978).

These neocortical columns number in the hundreds of millions, and because of the massive connectivity among them, the number of potential combinations between various cortical units is vast indeed. This notion has helped develop the concept of distributed systems in the brain that are composed of large numbers of extensively interlinked modular elements (Mountcastle, 1978). The idea of distributed systems has become so popular that it has largely supplanted the concept of cortical association areas. It should be evident, however, that the two notions are in fact quite compatible (Duffy, 1984), and the shift in terminology reflects advances in basic neuroscience more than a fundamental reconsideration of how the brain functions.

Also important in the elaboration of higher function are numerous structures below the cortical mantle. Gray matter nuclei within the diencephalon, basal ganglia, and brain stem play a special role in fundamental processes such as arousal, attention, mood, and motivation. Several important neurotransmitters—acetylcholine, dopamine, norepinephrine, and serotonin—are found in these areas and form part of the complex chemoanatomy of the brain that enables continuous synaptic transmission and interneuronal communication. Neurotransmitter systems arise from deep in the hemispheres or the brain stem and send projections to more rostral sites: the cholinergic system originating from the basal forebrain, the dopaminergic projections from the midbrain substantia nigra and adjacent ventral tegmental area, the noradrenergic system from the pontine locus ceruleus, and the serotonergic fibers from the raphe nuclei of the brain stem. Also important are many white matter tracts that serve to connect cortical and subcortical regions, facilitating rapid and efficient interregional communication. Intrahemispheric association fibers and interhemispheric commissural fibers link regions within and between the hemispheres, and deeper tracts including the fornix and medial forebrain bundle connect the cerebrum to the limbic system and the brain stem. All of these subcortical gray and white matter areas thus contribute to the multifocal cerebral ensembles that comprise the distributed networks dedicated to neurobehavioral functions.

It has recently become popular to compare the brain to the modern computer, which is increasingly capable of impressive computations that in some ways surpass the abilities of their creators. The field of artificial intelligence attempts to design machines that mimic if not duplicate the abilities of the human brain (Crevier, 1993). A consideration of computer science and artificial intelligence is beyond the scope of this book; however, it is instructive to note that the standard computer is known as a *serial* processor, whereas the brain has *parallel* as well as serial processing capacities (Dennett, 1991). Humans can simultaneously engage in multiple operations, but the typical computer, albeit at a very fast pace, must still perform only one task at a time. Thus a human can instantly recognize a familiar voice or face by simultaneously analyzing a flood of auditory or visual input; a typical computer must laboriously analyze each datum individually. The brain has the effortless capacity to weave disparate aspects of mental experience into a seamless unity. Undoubtedly its rich connectivity helps confer this advantage, enabling a greatly extended behavioral repertoire. The principle of parallel processing also helps explain the failure of early attempts to localize behaviors within strictly delineated brain regions; the higher functions involve networks of allied regions that each contribute a component to the final product. The next section demonstrates how an overly simplistic view of the brain and its activities can be highly deceptive.

The Excesses of Phrenology

The scientific attempt to localize mental functions in the brain had an inauspicious start. One need only look to the surprisingly popular doctrine in the late eighteenth and early nineteenth centuries known as phrenology to appreciate how a too literal approach to brain-behavior relationships can become absurd. Most strongly associated with the names of Franz Joseph Gall and Johann Kaspar Spurzheim, phrenology claimed to allow the assessment of behavioral traits by simple palpation of the skull, the bumps and ridges thereon allegedly corresponding to anatomical features of the underlying brain that had specific implications such as amativeness, wit, and destructiveness (Gall and Spurzheim, 1810–1818). It was thought that the centers for the various traits would develop with use and that this expansion would actually produce palpable protrusions in the overlying bony surface. Figure 1.4 illustrates the kind of cranial map that resulted from the phrenological point of view.

In its heyday, phrenology was widely practiced in Europe and America, and many phrenological societies and journals advocated the doctrine. Gall, an Austrian physician and neuroanatomist to whose credit legitimately goes the first distinction between gray and white matter in the brain, nevertheless assured himself a rather dubious place in medical history by the astonishing assertions of phrenology. Not only was his precise assignment of behavioral characteristics to discrete regions of the brain unsubstantiated, but his belief that cranial prominences could reveal these traits seems remarkably crude and naive to the modern observer.

Yet the phrenologists should be recognized for mounting formal opposition to the mind-brain dualism that prevailed in their day and for beginning to establish a legitimacy for considering the brain as the organ of behavior. Gall's error was in his extremism. The radical localizationism of phrenology was excessive, but the principle of assigning behaviors to

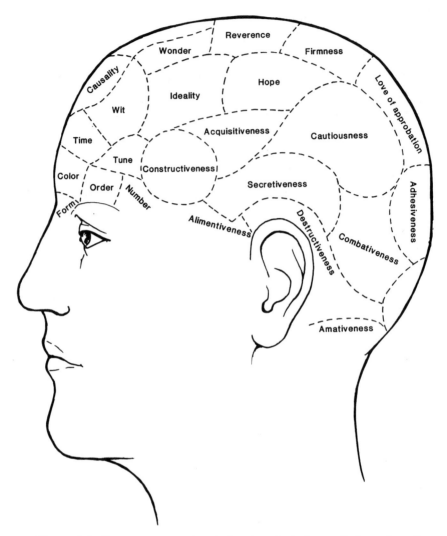

Figure 1.4 Contemporary portrayal of a phrenological map. Redrawn from Gregory, 1987

regions of the brain was not. As this book will attempt to illustrate, a reasonable view of the cerebral localization of behavior is one of the major goals of modern neuroscience.

Behavioral Neurology

This book is about the anatomy of human behavior. Use of the word "behavior" will signify the activities of the mind, or, more generally, the total of all the operations ordinarily regarded as mental acts. Neurologists sometimes refer to these as "higher functions," in order to distinguish them from the elemental sensory and motor functions that are also found in nonhuman species. Some authorities employ the term "higher cortical function" (Luria, 1980), although structures in the subcortex such as the thalamus, basal ganglia, and white matter clearly contribute to behavior, rendering this phrase misleading. As a general guideline, these higher *cerebral* functions can be usefully divided into the common sense categories of thoughts (cognition) and feelings (emotion), although in reality human behaviors usually involve components of both (Damasio, 1994). Our aim will be to review and summarize what is known or theorized about the localization of various behavioral capacities in the human brain. As less information exists regarding localization in children (Wilkening, 1989), this book will concentrate on the adult brain.

The specific approach herein will rely most heavily on *behavioral neurology* (Damasio, 1984), the subspecialty of neurology devoted to the behavioral effects of demonstrable brain disease or injury. Long an area of interest to neurologists, behavioral neurology has emerged in the past three decades as a vigorous discipline whose objective it is to correlate behavior with the structure and function of the brain (Geschwind, 1985). This recent development has been stimulated by many factors. First, the hugely influential tradition of Freudian psychoanalysis began to yield around the middle of this century to a more biological orientation in psychiatry and psychology and thus opened the door for a more quantitative approach to the study of behavior (Kandel, 1979). Second, advances in neuroscientific technology in the past 20 years have kindled the hope that sensitive neuroimaging methods (see page 17) will help disclose more about the complexities of behavior by clarifying the structure and function of the brain without the necessity for postmortem examination. Finally, behavioral neurology has come into its own as a formal discipline, largely through the efforts of Norman Geschwind, who in the 1960s established the importance of the field (Geschwind, 1965) and influenced a generation of clinician-investigators. Behavioral neurology now stands poised at the intersection of modern neuroscience and the detailed clinical observation of behavior. Through study of individuals with focal and diffuse brain lesions, the understanding of contributions made by regions of the brain to various behavioral functions is becoming increasingly more complete. Thus the analysis of mind can constructively proceed by way of a clinically based examination of the brain.

A central debate in behavioral neurology, to which there will be frequent reference throughout this book, is between localizationism and holism. An extreme example of the former is seen in phrenology, whose tradition remains something of an obstacle to a moderate localizationism. In contrast, the holistic viewpoint, also known as the organismic approach or the equipotentiality theory, assumes that the brain works as a unified whole to produce behavior, and that localization is an overly simplistic form of "diagram making." Two syndromes in regard to which holism has had vigorous support are aphasia and amnesia; it has been argued that language (Goldstein, 1948) and memory (Lashley, 1926) disturbances cannot be reliably related to discrete brain areas, but that widespread lesions can cause similar defects. The debate has not been entirely resolved, and it has surely promoted a healthy scientific exchange. However, a consensus has recently been reached that might be designated a modified localizationism. In this paradigm, widespread interconnected networks of cerebral areas participate in a given function (Mesulam, 1990); examples include the left perisylvian zone for language and the medial temporolimbic system for memory. These distributed neurobehavioral networks reflect a conception of brain-behavior relationships that maintains the principle of localizationism without falling prey to its excesses. These networks will be dealt with more completely at several points in this book.

The clinical discipline known as *neuropsychiatry* also deserves comment. Widely popular in nineteenth century Europe before the ascendancy of Sigmund Freud, neuropsychiatry has recently provoked new interest as a discipline having much in common with behavioral neurology (Cummings and Hegarty, 1994). Some confusion surrounds this term, however, as the field appears to be groping for a secure definition (Caine and Joynt, 1986; Yudofsky and Hales, 1989; Lishman, 1992; Trimble, 1993). The term "neuropsychiatry" may come to refer to a synthesis of many disciplines concerned with the evaluation and care of behaviorally disturbed individuals, but the field is still in a process of evolution. The critical point is that neurology and psychiatry are edging closer together in the effort to understand the neurobiological basis of behavior (Kandel, 1989). Such a trend is indeed welcome, both for the expanded insights that are likely to appear and for the pressing needs of many patients with disorders of the brain who have not been well understood by either specialty heretofore (Geschwind, 1975). Both behavioral neurology and neuropsychiatry have much to contribute to the understanding of behavior, and cooperation is clearly preferable to unproductive interdisciplinary disputes.

Although the clinical study of patients who harbor focal or diffuse brain lesions is the foundation of this book, it will also integrate information derived from the spectacular advances of neuroimaging in recent years (Raichle, 1994). It is now possible to study the higher functions in disease and health using safe and noninvasive techniques that produce elegant images of brain structure and function. The first advance of this kind was computerized tomography (CT), which appeared in the 1970s and quickly established its role in the examination of brain-behavior relationships (Naeser and Hayward, 1978). Then, in the 1980s, magnetic resonance imaging (MRI) offered a more sensitive structural imaging instrument, particularly for viewing the cerebral white matter (Goodkin et al., 1994). To complement these anatomical techniques, a variety of methods designed to image the physiology of the brain were developed. Regional cerebral blood flow (rCBF) studies (Lassen et al., 1978), single photon emission computed tomography (SPECT) (Alavi and Hirsch, 1991), and positron emission tomography (PET) (Roland, 1993) all utilize the principle that metabolic activity of the brain is coupled with blood flow, so that cerebral function during a given task can be assessed by the introduction into the bloodstream of an isotope emitting radiation.

Of all these techniques, PET has achieved the most impressive results, and "seeing the mind" in action is now possible (Posner, 1993). Most recently, interest has developed in functional MRI (fMRI), which exploits blood oxygenation to measure regional changes in brain metabolic activity during specified tasks. Elegant studies on the localization of elemental and higher brain functions are now appearing (Turner, 1994), and fMRI may improve on the spatial resolution that PET can offer. Neither PET nor fMRI, however, produces good temporal resolution, because changes in blood flow may occur seconds later than increases in neuronal activity (Raichle, 1994). A final technique, one that promises improved temporal resolution, is magnetoencephalography (MEG), a method similar to the familiar electroencephalography (EEG); MEG and EEG can measure magnetic fields and electrical activity at the same time that neuronal activity occurs (Crease, 1991). It may be that PET and fMRI combined with MEG and EEG will provide functional neuroimaging that succeeds in offering both spatial and temporal resolution (Raichle, 1994).

Relevant information from related disciplines including neuropsychology, cognitive science, and the basic neurosciences will also be integrated into this account. Neuropsychology is an active and growing field with major importance in terms of the precise characterization of behavioral disorders (Lezak, 1983). Cognitive science promises many new insights, particularly through its emphasis on computers and theoretical models of cognition (Gardner, 1987). Basic neuroscience, despite the lack of an animal model (almost by definition) for higher functions and their disorders, offers valuable information on such matters as neurotransmission and synaptic function (Kandel et al., 1991). An air of excitement pervades the exploration of behavior as interdisciplinary work produces new advances daily. Despite many uncertainties in all areas of neuroscience, a growing body of data is beginning to provide a cogent description of the roles played by brain structures in the wondrous array of human behaviors.

The study of how the higher functions are represented in the human brain is clearly a formidable task. Behavioral neurology can only proceed by analyzing abnormal behavior in the context of brain pathology and then theorizing about the normal behavior that has been disturbed (Benson, 1994). Difficulties arise both in the definition of neurobehavioral functions such as attention, memory, and language and in the accurate identification of damaged brain areas, so that both sides of the brain-behavior equation are subject to significant uncertainties. The lesion method, upon which behavioral neurology is based, should be used as a tool to explore the distributed networks of the brain subserving specific functions, and not in support of a supposed correspondence between the localization of a lesion and the dedicated site of a mental act (Damasio and Damasio, 1989). With this caveat in mind, it is hoped that a general sketch of the neuroanatomy of behavior will prove useful. The study of human beings is ultimately the only way to probe their unique behaviors, even though reliance on "nature's experiments"—due to stroke, trauma, degenerative disease, and the like—restricts the scope of such investigation more than tightly controlled experiments with laboratory animals.

The goal will be to examine in some detail the domains of mental activity that have been illuminated by clinical observation, demonstrating that such an endeavor not only has great value for the care of individuals with devastating afflictions of the brain but also contributes enormously to the understanding of how human behavior is neuroanatomically organized. As Geschwind wrote, with characteristic clarity: "It must be realized that every behavior has an anatomy" (Geschwind, 1975).

References

Alavi, A., and Hirsch, L.J. 1991. Studies of central nervous system disorders with single photon emission computed tomography and positron emission tomography. *Sem Nucl Med;* 21: 58–81.

Benson, D.F. 1994. *The Neurology of Thinking.* New York, Oxford.

Brodmann, K. 1909. *Vergleichende Lokalisationslehre der Grosshirnrinde in ihren Prinzipien dargestellt auf Grund des Zellenbaues.* Leipzig, Barth.

Caine, E.D., and Joynt, R.J. 1986. Neuropsychiatry . . . Again. *Arch Neurol;* 43: 325–327.

Churchland, P.S. 1986. *Neurophilosophy.* Cambridge, MIT Press.

Corsi, P. (ed.) 1991. *The Enchanted Loom. Chapters in the History of Neuroscience.* New York, Oxford.

Crease, R.P. 1991. Images of conflict: MEG vs. EEG. *Science,* 253: 374–375.

Crevier, D. 1993. *The Tumultuous History of the Search for Artificial Intelligence.* New York, Basic Books.

Cummings, J.L., and Hegarty, A. 1994. Neurology, psychiatry, and neuropsychiatry. *Neurology;* 44: 209–213.

Damasio, A.R. 1984. Behavioral neurology: theory and practice. *Sem Neurol;* 4: 117–119.

Damasio, A.R. 1994. *Decartes' Error: Emotion, Reason, and the Human Brain.* New York, Grosset/Putnam.

Damasio, H., and Damasio, A.R. 1989. *Lesion Analysis in Neuropsychology.* New York, Oxford.

Dennett, D.C. 1991. *Consciousness Explained.* Boston, Little, Brown.

Descartes, R. 1637. *Discourse on Method and the Meditations.* Sutcliffe, F. E. (trans.). 1968. London, Penguin Books.

Duffy, C.J. 1984. The legacy of association cortex. *Neurology;* 34: 192–197.

Gall, F.J., and Spurzheim, J.K. 1810–1818. *Anatomie et physiologie de système nerveux en général et du cerveau en particulier.* Paris, Schoell.

Gardner, H. 1987. *The Mind's New Science.* New York, Basic Books.

Geschwind, N. 1965. Disconnexion syndromes in animals and man. *Brain;* 88: 237–294, 585–644.

Geschwind, N. 1975. The borderland of neurology and psychiatry: some common misconceptions. In: Benson, D.F., and Blumer, D. (eds.). *Psychiatric Aspects of Neurologic Disease.* Vol. 1. New York, Grune and Stratton, pp. 1–8.

Geschwind, N. 1985. Brain disease and the mechanisms of mind. In: Coen, C.E. (ed.). *Functions of the Brain.* Oxford, Clarendon, pp. 160–180.

Goldstein, 1948. K. *Language and Language Disturbances.* New York, Grune and Stratton.

Goodkin, D.E., Rudick, R.A., and Ross, S.J. 1994. The use of brain magnetic resonance imaging in multiple sclerosis. *Arch Neurol;* 51: 505–516.

Gorman, D.G., and Unützer, J. 1993. Brodmann's "missing" numbers. *Neurology;* 43: 226–227.

Gregory, R.L. (ed.). 1987. *The Oxford Companion to the Mind.* New York, Oxford.

Horgan, J. 1994. Can science explain consciousness? *Sci Am;* 271(1): 88–94.

Hubel, D.H., and Wiesel, T.N. 1977. Functional architecture of macaque monkey visual cortex. *Proc R Soc Lond;* B198: 1–59.

James, W. 1890. *The Principles of Psychology.* New York, Henry Holt.

Kandel, E.R. 1979. Psychotherapy and the single synapse. *N Engl J Med;* 301: 1028–1037.

Kandel, E.R. 1989. Genes, nerve cells, and the remembrance of things past. *J Neuropsychiatry;* 1: 103–125.

Kandel, E.R., Schwartz, J.H., and Jessell, T.M. (eds.). 1991. *Principles of Neural Science.* 3rd ed. New York, Elsevier.

Lashley, K.S. 1926. Studies of cerebral function in learning VII: the relation between cerebral mass, learning and retention. *J Comp Neurol;* 41: 1–58.

Lassen, N.A., Ingvar, D.H., and Skinhoj, E. 1978. Brain function and blood flow. *Sci Am;* 239(4); 62–71.

Lezak, M.D. *Neuropsychological Assessment.* 1983. 2nd ed. New York, Oxford.

Lishman, W.A. 1992. What is neuropsychiatry? *J Neurol Neurosurg Psychiatry;* 55: 983–985.

Luria, A.R. 1980. *Higher Cortical Functions in Man.* New York, Consultants Bureau.

Mesulam, M.-M. 1985. Patterns in behavioral neuroanatomy: association areas, the limbic system, and hemispheric specialization. In: Mesulam, M.-M. *Principles of Behavioral Neurology.* Philadelphia, F. A. Davis.

Mesulam, M.-M. 1990. Large-scale neurocognitive networks and distributed processing for attention, language, and memory. *Ann Neurol;* 28: 597–613.

Mountcastle, V.B. 1978. An organizing principle for cerebral function: the unit module and the distributed system. In: Edelman, G.M., and Mountcastle, V.B. (eds.). *The Mindful Brain.* Cambridge, MIT Press, pp. 7–50.

Naeser, M.A., and Hayward, R.W. 1978. Lesion localization in aphasia with cranial computed tomography and the Boston Diagnostic Aphasia Exam. *Neurology;* 28: 545–551.

Nauta, W.J.H., and Fiertag, M. 1986. *Fundamental Neuroanatomy.* New York, W.H. Freeman.

Nolte, J. *The Human Brain.* 3rd ed. St. Louis, Mosby Year Book, 1993.

Penfield, W. *The Mystery of the Mind.* 1975. Princeton, Princeton University Press.

Popper, K.F., and Eccles, J.C. 1977. *The Self and Its Brain.* Berlin, Springer International.

Posner, M.I. 1993. Seeing the mind. *Science;* 262: 673–674.

Raichle, M.E. 1994. Visualizing the mind. *Sci Am;* 270(4): 58–64.

Roland, P.E. 1993. *Brain Activation.* New York, Wiley-Liss.

Ryle, G. 1949. *The Concept of Mind.* Chicago, University of Chicago Press.

Searle, J.R. 1984. *Minds, Brains and Science.* Cambridge, Harvard University Press.

Skinner, B.F. 1971. *Beyond Freedom and Dignity.* New York, Alfred A. Knopf.

Trimble, M.R. 1993. Neuropsychiatry or behavioural neurology. *Neuropsychiatry Neuropsychol Behav Neurol;* 6: 60–69.

Turner, R. 1994. Magnetic resonance imaging of brain function. *Ann Neurol;* 35: 637–638.

Wilkening, G.N. 1989. Techniques of localization in child neuropsychology. In: Reynolds, C.R., and Fletcher-Janzen, E. (eds.). *Handbook of Clinical Child Neuropsychology.* New York, Plenum, pp. 291–309.

Young, J.Z. 1987. *Philosophy and the Brain.* Oxford, Oxford University Press.

Yudofsky, S.C., and Hales, R.E. 1989. The reemergence of neuropsychiatry: definition and direction. *J Neuropsychiatry;* 1: 1–6.

CHAPTER 2

Mental Status Evaluation

The main purpose of the clinical interaction between physician and patient is the gathering of information that will contribute to the patient's proper evaluation and care. In the case of neurobehavioral disorders, deficits due to brain dysfunction can be recognized only after a thorough assessment of behavior has been made. Many of the clinical data, of course, are elicited with a medical history, physical examination, and elemental neurologic examination, but the assessment of mental status is a particularly revealing, if challenging, part of the clinical encounter. The mental status evaluation is, in fact, the foundation of behavioral neurology.

History and Interview

As a first step, much can be learned by simple observation of the patient during the initial greetings and history taking. The general appearance of the patient gives information about the degree of self-care and the quality of comportment, as well as providing evidence of movement disorders, gait disturbance, psychomotor retardation, catatonia, compulsive acts, anxiety, and hyperactivity. During the interview, anomalous thought characteristics such as loosened associations, tangentiality, flight of ideas, and grandiosity often become apparent in conversation. Delusions, the most notable disorders of thought content, may emerge. Abnormal perceptual phenomena, including hallucinations and illusions, may be obvious or easily elicited by appropriate questioning. Detection of disturbances such as these may suggest a behavioral disorder not clearly related to structural brain disease (a "psychiatric" disorder), and the remainder of the evaluation can be altered accordingly.

It is well to remember, however, that observations suggesting psychiatric disease may also reflect a neurologic illness. *Delusions*, or fixed false beliefs, have been reported in a great variety of neurologic conditions

(Cummings, 1985b) and appear to be more frequent when the pathologic process affects the limbic system (Cummings, 1992). Paranoid delusions are also common in Alzheimer's Disease, possibly due to medial temporal lobe involvement (Cummings and Victoroff, 1990). Two less common delusional syndromes are the *Capgras syndrome* (Alexander et al., 1979) and *reduplicative paramnesia* (Benson et al., 1976). Both are misidentification phenomena associated with a combination of bifrontal and right hemisphere pathology; in the Capgras syndrome, the patient believes that a close family member or friend has been replaced by an impostor, and in reduplicative paramnesia, there is a delusion that a familiar place has been relocated to a different site.

Hallucinations, sensory experiences without external stimulation, may occur in visual, auditory, tactile, olfactory, or gustatory modalities (Siegel, 1977). Some general rules guide the history taking. Visual hallucinations generally suggest neurologic involvement, whereas auditory hallucinations imply psychiatric disease (Cummings and Miller, 1987). Three settings predispose to visual hallucinations: perceptual release due to sensory system disease (Lepore, 1990), ictal discharge (King and Marsan, 1977), and toxic-metabolic disorders (Lipowski, 1980). Two types of release visual hallucination are the *Charles Bonnet syndrome*, visual hallucinations due to encroaching blindness from ocular pathology (Damas-Mora et al., 1982), and *palinopsia*, recurrence of a visual image after removal of the stimulus, associated with right parietooccipital lesions (Stagno and Gates, 1991). Visual hallucinations are more common with right hemisphere than left hemisphere lesions (Lessell, 1975; Hecaen and Albert, 1978), and, in general, unformed visual hallucinations suggest occipital lobe lesions, whereas formed images imply temporal lobe pathology (Cummings, 1985a). A peculiar type of visual hallucination is *peduncular hallucinosis*, formed hallucinations, often of people or animals, that are seen as benign or even entertaining; midbrain lesions in the vicinity of the cerebral peduncle are thought to be responsible (Dunn et al., 1983). Auditory hallucinations are very common in schizophrenia but may also occur in *schizophreniform psychosis* (Chapter 9) and *alcoholic hallucinosis* (Victor and Hope, 1958). *Palinacousis* is analogous to palinopsia, and the recurrent auditory experiences usually relate to a temporal lobe lesion (Jacobs et al., 1973). Tactile hallucinations occur mainly in psychiatric disorders but can also appear in toxic-metabolic disorders (Berrios, 1982); *formications,* the feeling of insects crawling on the skin, are common in drug withdrawal states. Olfactory, and rarely gustatory, hallucinations can be experienced with temporolimbic seizures (Daly, 1975), reflecting involvement of the medial temporal lobe and the insula.

Illusions are misperceptions or distortions of external stimuli. They occur most often in the visual realm, and they differ from hallucinations in that they do not arise spontaneously but are provoked by visual input. Common illusions include *micropsia* (the appearance of decreased size), *macropsia* (the appearance of increased size), and *metamorphopsia* (a change in shape or form). Clinical settings favoring the occurrence of illusions are temporolimbic seizures and classic migraine (Hecaen and Albert, 1978), but like hallucinations, they can be encountered in a variety of neurologic and psychiatric disorders.

Mental Status Examination

After the history taking, the mental status examination is carried out in a manner analogous to the remainder of the neurological examination, the objective being to assess specific functions systematically so that a syndrome diagnosis can be made; then alterations in underlying anatomy and physiology can be deduced and the cause of the problem ultimately discovered. It is therefore obvious that some sense of the neurobiological foundations of these functions is essential to the examiner. What follows is a relatively comprehensive review of the mental status examination (Table 2.1), which provides the organizational framework for considering the syndromes described in this book. The procedures listed in Table 2.1 allow for the detection of major neurobehavioral syndromes and should be carried out carefully in cases referred for neurobehavioral evaluation; additional comments on the assessment of specific syndromes can be found in the appropriate chapters. A brief screening mental status examination is also provided.

Certain principles should be remembered in conducting these examinations. First, clinical tests seldom assess a single neurobehavioral domain in isolation, although they can be fairly specific; the data collected must be analyzed as a whole to detect the salient deficits. Another point is that many aspects of a patient's performance are significantly influenced by life experiences, cultural background, age, and education, necessitating a certain flexibility on the part of the examiner. Finally, it should be

Table 2.1   Mental status examination

I. Arousal, attention, and motivation	IV. Visuospatial function
A. Arousal	A. Directed attention
1. Hyperarousal	B. Spatial orientation
2. Hypoarousal	C. Dressing
B. Attention	D. Drawing
1. Digit span	V. Complex cognition
2. Serial sevens	A. Idioms and proverbs
3. Random letter test	B. Similarities
4. Double simultaneous stimulation	C. Multistep arithmetic
C. Motivation	D. Word list generation
1. Cooperation	E. Alternating sequences
2. Perseverance	F. Insight
II. Memory	G. Judgment
A. Immediate	VI. Mood and affect
B. Recent	A. Mood
1. Verbal	1. Inquiry to patient
2. Visual	2. Inquiries to family and friends
C. Remote	B. Affect
III. Language	1. Facial expression
A. Spontaneous speech	2. Tone of voice
B. Auditory comprehension	3. Latency of response
C. Repetition	4. Gesture and body posture
D. Naming	
E. Reading	
F. Writing	

stressed that keen observation is of paramount importance; neurology, particularly behavioral neurology, remains heavily dependent on the clinician's skill in detecting the subtle, often nonverbal, manifestations of central nervous system function and dysfunction. Even powerful new imaging techniques are no substitute for the careful and sensitive evaluation of an experienced clinician.

Arousal, Attention, and Motivation

The formal mental status examination logically begins with a consideration of the fundamental functions of arousal, attention, and motivation. Assessment of these phenomena is a necessary first step in judging mentation because if any one is sufficiently compromised, the remainder of the examination is uninformative. Individuals who are not fully awake, who do not adequately pay attention, or who simply fail to put forth satisfactory effort cannot be formally assessed in neurobehavioral terms, although of course much can still be learned in other ways about their mental state.

Arousal is a physiologic concept describing the wakefulness of the individual. It is useful to regard arousal in terms of the *level of consciousness*, which is best viewed as dependent on the integrity of the ascending reticular activating system (ARAS) in the brain stem and diencephalon (Plum and Posner, 1982). *Alertness* is an alternate designation for this important domain. In contrast, the *content of consciousness*—the sum of all the operations of cognition and emotion—is mediated primarily by the cerebral hemispheres (Plum and Posner, 1982). It is evident that an appropriate degree of arousal is required for the engagement of cognitive and emotional processes; in anatomic terms, the ARAS must be functional for the hemispheres to operate effectively.

Disorders of arousal are identified by simple recognition of abnormal states, be they those of hyperarousal (restlessness, agitation, delirium) or hypoarousal (drowsiness, lethargy, stupor, coma). The use of many of these terms is not standardized, and if doubt or the possibility of poor communication exists, a wise course is simply to describe a patient's level of consciousness rather than attach to it an ambiguous label.

Attention is a more complicated phenomenon, and its many different definitions by various authorities have led to considerable confusion. Nevertheless, there is no question that inattention in a neurological sense carries important diagnostic and therapeutic implications. For the purposes of this book, attention will be considered in light of the many disorders that have been noted to lead to some aspect of attentional dysfunction.

This approach will then permit a practical, albeit preliminary, formulation of how the complex attentional network in the brain is organized.

Three aspects of attention have neurobehavioral implications. The first is the general category of *selective attention*, a capacity that permits the focusing of awareness on biologically relevant stimuli in the external environment. This crucial ability is reliably judged by the digit span test, in which the patient is asked to repeat lists of single digits dictated by the examiner; normal performance ranges are seven plus or minus two numbers repeated in the order dictated, and five plus or minus one numbers recited in reverse order (Cummings, 1985a). Second, there is *sustained attention*, also called "vigilance" or "concentration," which involves selective attention to a task longer than the few seconds necessary to perform the digit span task. Sustained attention can be evaluated by the serial sevens test, having the patient count backward from 100 by sevens, or by the random letter test (Strub and Black, 1993), in which the patient responds by lifting a hand each time the examiner says the letter "A" in a long random list of letters. Finally, the aspect known as *directed attention* is a lateralized function that is organized in such a fashion that the right hemisphere attends to the left hemispace and vice versa. Hemiattentional disorders, most importantly hemineglect—often referred to simply as "neglect"— are sought by testing for *extinction* to double simultaneous stimulation in the tactile, visual, and auditory modalities. Affected patients will fail to detect one of two stimuli that are simultaneously applied to both sides of the body, but they have no difficulty with unilateral stimulation. Neglect is generally much more common on the left side of the body than on the right, and the demonstration of left side neglect should prompt a particularly assiduous search for other signs of right hemisphere dysfunction.

Motivation refers to the level of effort a patient puts forth during the examination and is subjectively but reliably assessed by noting the degree of cooperation and perseverance. The patient's underlying personality clearly plays a major role in motivation, but this aspect of behavior is also dependent on the integrity of frontal, subcortical, and limbic structures (Mesulam, 1985). Amotivational states often imply bilateral frontal lobe dysfunction, and depression is another potential cause. Malingering with symptom magnification and other psychiatric conditions need also be considered in this context.

Memory

The word *memory* has been employed to refer to members of a complex group of psychological functions, and the study of memory has taken many different approaches depending on the discipline investigating it. One source of continuing confusion is the difference between short-term and long-term memory, a distinction accepted in the psychological literature between temporary and permanent storage of memory. This is indeed a meaningful difference, but does "long-term memory" refer to new learning within minutes or to stable memories over months or years? Clinicians have tended to divide long-term memory into the categories of "recent" and "remote," retaining a form of short-term memory in the category designated as "immediate." For clinical purposes, therefore, it is most useful to consider memory under the headings of immediate, recent, and remote (Kirshner, 1986; Strub and Black, 1993).

Immediate memory is intimately related to selective attention, which enables the performance of tasks such as recalling a phone number long enough to use it correctly without the need to write it down. An older formulation of this general phenomenon is *primary memory* (James, 1890), and a newer term for this capacity is *working memory* (Baddeley, 1992). Whatever terminology is used, this kind of memory is adequately tested clinically with the digit span test. Alternatively, recitation in reverse order of the months of the year or the days of the week is a satisfactory procedure.

Recent memory refers to the ability to accomplish new learning. Information retained for a period of minutes to hours is regarded as being held in recent memory. Testing of recent memory involves asking the patient to remember three or four unrelated words for five to ten minutes, during which time other components of the evaluation are carried out to prevent mental rehearsal. If this task is failed, provision of a semantic cue (such as the category for the forgotten item) or a phonemic cue (the first phoneme of the word) may help certain patients, and offering a list of words from which the correct one can be recognized can assist others. Individuals whose performance improves with these procedures generally have more difficulty with retrieval than with encoding and may have primarily subcortical pathology. As it is known that left and right side lesions may cause selective verbal and visual memory deficits, respectively, it is often worthwhile to use the same format with pictures, designs, or objects in the room. The "Three Words–Three Shapes" test, for example, allows simultaneous evaluation of verbal and nonverbal recent memory (Weintraub and Mesulam, 1985). Other tests of recent memory involve orientation to locale and date, as well as details of the present illness or current political or sports events.

Remote memory, commonly known as knowledge, involves the storage of material learned days, months, or years past and is tested by asking about significant occasions in the patient's life or important historical events. This component of memory is assumed to depend on diffuse, probably redundant representation of information in the neocortex. As such, it is typically better preserved than recent memory in neurologic disease, a feature strikingly apparent in many cases of early dementia.

Language

Language is the verbal or written representation of thought that permits symbolic communication with other individuals. It is to be distinguished from *speech*, the motor capacity for the articulation of oral language, and *voice*, the laryngeal function of producing sound by phonation. Disorders of speech (dysarthrias) and voice (dysphonias) may or may not be associated with disorders of language (aphasias, or, as some authorities prefer, dysphasias) and require separate consideration.

In testing for aphasia, six aspects of language should always be sampled if the patient is capable of performing the requested tasks.

1. *Spontaneous speech* is assessed during conversation in the history taking, and the major distinction to be made is between *fluency* and *nonfluency;* the latter is characterized by reduced phrase length (a maximum of five words or less between pauses), agrammatism (incorrect grammatical structure), impaired linguistic prosody (abnormal rhythm and stress), and articulatory struggle (dysarthria).

2. *Auditory comprehension* is probed by the presentation of increasingly complex directions: pointing to body parts, pointing to objects in the room, pointing to two, three, or four objects in sequence, pointing to objects functionally described ("Show me the device I have on to tell time"), answering sentence-length yes-no questions ("Am I wearing a hat?" "Is a fork good for eating soup?"), and answering questions that employ more complex grammar and syntax ("A lion was killed by a tiger; which animal died?").

3. *Repetition* is tested by having the patient repeat single content words ("house," "baseball"), sentences with content words ("The train entered the station"), and sentences with many small functor words ("He is the one who did it").

4. *Naming* is done by the method of confrontation, so that the patient is asked to name common and uncommon items in the classes of objects, body parts, and colors.

5. *Reading* is tested by having the patient read aloud and silently for comprehension; both are performed using letters, words, sentences, and paragraphs.

6. *Writing* involves the patient producing a signature (a highly resistant, overlearned skill), writing to dictation (words, short sentences), and writing a narrative sentence about some familiar topic, such as the current weather conditions. The last two of these tasks clearly depend on the literacy of the individual being examined.

In addition to the findings elicited by this basic core of tests, the presence of *paraphasias* should be noted. These are errors made in speech characterized by letter or word substitutions; they are classified as phonemic or literal (e.g., "bree" for "tree"), semantic or verbal (e.g., "house" for "tree"), or neologistic (a *neologism* is a meaningless word such as "stribenlug"). Paraphasic speech is characteristic of all aphasias, but it is easier to detect in fluent aphasias in which there is more abundant speech production. The term *jargon aphasia* refers to severe fluent aphasia with heavily paraphasic speech that is difficult or impossible to follow.

In selected patients, other procedures may be useful. Evaluation of singing can demonstrate musical ability that may be advantageous in the rehabilitation of nonfluent aphasics (Chapter 8). The finding that serial speech (days of the week, the pledge of allegiance) is preserved assists in the diagnosis of the transcortical aphasias. Spelling errors can accompany the abnormal written output of aphasia (agraphia) or be associated with developmental reading syndromes.

It is often appropriate after the assessment of language to examine for *apraxia*, a disorder of the ability to carry out learned motor activity. Apraxia often accompanies aphasia and may exacerbate deficits from which aphasic patients already suffer. Furthermore, apraxia provides localizing information in addition to that revealed by language disturbances. Apraxia is discussed as a disorder of higher motor function in Chapter 6.

Finally, the testing for *Gerstmann's syndrome* (agraphia, acalculia, right-left disorientation, and finger agnosia) fits into the examination conveniently at this point. After a writing sample is obtained, calculating ability is probed using simple arithmetic problems. Next, the patient is asked to identify the right and left hands on him- or herself and the examiner. Finally, recognition of fingers (thumb, index finger, middle finger, ring finger, and little finger) on the patient and on the examiner is tested. This peculiar combination of deficits often localizes a lesion to the left angular gyrus. "Finger agnosia" is one way in which the word "agnosia" finds use, but the classic agnosias refer more properly to modality-specific recognition deficits. *Agnosia* as a disorder of higher sensory function can be suspected when complex deficits in vision, audition, and tactile sensation are detected, and the agnosias will be considered in Chapter 7.

Visuospatial Function

This broad category includes the ability to attend to visually presented material, to analyze it, to remember it, and to represent it accurately by means of integrated motor output. Traditionally, these abilities are assigned to the right hemisphere, and a large body of data supports the central role of this hemisphere in visuospatial processing. Tests probing various aspects of visuospatial ability offer the most convenient means of surveying the neurobehavioral integrity of the right hemisphere. The parietal lobe, however, is considered the most important single lobe for the performance of visuospatial tasks.

The first step is to search for *neglect*, which may be elicited by the method of double simultaneous stimulation (described on page 28) or by tests of line cancellation (asking the patient to cross out all the randomly placed lines on a sheet of paper) and line bisection (asking for a mark to be made exactly in the middle of each of several horizontal lines of differing length). *Spatial orientation* can be tested by having the patient place major cities or other sites on a sketch of a familiar country. The patient may then be asked how one would travel to some familiar place from the hospital or clinic, or how to get to the nurses' station or the receptionist's desk. *Dressing* can also be judged, and if deficient, can provide useful information pertaining to right parietal dysfunction.

Finally, the traditional test of visuospatial function is *drawing*. First, drawing to the examiner's direction is conducted: simple geometric shapes (square, triangle, cross), three-dimensional shapes (cube, house), a daisy, a clock face. Then it is often helpful to ask the patient to make copies next to the examiner's drawings: objects, if any, that were previously failed and any new ones that may be instructive. The clock face with the hands set at 11:10 is particularly helpful because it may disclose additional evidence of visuospatial disturbance. Errors that are typically made by patients with right hemisphere lesions include left side hemineglect, loss of perspective, impairment of the overall contour, a tendency to work from right to left, and "closing in" of the copy too close to the original. Lesions of the left hemisphere are more likely to result in simplification, loss of internal detail, and perseveration.

Complex Cognition

Derived from the Latin verb *cognoscere* (to know), "cognition" is a word with many meanings. For our purposes, *cognition* will refer broadly to the various mental operations participating in the acquisition and utilization of information that permits the organism to generate an adaptive response to environmental or internal needs. It is more or less synonymous with the common use of the word "thinking," and it will be distinguished herein from the category of emotions or "feelings." A subset of cognitive operations is what might be called *complex cognition*—distinct from attention, memory, language, and visuospatial ability—and includes such capacities as reasoning, insight, judgment, multistep calculations, problem solving, and impulse control. These abilities, often referred to as the brain's "highest" functions, are the most difficult to evaluate in neurobehavioral terms because they involve extremely complicated computations with ill-defined cerebral correlates. Complex cognitive skills are very likely represented throughout the cerebrum, with specialized regions participating preferentially in selected domains. As will be seen in Chapter 10, it is appropriate to consider the frontal lobes as playing a unique role in directing these activities (Luria, 1973; Stuss and Benson, 1986), although many aspects of complex cognition—including the problematic concept of intelligence—are strongly associated with more posterior regions.

The examination of complex cognition attempts to assess the patient's capacity to adapt to novel situations, to manipulate knowledge, to reason, to innovate, and to integrate emotional drives into an appropriate behavioral repertoire. Tests frequently given include:

1. interpretation of *idioms* ("a loud tie"; "a heavy heart") and *proverbs* ("Don't cry over spilled milk"; "You can't tell a book by its cover"), which taps reasoning skills

2. recognition of *similarities* (table and chair, coal and paper), which assesses metaphorical capacity

3. *multistep arithmetic problems* that require challenging calculations

4. *word list generation*, a verbal fluency task requiring the patient to list aloud in 60 seconds as many words as possible within a given category, such as animals or fruits and vegetables (normal is 18 or more per category) and as many words as possible that begin with a specific letter such as F, A, or S (normal is 12 or more per letter) (Strub and Black, 1993)

5. *alternating sequence tasks*, in which the patient is asked to copy a continuous series of alternating m's and n's in cursive, or alternating squares and triangles (after a short sequence to copy, the patient continues to the end of the page, and perseveration may be demonstrated if the alternating sequence is not maintained)

These tests are primarily mediated through language and therefore tend to reflect left hemisphere function more than right. The behavioral neurology of the right hemisphere is relatively obscure in comparison, and complex cognitive deficits associated with unilateral right hemisphere lesions may prove quite difficult to detect. The right frontal lobe can be particularly problematic to the examiner attempting to identify or exclude lesions in this region. However, deficits in attention, vigilance, visuospatial skills, and comportment can serve as indicators of possible right hemisphere dysfunction.

Insight and judgment probably reflect bifrontal function to a large extent, as they require the integration of emotional as well as cognitive components. Much can be learned about emotional adjustment by inquiring about *insight* into the illness at hand and its potential effect on the patient and family. In addition, simple questions regarding *judgment* ("What would you do in a crowded theater if you smelled smoke?") may reveal evidence of disturbed social and ethical behavior. Other features of impairment in the integration of emotional behavior are sometimes more obvious; abulia, facetiousness, inappropriate sexual behavior, unconcern, apathy, and irritability are all associated with bifrontal pathology.

Finally, the functions that are truly the highest in the human repertoire—creativity, imagination, tolerance, love, altruism, and aesthetic sensibility—cannot be tested directly. At best, only a general sense of alteration in these traits can be suspected after some time is spent with a patient. Information from family or friends may be very helpful in this regard. It is paradoxical, although not surprising, that the qualities that are most distinctly human prove to be the most difficult to describe and quantify.

Mood and Affect

This part of the mental status examination specifically focuses on emotional behavior. Mood and affect are the key areas to assess, and important information on changes in personality and comportment may also emerge during this process. Although these aspects of the clinical evaluation are often viewed as properly assigned to psychiatrists or psychologists, mood and affect have important neurobehavioral implications. The assessment of mood and affect is necessarily subjective, and considerable clinical experience is often needed to detect subtle alterations. *Mood* is best considered the content of an individual's emotional experience, or the inner feeling state, and is quite inaccessible to the examiner except through the patient's own statements. *Affect*, on the other hand, is a more observable phenomenon, consisting of the outward manifestations of emotions— facial expressions, tone of voice, latency of response, and paralinguistic communication such as gesture and body posture.

The anatomical substrate of emotion is exceedingly complex and poorly defined. The limbic system clearly plays a pivotal role, mediating the drives or instincts that assist in the attainment of fundamental biological needs. Limbic cortical regions, especially the cingulate gyrus, participate in the experience of emotion, and the hypothalamus is responsible for directing the autonomic and endocrine effectors of emotion. The activity of these systems is then modified by the influence of neocortical areas, especially the frontal lobes, which act, as reviewed above, to modulate basic drives into acceptable social patterns. Also important in emotional behavior is the right hemisphere, which acts in little-understood ways to confer elements such as interpersonal competence, prosodic and musical skills, and humor upon the behavioral profile. Emotional disorders may thus result from damage to a variety of areas.

In regard to mood, the patient's own comments are often verified or contradicted by observations of family or friends, and interviews with these outside sources are often quite helpful. Detection of the vegetative signs of depression—weight loss, insomnia, anhedonia—is obviously critical at this point. Affect is most often congruent with mood, so that a patient with a sad affect usually does feel depressed and an elated, euphoric patient usually feels manic. One must bear in mind, however, that affect may not accurately reflect mood, particularly in patients with cerebral disease. The pathologic weeping or laughter of patients with *pseudobulbar affect* from bifrontal disease, for example, is often incongruent with their mood, and patients with right hemisphere lesions may appear indifferent but actually be depressed. A final point is that primary motor disorders must not be mistaken for an affective disturbance; the masked facies of Parkinson's Disease, for example, is not indicative of flat affect.

A Brief Screening Examination

The use of an abbreviated mental status examination is indicated for patients in whom neurobehavioral function is suspected, but not known, to be intact. Such an exam should consist of

1. assessment of arousal and attention from the history taking,

2. memory testing by verifying events of the medical history and asking for three words to be recalled after five minutes,

3. probing language in terms of fluency, comprehension, repetition, and naming,

4. having the patient draw a clock with the hands at 11:10,

5. assessing complex cognition with an idiom, a proverb, and a relatively difficult arithmetic problem, and

6. asking about mood and judging affect.

Standardized Mental Status Testing

The procedures described above for evaluating mental status offer a general framework to help organize the practical testing of extremely complex clinical phenomena. This kind of evaluation allows the clinician to be comprehensive enough to sample all major neurobehavioral domains yet flexible enough to adapt the process to focus on salient problems that may appear. The result is a clinical impression that does not produce a single score for a patient's performance, but rather a richly descriptive portrayal of deficits and strengths that captures the essence of the individual's neurobehavioral profile.

There are times, however, when this somewhat subjective approach can be complemented by more objective evaluation, and the use of standardized tests that generate comparative scores is often helpful. One popular test of this type is the Mini Mental State Examination (MMSE) (Folstein et al., 1975), which yields a score between 0 and 30 and requires only five to ten minutes for administration (see Table 2.2).

Despite the advantage of its brevity and the fact that patients with neurologic conditions usually score lower than those with psychiatric illnesses (Lezak, 1983), this test is not a substitute for careful mental status examination as previously described because it is simply too limited. For example, the MMSE is heavily weighted to assess language, allocating only one point for visuospatial skills, so that a patient with a large right hemisphere lesion might well be misdiagnosed as normal because of a near-perfect score of 29. The MMSE and similar tests, however, are useful in the longitudinal evaluation of dementia patients; in general, patients with Alzheimer's Disease can be expected to decline by three points per year on the MMSE (Salmon et al., 1990).

More detailed standardized testing, of course, is available by referral to a neuropsychologist. Neuropsychological testing extends and elaborates the mental status evaluation but, as with the MMSE, does not replace it. The information gathered by neuropsychological assessment is particularly helpful if it is unclear whether the patient has neurologic or psychiatric illness and is also helpful in establishing the pattern and severity of deficits in patients with known structural damage. These data may assist greatly in rehabilitation, counseling, and litigation issues.

Although it is not our purpose in this book to discuss neuropsychology in detail, a brief comment on its methods is helpful. Two

Table 2.2 Mini Mental State Examination[*]

Maximum Score	Score	
		Orientation
5	( )	What is the (year) (season) (date) (day) (month)?
5	( )	Where are we: (state) (county) (town) (hospital) (floor)?
		Registration
3	( )	Name three objects, one second to say each, then ask the patient to repeat all three after you have said them. Give one point for each correct answer. Continue repeating all three objects until the patient learns all three.
		Attention and Calculation
5	( )	Serial sevens. One point for each correct response. Stop after five answers. Alternatively, spell "world" backward.
		Recall
3	( )	Ask for the three objects named in *Registration.* Give one point for each correct answer.
		Language
2	( )	Name a pencil and watch.
1	( )	Repeat the following: "No ifs, ands, or buts."
3	( )	Follow a three-stage command: "Take this paper in your right hand, fold it in half, and put it on the floor."
1	( )	Read and obey the following: CLOSE YOUR EYES.
1	( )	Write a sentence.
1	( )	Copy a design.

30	Total

[*] Source: M. F. Folstein, S.E. Folstein, and P. R. McHugh. 1975. "Mini-mental state." A practical method for grading the cognitive state of patients for the clinician. *J. Psychiatr Res;* 12: 189–198. Reprinted with permission from Elsevier Science Ltd., Pergamon Imprint, Oxford, England.

broad philosophies are represented in the field, one adhering to highly structured batteries of tests such as the Halstead-Reitan Battery (Russell et al., 1970) and the Luria-Nebraska Battery (Golden, 1981), from which a myriad of scores are generated, and the other advocating a "process approach" in which the way a patient carries out a task is given particular attention (Kaplan, 1983). In the former, a quantitative evaluation is considered paramount, whereas the latter stresses qualitative assessment as most revealing. Neuropsychologists usually adopt an intermediate position, considering both scores, which allows comparison of a patient to many others who have been similarly tested, and individualized assessments of performance to characterize particular neuropsychological features.

An impressive number of tests has been assembled by neuropsychologists to probe the various areas of neurobehavioral function (Lezak, 1983). Table 2.3 lists some of the more commonly used neuropsychological measures, grouped by the major functional domain they assess. This is far from an exhaustive list, and it emphasizes measures that correspond reasonably well to the cognitive and emotional domains established in this book; many other neuropsychological tests may yield useful information, depending on the individual patient under consideration.

Table 2.3 Popular neuropsychological tests

General intellectual ability
Wechsler Adult Intelligence Scale—Revised (WAIS-R)
(Wechsler, 1981)
Dementia Rating Scale (Mattis, 1988)
Mini Mental State Examination (Folstein et al., 1975)

Attention
Digit Span (from WAIS-R) (Wechsler, 1981)
Digit Vigilance Test (Lewis and Rennick, 1979)
Trail Making Test (Reitan and Davison, 1974)
Paced Auditory Serial Addition Test (Gronwall, 1977)

Memory
Wechsler Memory Scale—Revised (WMS-R) (Wechsler, 1987)
California Verbal Learning Test (Delis et al., 1987)
Rey Auditory Verbal Learning Test (Lezak, 1983)

Table 2.3 Popular neuropsychological tests (Continued)

Language
Aphasia Screening Test (Reitan, 1984)
Boston Diagnostic Aphasia Examination (Goodglass and Kaplan, 1983)
Boston Diagnostic Aphasia Examination (Goodglass and Kaplan, 1983)
Boston Naming Test (Kaplan et al., 1983)
Verbal Associative Fluency Test (Benton, 1968)

Visuospatial ability
Rey-Osterrieth Complex Figure Test (Lezak, 1983)
Boston Parietal Drawings (Goodglass and Kaplan, 1983)
Hooper Visual Organization Test (Hooper, 1958)
Judgment of Line Orientation Test (Benton et al., 1978)

Complex cognition
Wisconsin Card Sorting Test (Grant and Berg, 1948)
Category Test (Reitan and Davison, 1974)
Stroop Test (Stroop, 1935)
Raven's Progressive Matrices (Raven, 1960)

Emotion and personality
Beck Depression Inventory (Beck et al., 1961)
Minnesota Multiphasic Personality Inventory (MMPI) (Hathaway and McKinley, 1967)

References

Alexander, M.P., Stuss, D.T., and Benson, D.F. 1979. Capgras syndrome: a reduplicative phenomenon. *Neurology;* 29: 334–339.

Baddeley, A. 1992. Working memory. *Science;* 255: 556–559.

Beck, A.T., Ward, C.H., Mendelson, M., et al. 1961. An inventory for measuring depression. *Arch Gen Psychiat;* 4: 561–571.

Benson, D.F., Gardner, H., and Meadows, J.C. 1976. Reduplicative paramnesia. *Neurology;* 26: 147–151.

Benton, A.L. 1968. Differential behavioral effects in frontal lobe disease. *Neuropsychologia;* 6: 53–60.

Benton, A.L., Varney, N.R., and Hamsher, K. deS. 1978. Visuospatial judgement. A clinical test. *Arch Neurol;* 35: 364–367.

Berrios, G.E. 1982. Tactile hallucinations: conceptual and historical aspects. *J Neurol Neurosurg Psychiatry;* 45: 285–293.

Cummings, J.L. 1985a. *Clinical Neuropsychiatry.* Orlando, Fla., Grune and Stratton.

Cummings, J.L. 1985b. Organic delusions: phenomenology, anatomical correlations, and review. *Br J Psychiat;* 146: 184–197.

Cummings, J.L. 1992. Psychosis in neurologic disease. *Neuropsychiatry Neuropsychol Behav Neurol;* 5: 144–150.

Cummings, J.L., and Miller, B.L. 1987. Visual hallucinations. Clinical occurrence and use in differential diagnosis. *West J Med;* 146: 46–51.

Cummings, J.L., and Victoroff, J.I. 1990. Noncognitive neuropsychiatric syndromes in Alzheimer's Disease. *Neuropsychiatry Neuropsychol Behav Neurol;* 3: 140–158.

Daly, D.D. 1975. Ictal clinical manifestations of complex partial seizures. *Adv Neurol;* 11: 57–82.

Damas-Mora, J., Skelton-Robinson, M., and Jenner, F.A. 1982. The Charles Bonnet syndrome in perspective. *Psychol Med;* 12: 251–261.

Delis, D.C., Kramer, J.H., Kaplan, E., and Ober, B.A. 1987. *California Verbal Learning Test.* San Antonio, Psychological Corporation.

Dunn, D.W., Weisberg, L.A., and Nadell, J. 1983. Peduncular hallucinations caused by brain stem compression. *Neurology;* 33: 1360–1361.

Folstein, M.F., Folstein, S.E., and McHugh, P.R. 1975. "Mini-mental state." A practical method for grading the cognitive state of patients for the clinician. *J Psychiatr Res;* 12: 189–198.

Golden, C.J. 1981. A standardized version of Luria's neuropsychological tests: a quantitative and qualitative approach to neuropsychological evaluation. In: Filskov, S.B., and Boll, T.J. (eds). *Handbook of Clinical Neuropsychology.* New York, Wiley-Interscience, pp. 608–642.

Goodglass, H., and Kaplan, E. 1983. *The Assessment of Aphasia and Related Disorders.* 2nd ed. Philadelphia, Lea and Febiger.

Grant, D.A., and Berg, E.A. 1948. A behavioral analysis of degree of reinforcement and ease of shifting to new responses in a Weigl-type cart-sorting problem. *J Exp Psychol;* 38: 404–411.

Gronwall, D.M.A. 1977. Paced auditory serial addition task: a measure of recovery from concussion. *Percep Motor Skills;* 44: 367–373.

Hathaway, S.R., and McKinley, J.C. 1951. *The Minnesota Multiphasic Personality Inventory Manual* (revised). New York, Psychological Corporation.

Hecaen, H., and Albert, M.L. 1978. *Human Neuropsychology.* New York, John Wiley and Sons.

Hooper, H.E. 1958. *The Hooper Visual Organization Test Manual.* Los Angeles, Western Psychological Services.

Jacobs, L., Feldman, M., Diamond, S.P., and Bender, M.B. 1973. Palinacousis: persistent or recurring auditory sensations. *Cortex;* 9: 275–287.

James, W. *The Principles of Psychology.* New York, Henry Holt.

Kaplan, E. 1983. Process and achievement revisited. In: Wapner, S., and Kaplan, B. (eds.). *Toward a Holistic Developmental Psychology.* Hillsdale, N.J., Lawrence Erlbaum, pp. 143–156.

Kaplan, E., Goodglass, H., and Weintraub, S. 1983. *Boston Naming Test*. Philadelphia, Lea and Febiger.

King, D.W., and Marsan, C.A. 1977. Clinical features and ictal patterns in epileptic patients with EEG temporal lobe foci. *Ann Neurol;* 2: 138–147.

Kirshner, H.S. 1986. *Behavioral Neurology. A Practical Approach*. New York, Churchill Livingstone.

Lepore, F.E. 1990. Spontaneous visual phenomena with visual loss: 104 patients with lesions of retinal and neural afferent pathways. *Neurology;* 40: 444–447.

Lessell, S. 1975. Higher disorders of visual function; positive phenomena. In: Glaser, J.S., and Smith, J.L. (eds.). *Neuro-ophthalmology*. Vol. VIII. St. Louis, C.V. Mosby, pp. 27–44.

Lewis, R.F., and Rennick, P.M. 1979. *Manual for the Repeatable Cognitive-Perceptual-Motor Battery*. Grosse Pointe Park, MI, Axon Publishing Co.

Lezak, M.D. 1983. *Neuropsychological Assessment*. 2nd ed. New York, Oxford.

Lipowski, Z.J. 1980. *Delirium. Acute Brain Failure in Man*. Springfield, Charles C. Thomas.

Luria, A.R. 1973. *The Working Brain*. New York, Basic Books, pp. 187–225.

Mattis, S. 1988. *Dementia Rating Scale*. Odessa, FL, Psychological Assessment Resources.

Mesulam, M.-M. 1985. Patterns in behavioral anatomy: association areas, the limbic system, and hemispheric specialization. In: Mesulam, M.-M. *Principles of Behavioral Neurology*. Philadelphia, F.A. Davis.

Plum, F., and Posner, J.B. 1982. *The Diagnosis of Stupor and Coma*. 3rd ed. Philadelphia, F.A. Davis.

Raven, J.C. 1960. *Guide to the Standard Progressive Matrices*. London, H.K. Lewis.

Reitan, R.M. 1984. *Aphasia and Sensory-Perceptual Deficits in Adults*. Tucson, Reitan Neuropsychology Laboratories.

Reitan, R.M., and Davison, L.A. 1974. *Clinical Neuropsychology: Current Status and Applications*. New York, Hemisphere.

Russell, E.W., Neuringer, C., and Goldstein, G. 1970. *Assessment of Brain Damage: A Neuropsychological Key Approach*. New York, Wiley Interscience.

Salmon, D.P., Thal, L.J., Butters, N., and Heindel, W.C. 1990. Longitudinal evaluation of dementia of the Alzheimer type: a comparison of 3 standardized mental status examinations. *Neurology;* 40: 1225–1230.

Siegel, R.K. 1977. Hallucinations. *Sci Am;* 237(4): 132–140.

Stagno, S.J., and Gates, T.J. 1991. Palinopsia: a review of the literature. *Behav Neurol;* 4: 67–74.

Stroop, J.R. 1935. Studies of interference in serial verbal reactions. *J Exp Psychol;* 18: 643–662.

Strub, R.L., and Black, F.W. 1993. *The Mental Status Examination in Neurology* 3rd ed. Philadelphia, F.A. Davis.

Stuss, D.T., and Benson, D.F. 1986. *The Frontal Lobes*. New York, Raven.

Victor, M., and Hope, J.M. 1958. The phenomenon of auditory hallucinations in chronic alcoholism. *J Nerv Ment Dis;* 126: 451–481.

Wechsler, D.A. 1981. *Wechsler Adult Intelligence Scale—Revised (WAIS-R)*. New York, Psychological Corporation.

Wechsler, D.A. 1987. *Wechsler Memory Scale—Revised*. New York, Psychological Corporation.

Weintraub, S., and Mesulam, M.-M. 1985. Mental state assessment in young and elderly adults in behavioral neurology. In: Mesulam, M.-M. *Principles of Behavioral Neurology*. Philadelphia, F.A. Davis, pp. 71–123.

CHAPTER 3

Disorders of Arousal and Attention

Disturbances of arousal and attention comprise a heterogeneous and challenging group of neurobehavioral syndromes. Ranging in severity from coma after brain stem infarction to subtle acute confusional states related to drug intoxication, these disorders are not only common clinically but provide many insights into the brain's capacity to enable uniquely human mental life. Moreover, they bear directly upon the fundamental question of the nature of consciousness, an ancient philosophical conundrum that can now be usefully addressed in a neuroscientific context. This chapter will jointly consider the arousal and attentional disorders in some detail, as they are closely linked in the mental status examination and have several clinical and neuroanatomic similarities. First, however, some general background related to these topics merits consideration.

In order for any higher mental function to occur, the human brain must possess a mechanism that can maintain the waking state as well as a means to permits the ability to focus awareness on behaviorally relevant external stimuli. Both of these systems are indeed present, and it is useful and widely accepted to refer to them respectively as the arousal system and the attentional system. In everyday terms, the simple observation that one can be awake without being attentive suggests that arousal and attention are in fact separable. In a neurologic context, individuals who are in a vegetative state provide a dramatic example of this distinction: there is massive bilateral hemispheric damage, with sparing of the brain stem, leaving a patient with intact arousal but absent attention (Multi-Society Task Force on PVS, 1994).

Arousal refers to the phenomenon of wakefulness, and comparable terms include "awareness" and "alertness." Disorders of arousal therefore imply a departure from normal wakefulness, excluding, of course, the physiologic process of sleep. *Attention* is a complex concept that has been given many meanings, but in general it refers specifically to *selective attention,* the capacity to direct awareness to specific aspects of the extrapersonal space and simultaneously screen out competing but irrelevant information. When selective attention is operative over an extended period, *sustained attention* is said to be active, and alternative terms for this phenomenon are "vigilance" and "concentration." Another pertinent concept is *directed attention,* which refers to selective attention directed to the contralateral hemispace.

It is apparent that these disorders all imply some form of dysfunction in the realm of consciousness, which has recently been the subject of renewed neuroscientific interest despite its enigmatic philosophical reputation. Neurologists have found it useful to distinguish between the *level* of consciousness, or the degree of arousal, and the *content* of consciousness, the sum of all mental functions (Plum and Posner, 1982); attention as reviewed in the previous paragraph would thus be one aspect of the content of consciousness. Arousal can be envisioned figuratively as the source of the neural energy that powers the mental apparatus; this requirement met, the full expression of consciousness then involves the participation of all cognitive and emotional domains. As will be seen, disorders of the level and content of consciousness can be clinically dissociated, and each has a relatively secure, although often overlapping, neuroanatomy. Coma, the prototype syndrome of impaired arousal, results most directly from discrete lesions of the brain stem and thalamus, whereas acute confusional state, the classic syndrome of impaired attention, generally follows hemispheric dysfunction. It follows that a disorder of arousal always involves an attentional disorder as well, but the converse is not true; an acute confusional state may affect attention while largely sparing arousal.

Implicit in all these issues, of course, is the notion of consciousness itself. Many would take consciousness to mean the awareness of self, a notion highlighting the self-reflective aspect of human consciousness that seems characteristic. Yet despite this sturdy conception, and the convenient classifications of impaired consciousness that clinicians and researchers have put to good use, there is still something unfathomable about this most important property of the human mind. There is, to be sure, no reason to doubt that the structure and function of the brain account in some way for the phenomenon of consciousness, but the

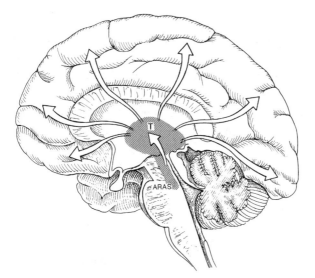

Figure 3.1 Midsagittal view of the brain illustrating structures responsible for arousal: the ascending reticular activating system (ARAS) and the thalamus (T).

actual means by which neuronal activity is transformed into subjective conscious experience remains as yet an impenetrable mystery.

Arousal Dysfunction

The anatomy of arousal has been elucidated in considerable detail, although uncertainties remain. Classic experiments using laboratory animals in the mid-twentieth century (Moruzzi and Magoun, 1949) convincingly established that arousal is dependent on a widely distributed structure in the rostral brain stem that has come to be called the ascending reticular activating system (ARAS). Because it has indistinct boundaries throughout its extent, the ARAS is more a physiologic concept than an anatomic entity; it can be visualized, however, as a portion of the reticular formation in the core of the brain stem extending from the pons to the thalamus via the midbrain (Figure 3.1). Although the ARAS receives important input from all sensory modalities—accounting for the rapid arousal that ensues when, for example, one touches a hot stove—there are endogenous mechanisms for arousal as well. One example of such an intrinsic mechanism is the cyclical alternation between wakefulness and sleep, which, although still poorly understood, clearly depends in large measure on an active neurochemical process occurring in the ARAS (Hobson, 1990). From the thalamus, further connections to the hemispheres are made (Morison and Dempsey, 1942). The ARAS ascends to the intralaminar nuclei of the thalamus, the two largest of which are the centromedian and parafascicular nuclei, and from these midline relay stations originate diffuse projections to widespread areas of the cortex (Figure 3.1). The graphic record of brain electrical activity known as the electroencephalogram (EEG) depends on the integrity of the ARAS and the thalamocortical projection system working in synchrony to produce the rhythmic oscillations recorded from the scalp (Plum and Posner, 1982).

Clinical disorders of arousal may take a number of forms, resulting either in hyperaroused or, more commonly, hypoaroused states. Hyperarousal can appear as restlessness, agitation, or delirium, all presumably due to some loss of inhibitory control in the hemispheres that releases lower structures from normal regulation. Hypoarousal can take many forms, depending on the severity of the causative condition. Less severe deficits can be roughly described by use of a spectrum of descriptors ranging from drowsiness and somnolence to lethargy and obtundation. More dramatic are the two syndromes of *stupor*, a state of unresponsiveness from which arousal can be achieved only by vigorous and repeated stimulation, and *coma*, a state of unarousable unresponsiveness (Plum and Posner, 1982). The clinical neurologic literature supports the thesis that the arousal system in the upper brain stem and thalamus does indeed maintain alertness (Brain, 1958; Katz et al., 1987), and a variety of structural lesions in these regions, including infarcts, hemorrhages, tumors, and abscesses, have caused stupor and coma. As a general rule, small and restricted lesions in the arousal system can be sufficient to result in stupor or coma, whereas hemispheric lesions must be extensive and bilateral to produce the same picture. Deep midline lesions of the brain stem and diencephalon, therefore, are most clearly associated with disorders of arousal.

Three conditions require brief consideration before leaving the topic of arousal dysfunction. These are all disorders in which the absence of movement and speech suggests an arousal disorder but which in fact do not involve this kind of disturbance. The devastating syndrome of the *persistent vegetative state* (PVS) implies massive bilateral hemispheric insult from trauma, anoxia, degenerative disease, or other etiologies and leaves the patient with absent mentation but normal arousal (Multi-Society Task

Force on PVS, 1994). Such a patient has preserved sleep-wake cycles and appears, during waking, to be alert, but has no self-awareness or other evidence of higher function. *Akinetic mutism* is similar to PVS but involves less widespread destruction, often in medial frontal areas, and patients display an extreme form of abulia (Chapter 10). Arousal and sleep-wake cycles are normal, but motivation is absent to perform any motor or mental action. Finally, the *locked-in syndrome* involves no mental deficit at all, but patients are "de-efferented" by a lesion in the pons that spares the ARAS but causes quadriplegia. Only by careful examination using vertical eye movements and eye opening—which are preserved because they are mediated by the midbrain—will it be apparent that no alteration of consciousness is present. All three of these conditions need to be distinguished from stupor and coma.

The arousal system deep in the brain is clearly necessary for human mental life, but it is far from sufficient. The hemispheres, in contrast, are dedicated to the content of consciousness—the total of all the human cognitive and emotional functions. The remainder of this book deals with disorders in which the content of consciousness is specifically affected.

Attentional Dysfunction

Attention, a complex psychological concept, is more difficult to relate to brain structure than arousal. Because attentional competence underlies all higher function, attention plays a role in every conscious action and is therefore widely distributed across the entire brain. Still, clinical observations and recent functional imaging data indicate that certain regions play a special role in this fundamental neurobehavioral domain. Having seen how brain stem and thalamic structures regulate arousal, we now proceed to the cerebral hemispheres as areas more involved in attention. The common neurobehavioral syndrome known as the acute confusional state will serve as a vivid illustration of the clinical importance and neuroanatomic basis of disordered attention.

The *acute confusional state* is one of the most common conditions encountered in medical and neurologic practice (Taylor and Lewis, 1993). The abrupt appearance of confusion in a previously healthy person signifies a serious disturbance of the brain that can have any of one or more numerous causes. Recognition of the acute confusional state is crucial because most of its etiologies are reversible if treated promptly (Taylor and Lewis,

1993). The reversibility of this syndrome is due to the fact that most cases involve toxic or metabolic disorders that exert a widespread but not initially destructive effect upon the brain. Only if the insult persists without treatment for an extended period is there the possibility of irreversible structural damage. In the less common cases in which structural damage is the immediate cause of the syndrome, the outcome may be less favorable.

"Confusion" is a somewhat problematic word because its strong ordinary meaning interferes with its medical specificity. In neurobehavioral terms, *confusion* is best thought of as the inability to maintain a coherent line of thought (Geschwind, 1982). There is difficulty attending to meaningful environmental stimuli, and at the same time distractibility results from undue attention to irrelevant external material. The acute confusional state refers to a rapidly evolving disorder of selective attention that precludes the adequate performance of other neurobehavioral operations in the domains of memory, language, visuospatial skills, and the like (Chedru and Geschwind, 1972a). To a lesser extent, arousal is also affected, and, in practice, arousal and attentional deficits are often commingled. Some cases, in fact, evolve from acute arousal deficits to persistent attentional disturbances (Katz et al., 1987).

There are some alternate designations for the acute confusional state. Some authorities, usually from the perspective of internal medicine, use the term *toxic-metabolic encephalopathy*, which has the advantage of indicating the most common causes of the syndrome and the fact that they affect the brain diffusely. Others follow the psychiatric practice and prefer the colorful word *delirium*, implying a state of agitated confusion with associated autonomic overactivity (American Psychiatric Association, 1994). In the context of behavioral neurology, however, "acute confusional state" is preferred because it identifies the fundamental clinical impairment that is invariably present: the disorder of attention known as confusion. Furthermore, the term "toxic-metabolic encephalopathy" fails to include other causes of the syndrome, such as trauma, seizures, and stroke, and the term "delirium" neglects the hypoactive or lethargic confusional states without autonomic overactivity that are in fact more common than the hyperactive and agitated states of delirium. The term "acute organic brain syndrome" is too vague and nonspecific to be of any use and is not recommended.

Clinical features of the acute confusional state are usually quite readily apparent. *Inattention* with poor mental control, concentration, and vigilance is the central deficit, and *distractibility* and *disorientation* are also typically present. Performance on the digit span test is reduced, reflecting an impairment in the brain's normal capacity to process information (Miller, 1956). A frequent finding is a fluctuating level of consciousness, which is not ordinarily seen in dementia, aphasia, and psychiatric disorders (Cummings, 1985). Other prominent problems that may appear are bizarre, confabulated naming errors known as *nonaphasic misnaming* (Weinstein and Keller, 1963), and disordered writing with spatial aberrations and spelling errors (Chedru and Geschwind, 1972b). Memory deficits, insofar as they are testable, are present. Aphasia in the usual sense (Chapter 5) is not seen, although mild anomia, verbal paraphasias, and dysarthria are common. Visuospatial dysfunction is usually encountered. In *delirium tremens*, the most dramatic of the acute confusional states, there is profound agitation associated with hallucinations, delusions, insomnia, tachycardia, hypertension, fever, diaphoresis, and tremor (Charness et al., 1989). The acute confusional state is particularly common in the elderly (Lipowski, 1983), and manifestations in the evening hours ("sundowning") may be especially troublesome. Individuals with pre-existing neurobehavioral impairment are also more prone to develop the syndrome (Lipowski, 1980). The EEG is useful in diagnosis because of the typical appearance of generalized theta (four to seven Hertz) or delta (one to three Hertz) range slowing (Obrecht et al., 1979).

The causes of acute confusional state constitute a very long list (Table 3.1). A great variety of intoxicants, metabolic disorders, infections, epileptic conditions, vascular events, traumatic injuries, and neoplasms can prove to be responsible, and the postsurgical state is a frequent setting for its appearance (Strub, 1982). The vascular syndromes are less well recognized but important: infarctions in the distribution of the posterior cerebral arteries (Medina et al., 1974), the anterior communicating artery (Alexander and Freedman, 1984), and the right middle cerebral artery (Mesulam et al., 1976) may all cause an acute confusional state. In the last example, destruction of the right parietal lobe—important in directed attention—is a plausible cause of the syndrome; the other locations are more difficult to explain, although any high-order association cortex could be selectively vulnerable (Mesulam, 1985). Psychiatric disorders

Table 3.1 Major etiologies of the acute confusional state

Toxic	**Vascular**
Prescription drugs	Stroke
Nonprescription drugs	Subarachnoid hemorrhage
Drug withdrawal	**Traumatic**
Metabolic	Concussion
Hypoxia	Severe traumatic brain injury
Hypoglycemia	**Neoplastic**
Uremia	Deep midline tumors
Hepatic disease	Increased intracranial pressure
Thiamine deficiency	**Postsurgical**
Electrolyte disturbances	Preoperative atropine
Endocrinopathies	Hypoxia
Infectious and inflammatory	Analgesics
Meningitis	Electrolyte imbalance
Encephalitis	Fever
Vasculitis	
Abscess	
Epileptic	
Postictal state	
Complex partial status epilepticus	
Absence status epilepticus	

such as schizophrenia or mania may present with features that mimic but are distinct from those that characterize the acute confusional state, and a patient with acute Wernicke's aphasia can be mistakenly diagnosed as acutely confused. Mental status evaluation proves invaluable in distinguishing between these possibilities, and the appropriate use of laboratory and neuroradiologic tests is also indispensable.

Treatment of the acute confusional state depends on its cause, which must be sought by a prompt and comprehensive neurologic and medical evaluation. While the cause is being sought and addressed, supportive care is also important (Lipowski, 1987). In most cases the syndrome will be partially or completely reversible; often a simple dosage reduction or withdrawal of psychoactive medications—especially in older persons—results in a gratifying recovery. It is well to bear in mind, however, that recovery may require days to weeks in the elderly, particularly if more than one causative factor has been involved. Finally, it should be added that the acute confusional state can be fatal if the underlying conditions are sufficiently serious (Liston, 1982).

Another syndrome that appears to involve attentional dysfunction is the controversial disorder known as *attention-deficit/hyperactivity disorder* (ADHD). Originally described in children of school age, ADHD has recently been postulated to occur also in adulthood as a so-called "residual type" (Denckla, 1991). This syndrome essentially refers to individuals who have difficulty paying attention, completing tasks, organizing activity, and planning ahead; many are hyperactive, impulsive, and restless, leading to a formal distinction between "inattentive" and "hyperactive-impulsive" subtypes (American Psychiatric Association, 1994). Although there are as yet no demonstrable brain abnormalities in these individuals, recent findings have implicated dysfunction of both frontal lobes and right hemisphere systems. Neuropsychological evidence suggesting frontal but not temporal lobe dysfunction has been found in ADHD children (Shue and Douglas, 1992). In addition, functional imaging studies have found bilateral premotor and prefrontal hypometabolism in adults with hyperactivity of childhood onset (Zametkin et al., 1990). In contrast, children with right hemisphere lesions have been found to have a high incidence of attention deficit disorder (Voeller, 1986). Moreover, findings of hemineglect in children with attention deficit disorder have suggested right hemisphere dysfunction (Voeller and Heilman, 1988). By analogy with studies in adults showing a tendency of right frontal lesions to cause motor impersistence (Kertesz et al., 1985), it may be that ADHD represents a nonstructural deficit in right frontal function.

It would be premature to suggest that there is an established neuroanatomy for attention. As mentioned previously, attention is required for all higher functions and thus can be said to be associated with all brain areas. However, certain regions do appear to be particularly affiliated with attention. A substantial literature exists on the prominent role of the right hemisphere in attention, and Chapter 8 will take up this topic in detail. There is also good reason to believe that the frontal lobes and their connections play a complementary role in this function. This frontal lobe contribution will now be considered at some length, with the aim of proposing that the right frontal lobe may represent the intersection of the right hemisphere and frontal attentional systems.

The frontal lobes appear to be particularly crucial to many aspects of attentional function (Luria, 1973; Stuss and Benson, 1984; Mesulam, 1985). Receiving extensive projections from the brain stem and thalamus,

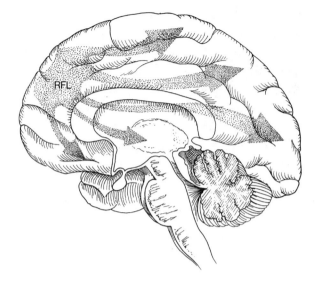

Figure 3.2 Midsagittal view of the brain illustrating the role of the frontal lobes in attention. RFL—right frontal lobe.

the frontal lobes themselves send dense projections to posterior cortical and subcortical regions and conversely receive reciprocal connections in return. It is clear that the frontal lobes are richly connected with all other regions of the hemispheres (Figure 3.2), and are thus anatomically situated to exert a regulatory and organizing influence upon the rest of the brain (Chapter 10). Numerous case studies from the clinical literature amply verify that frontal lesions can have a profound effect on the attentional abilities of affected patients (Stuss and Benson, 1984).

The prefrontal areas may be of particular importance with regard to attention (Weinberger, 1993). In keeping with the "executive" role of the dorsolateral frontal regions (Chapter 10), the prefrontal areas are intimately involved with the mediation of attention and the performance of purposeful activity (Weinberger, 1993). Functional imaging studies have consistently found that normal individuals responding to incoming stimuli or performing mental operations activate prefrontal areas regardless of what posterior sensory or cognitive region is also activated. Risberg and Ingvar (1973) found that the greatest increase in regional cerebral blood flow during a reverse digit span task was in the prefrontal areas. Roland (1982) noted that the prefrontal cortex was strongly activated whether subjects were attending to visual, auditory, or tactile stimuli. Mazziotta et al. (1982) found that prefrontal regions were activated by both verbal and nonverbal auditory stimuli.

Although both frontal lobes clearly play a role in attention, there may be an advantage for the right frontal lobe in this capacity. This advantage may be most apparent in terms of sustained attention or vigilance. Motor impersistence, as we have seen, is most typically seen after right frontal lesions (Kertesz et al., 1985). Recent neuropsychological evidence suggests that right frontal lesions are particularly detrimental to sustained attention (Wilkins et al., 1987). Positron emission tomography (PET) data from normal subjects engaged in vigilance tasks (Cohen et al., 1988) and tasks requiring heightened effort (Bench et al., 1993) also implicate the right frontal lobe. Another PET study found both the right prefrontal and parietal areas to be active under similar conditions (Pardo et al., 1991), leading to the idea that a network of right hemisphere structures is uniquely designed for the maintenance of sustained attention. Although it is unclear precisely how the frontal lobes and right hemisphere interact in the phenomena of attention, the right frontal lobe may represent the anatomic overlap of two distributed networks subserving attentional function. Further clinical study of patients with right frontal lesions in this light would be highly informative.

Finally, the cerebral white matter is likely to have a role in the regulation of attention. Because of the extensive white matter connections between the frontal lobes and the remainder of the cerebrum (Chapter 12), myelinated axons in the hemispheres play an important part in the regulatory functions of the frontal lobes that enable other cognitive and emotional operations of the brain. It is noteworthy that cortical deficits such as aphasia, apraxia, and agnosia are not typical of acute confusional states (Chedru and Geschwind, 1972a), implying that dysfunction in structures underlying the cortex is more implicated in the genesis of attentional deficits. A wide variety of cerebral white matter disorders have a prominent impact on attention, leading to the idea that white matter plays a crucial role in the cerebral networks mediating attention (Filley, in press). Reduced size of the corpus callosum, for example, has been linked with vigilance deficits in adults with multiple sclerosis (Rao et al., 1989) and has also been found in ADHD (Giedd et al., 1994), implying that frontal interhemispheric communication may be critical in the maintenance of sustained attention. The importance of the cerebral white matter in this and other areas of behavioral neurology will be considered more thoroughly in Chapter 12.

This discussion should not be interpreted as suggesting that the frontal lobes are dedicated centers for attention or even that attentional disorders are reliably encountered after any frontal lobe lesion. Attention is a widely distributed phenomenon (Mesulam, 1985; Posner and Peterson, 1990), and, as we have seen, a wide variety of lesions can disrupt it. Instead, the intent has been to illustrate how selective attention can be theoretically linked to the frontal regions with the aid of increasingly sophisticated clinical and experimental techniques. Although clearly not reducible to one cerebral area, attention will likely be found to have a special affiliation with the frontal lobes, perhaps the right in particular, in keeping with the powerful organizational influence of the frontal lobes in general.

References

Alexander, M.P., and Freedman, M. 1984. Amnesia after anterior communicating artery aneurysm rupture. *Neurology;* 34: 752–757.

American Psychiatric Association. 1994. *Diagnostic and Statistical Manual of Mental Disorders.* 4th ed. Washington, D.C., American Psychiatric Association.

Bench, C.J., Frith, C.D., Grasby, P.M., et al. 1993. Investigations of the functional anatomy of attention using the Stroop test. *Neuropsychologia;* 31: 907–922.

Brain, R. 1958. The physiological basis of consciousness. *Brain;* 81: 426–455.

Charness, M.E., Simon, R.P., and Greenberg, D.A. 1989. Ethanol and the nervous system. *N Engl J Med;* 321: 442–454.

Chedru, F., and Geschwind, N. 1972a. Disorders of higher cortical functions in acute confusional states. *Cortex;* 8: 395–411.

Chedru, F., and Geschwind, N. 1972b. Writing disturbances in acute confusional states. *Neuropsychologia;* 10: 343–354.

Cohen, R.M., Semple, W.E., Gross, M., et al. 1988. Functional localization of sustained attention: comparison to sensory stimulation in the absence of instruction. *Neuropsychiatry Neuropsychol Behav Neurol;* 1: 3–20.

Cummings, J.L. 1985. *Clinical Neuropsychiatry.* Orlando, Grune and Stratton.

Denckla, M.B. 1991. Attention deficit hyperactivity disorder—residual type. *J Child Neurol;* 6: S44-S48.

Filley, C.M. In press. Neurobehavioral aspects of cerebral white matter disorders. In: Fogel, B.S., Schiffer, R.B., and Rao, S.M. (eds.). *Comprehensive Neuropsychiatry.* Baltimore, Williams and Wilkins.

Geschwind, N. 1982. Disorders of attention: a frontier in neuropsychology. *Phil Trans R Soc Lond;* 298: 173–185.

Giedd, J.N., Castellanos, F.X., Casey, B.J., et al. 1994. Quantitative morphology of the corpus callosum in attention deficit hyperactivity disorder. *Am J Psychiatry;* 151: 665–669.

Hobson, J.A. 1990. Sleep and dreaming. *J Neurosci;* 10: 371–382.

Katz, D.I., Alexander, M.P., and Mandell, A.M. 1987. Dementia following strokes in the mesencephalon and diencephalon. *Arch Neurol;* 44: 1127–1133.

Kertesz, A., Nicholson, I., Cancilliere, A., et al. 1985. Motor impersistence: a right hemisphere syndrome. *Neurology;* 35: 662–666.

Lipowski, Z.J. 1980. *Delirium: Acute Brain Failure in Man.* Springfield, Charles C. Thomas.

Lipowski, Z.J. 1983. Transient cognitive disorders (delirium, acute confusional states) in the elderly. *Am J Psychiatry;* 140: 1426–1436.

Lipowski, Z.J. 1987. Delirium (acute confusional states). *J Am Med Assoc;* 258: 1789–1792.

Liston, E.H. 1982. Delirium in the aged. *Psychiat Clin N Am;* 5(1): 49–66.

Luria, A.R. 1973. *The Working Brain.* New York, Basic Books.

Mazziotta, J.C., Phelps, M.E., Carson, R.E., and Kuhl, D.E. 1982. Tomographic mapping of human cerebral metabolism: auditory stimulation. *Neurology;* 32: 921–937.

Medina, J.L., Rubino, F.A., and Ross, E. 1974. Agitated delirium caused by infarction of the hippocampal formation and fusiform and lingual gyri: a case report. *Neurology;* 24: 1181–1183.

Mesulam, M.-M. 1985. Attention, confusional states, and neglect. In: Mesulam, M.-M. *Principles of Behavioral Neurology.* Philadelphia, F.A. Davis, pp. 125–168.

Mesulam, M.-M., Waxman, S.G., Geschwind, N., and Sabin, T.D. 1976. Acute confusional states with right middle cerebral artery infarctions. *J Neurol Neurosurg Psychiatry;* 39: 84–89.

Miller, G.A. 1956. The magical number seven, plus or minus two: some limits on our capacity for processing information. *Psychol Bull;* 63: 81–97.

Morison, R.S., and Dempsey, E.W. 1942. A study of thalamo-cortical relations. *Am J Physiol;* 135: 281–292.

Moruzzi, G., and Magoun H.W. 1949. Brain stem reticular formation and activation of the EEG. *Electroencephalogr Clin Neurophysiol;* 1: 455–473.

Multi-Society Task Force on PVS. 1994. Medical aspects of the persistent vegetative state. *N Engl J Med;* 330: 1499–1508, 1572–1579.

Obrecht, R., Okhomina, F.O.A., and Scott, D.F. 1979. Value of EEG in acute confusional states. *J Neurol Neurosurg Psychiatry;* 42: 75–77.

Pardo, J.V., Fox, P.T., and Raichle, M.E. 1991. Localization of a human system for sustained attention by positron emission tomography. *Nature;* 349: 61–64.

Plum, F., and Posner, J.B. 1982. *The Diagnosis of Stupor and Coma.* 3rd ed. Philadelphia, F.A. Davis.

Posner, M.I., and Peterson, S.E. 1990. The attention system of the human brain. *Ann Rev Neurosci;* 13: 25–42.

Rao, S.M., Leo, G.J., Haughton, V.M., et al. 1989. Correlation of magnetic resonance imaging with neuropsychological testing in multiple sclerosis. *Neurology;* 39: 161–166.

Risberg J., and Ingvar, D.H. 1973. Patterns of activation in the grey matter of the dominant hemisphere during memorizing and reasoning. *Brain;* 96: 737–756.

Roland, P.E. 1982. Cortical regulation of selective attention in man. A regional cerebral blood flow study. *J Neurophysiol;* 48: 1059–1078.

Shue, K.L., and Douglas, V.I. 1992. Attention deficit hyperactivity disorder and the frontal lobe syndrome. *Brain and Cognition;* 20: 104–124.

Strub, R.L. 1982. Acute confusional state. In: Benson, D.F., and Blumer, D. (eds.). *Psychiatric Aspects of Neurologic Disease.* Vol. 2. New York, Grune and Stratton, pp. 1–23.

Stuss, D.T., and Benson, D.F. 1984. Neuropsychological studies of the frontal lobes. *Psychol Bull;* 95: 3–28.

Taylor, D., and Lewis, S. 1993. Delirium. *J Neurol Neurosurg Psychiatry;* 56: 742–751.

Voeller, K.K.S. 1986. Right-hemisphere deficit syndrome in children. *Am J Psychiatry;* 143: 1004–1009.

Voeller, K.K.S., and Heilman, K.M. 1988. Attention deficit disorder in children: a neglect syndrome? *Neurology;* 38: 806–808.

Weinberger, D.R. 1993. A connectionist approach to the prefrontal cortex. *J Neuropsychiatry;* 5: 241–253.

Weinstein, E.A., and Keller, N.J.A. 1963. Linguistic patterns of misnaming in brain injury. *Neuropsychologia;* 1: 79–90.

Wilkins, A.J., Shallice, T., and McCarthy, R. 1987. Frontal lesions and sustained attention. *Neuropsychologia;* 25: 359–365.

Zametkin, A.J., Nordahl, T.E., Gross, M., et al. 1990. Cerebral glucose metabolism in adults with hyperactivity of childhood onset. *N Engl J Med;* 323: 1361–1366.

CHAPTER 4

Memory Disorders

Memory is a vital neurobehavioral domain that has long challenged students of behavior. Without an intact mnemonic system, past experience cannot be called upon to deal with present contingencies or to formulate future plans. Many different disciplines have made contributions to the study of memory, which now encompasses organisms as simple as the mollusk (Kandel and Hawkins, 1992) in addition to the higher primates and humans (Squire, 1982). This chapter will concentrate on those aspects of memory that have particular neurobehavioral significance, recognizing that many important memory phenomena have no established neuroanatomic correlates. Nevertheless, much has been learned about the neuroanatomy of clinically apparent memory disorders. In precise terms, "memory" refers to the retention of information, whereas "learning" indicates the acquisition of that information (Squire, 1987). For the sake of conciseness, memory disorders will be regarded here as including both learning and memory deficits.

Three temporally distinct types of memory will form the basis for the consideration of memory disorders. These varieties, also designated as primary, secondary, and tertiary memory, are based on approximate but still useful distinctions in time: *immediate memory*, which functions over a period of seconds; *recent memory*, in which material is held for minutes to days; and *remote memory*, referring to memory storage over months or years. Each of these can be tested conveniently during the mental status examination (Strub and Black, 1993), and each has meaningful neuroanatomic and clinical implications (Kirshner, 1986). This scheme is not meant to imply the irrelevance of other taxonomic categories of memory, but it does indicate that the most helpful clinical information can be gathered by operating within this framework.

Inattention

The most obvious manifestation of memory dysfunction in a broad sense is failure of immediate memory, which signifies the inability to register information because of *inattention*. Patients with acute confusional states (Chapter 3) clearly exemplify this kind of deficit. Most authorities prefer not to designate such a condition as an amnesia, and indeed the primary problem is in the fundamental process of attention and not in the act of new learning. The neuroanatomy of attention as described in Chapter 3 is pertinent to this section.

A related concept currently receiving much study is *working memory*, the ability to hold information in short-term storage while permitting other cognitive operations to take place; a good example is the carryover operation in mental arithmetic (Baddeley, 1992). Working memory emphasizes the capacity of immediate memory to retain information so that further manipulation of this material by other cognitive processes can take place. It is thought that working memory oversees two major systems, phonological and visuospatial (Baddeley, 1992). In an intuitively satisfying manner, recent functional imaging studies have indicated that these two systems correspond to the left and right hemispheres, respectively (Frackowiak, 1994). Closely associated with attention, it is not surprising that working memory is thought to depend on the prefrontal cortex (Goldman-Rakic, 1992), specifically Brodmann areas 46 and 9 (see Figure 1.3; Petrides et al., 1993). The prefrontal cortex has also been shown to be activated during the performance of neuropsychological tasks that place strong demands on attention (Rezai et al., 1993).

Amnesia

The ability to learn new information is of central importance in human existence, and disorders of recent memory provide striking examples of the disability produced by impairment in this realm. *Amnesia* is the word used most often to describe this syndrome, one of the most important in behavioral neurology and clinical medicine in general.

Amnesia is not a unitary phenomenon, and it can be considered clinically in a number of ways. One familiar contrast is between failure of new learning—*anterograde amnesia*—and failure to consolidate recently formed memories—*retrograde amnesia*. Both types of amnesia are vividly demonstrated in patients with traumatic brain injury, for example, in whom there is a gap in memories of events that took place before the injury and a longer period thereafter during which new learning is impaired (Levin et al., 1982). These deficits can accompany any amnesia, however, and the anterograde component is typically more severe and incapacitating (Hirst, 1982). The inability to acquire new learning as a result of anterograde amnesia is often accompanied by the interesting feature of *confabulation*, the fabrication of information in response to questioning, which has been associated with perseveration, impaired self-monitoring, and failure to inhibit incorrect responses (Shapiro et al., 1981).

In addition to these temporal components of amnesia, other distinctions are useful. One of the major advances of recent years is the characterization of declarative and procedural memory (Squire, 1982). *Declarative memory* refers to the retention of facts and events encountered in experience, or what might be called the memory of *what* has occurred, and *procedural memory* designates the learning of skills and habits, or what can be viewed as the memory of *how* something is done. The terms "explicit memory" and "implicit memory" have been used by others to describe a similar distinction, emphasizing the contrast between intentional recollection of previous experience in the former and the more automatic recall of learned skills in the latter (Schacter et al., 1993). In clinical practice, the assessment of amnesia is ordinarily restricted to the detection of deficits in declarative memory, which is much more completely understood in neurobehavioral terms, but procedural memory offers an exciting new opportunity to examine the neural basis of other types of learning that also contribute to effective human activity.

With respect to the neuroanatomy of amnesia, the medial temporal lobe, selected nuclei of the diencephalon, and the basal forebrain are crucial (Zola-Morgan and Squire, 1993). Each of these interconnected regions will be considered in turn. Figure 4.1 illustrates the general anatomic relationships of the components of this complex network: the hippocampus, in the depths of the temporal lobe; the thalamus, a diencephalic structure containing important nuclei of the memory system; and the basal forebrain, a group of cell bodies that supply acetylcholine to the entire cortical mantle.

Within the temporal lobe, the hippocampus, a term that for our purposes will serve as shorthand for the hippocampal formation (hippocampus proper, dentate gyrus, and subiculum), has emerged as the key

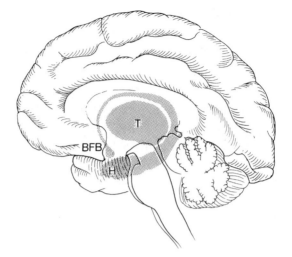

Figure 4.1 The hippocampus (H), thalamus (T), and basal forebrain (BFB) in relation to the right cerebral hemisphere.

structure. The current understanding of amnesia can be traced to a seminal case study that has been in progress for over 40 years and revealed more about human memory than any other single project. The widely known subject, referred to as H.M., is a man who at age 27 was subjected to bilateral anterior temporal lobectomies in an effort to control intractable posttraumatic epilepsy. By virtue of their position deep in the temporal lobes, both hippocampi and both amygdalae were resected, along with the epileptogenic cortex of the anterior temporal lobes (Scoville and Milner, 1957). Despite the good control of seizures that was achieved, H.M. was rendered permanently amnesic by the procedure and has henceforth been essentially unable to learn any new verbal or nonverbal declarative information (Corkin, 1984). Intriguingly, his ability to acquire procedural knowledge—his skill learning—is much better preserved (Milner et al., 1968; Corkin, 1968), an observation that has influenced the acceptance of the declarative-procedural distinction. This remarkable case has stimulated a generation of research on the role of the medial temporal lobe in recent memory, and it is now securely established that the hippocampus plays an essential role in new learning (Squire and Zola-Morgan, 1991).

Two challenges to this "hippocampal hypothesis" have been mounted. An interesting proposal was made by Horel (1978), who suggested that lesions of the temporal stem—the white matter tracts containing temporal

Neurobehavioral Anatomy

lobe afferent and efferent fibers—were essential for amnesia. In the same year, Mishkin (1978) argued that combined involvement of the hippocampus and amygdala was necessary for amnesia. It seems likely, however, that hippocampal lesions are sufficient, as recent cases of amnesia due to anoxic injury have been reported to damage the hippocampus but spare both white matter (Cummings et al., 1984) and the amygdalae (Zola-Morgan et al., 1986).

There is also evidence of lateralization of recent memory function, such that verbal memory is more dependent on the left hippocampus and its connections, whereas nonverbal memory is more dependent on the right side (Milner, 1971; Helmstaedter et al., 1991). Such a dichotomy is in keeping with hemispheric lateralization evidence in other areas of behavioral neurology (Chapters 5 and 8). It should be noted, however, that unilateral excision of medial temporal structures, as is often performed for intractable temporolimbic epilepsy, is rarely associated with significant amnesia (Glaser, 1980). Deficits related to the side of the resection can be detected—that is, verbal with the left and nonverbal with the right—but the intact side can compensate to a considerable extent, and clinical impairment is mild.

Two other fertile areas of clinical research into recent memory have contributed to an emerging understanding of the neuroanatomy of memory. The first is the problem of Korsakoff's psychosis in alcoholism affecting recent memory by damaging thalamic and limbic structures anatomically connected with the medial temporal lobe. More recently, attention has also focused on the dementia of Alzheimer's Disease (AD), in which memory and other cognitive deficits have been correlated with loss of neurons in the basal forebrain.

Korsakoff's psychosis, an unfortunate misnomer that has become entrenched in the literature, is in fact an amnesia due to dietary deficiency of thiamine. Evolving out of the syndrome of *Wernicke's encephalopathy* (consisting of a lethargic acute confusional state, ophthalmoplegia, and gait ataxia) in chronic alcoholics, Korsakoff's psychosis completes the full *Wernicke-Korsakoff syndrome* (Victor et al., 1989). In addition to severe anterograde and variable retrograde amnesia, these patients may display confabulation, the recitation of fictitious experiences, in response to the examiner's questions. Despite the implausible, even bizarre content of many confabulated responses that may suggest a psychotic illness, confabulation is not a constant feature in these patients (Victor et al., 1989), and a more accurate name for Korsakoff's psychosis would be "Korsakoff's amnesia." Pathologic changes are regularly found in the dorsal medial nucleus of the thalamus and the mammillary bodies, and Victor et al. (1989) have emphasized the importance of the dorsal medial nucleus lesions in the pathogenesis of amnesia. Supporting the validity of diencephalic amnesia is the notable case of N.A., who sustained a penetrating injury to the left dorsal medial nucleus with a miniature fencing foil; the memory deficit in this individual is characterized by selective verbal amnesia (Squire and Moore, 1979). Additional evidence for the involvement of thalamic nuclei in memory function comes from studies of amnesia in patients with infarction due to occlusion of small arteries derived from the posterior cerebral or posterior communicating arteries that supply the thalamus (Graff-Radford et al., 1990). As a general rule, amnesia follows stroke in the anterior but not the posterior thalamus; furthermore, elegant neuroanatomic studies have suggested that interruption of fibers connecting the dorsal medial and the anterior thalamic nuclei with the medial temporal lobe may be crucial in diencephalic amnesia (Graff-Radford et al., 1990).

The memory deficit of AD is of course the central problem in this very prevalent affliction, which will be discussed further in Chapter 12. Here the basal forebrain, a collection of interdigitated cell groups inferior to the basal ganglia consisting of the medial septal nucleus, the vertical and horizontal limb nuclei of the diagonal band of Broca, and the nucleus basalis of Meynert, plays a key role. With regard to amnesia, it seems clear that loss of cholinergic cells in the basal forebrain is both severe (Whitehouse et al., 1982) and linked with memory dysfunction in the disease (Perry et al., 1978). Basal forebrain cholinergic projections to the hippocampus and neocortex are well known (Mesulam and Geula, 1988), and it is reasonable that damage in the basal forebrain would impair memory and other cognitive functions. Supportive evidence for the role of the basal forebrain in recent memory comes from descriptions of patients with destructive lesions of this region who developed amnesia (Damasio et al., 1985; Morris et al., 1992). The disappointing efficacy of cholinergic drugs for AD suggests, however, that more than basal forebrain damage is necessary to explain the neurobehavioral devastation of AD.

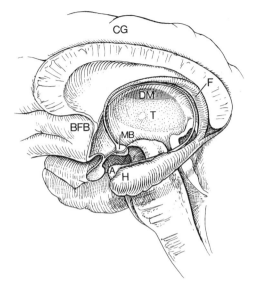

Figure 4.2 Detailed illustration of structures important in recent memory. H—hippocampus; A—amygdala; F—fornix; MB—mammillary body; T—thalamus; DM—dorsal medial thalamic nucleus; BFB—basal forebrain; CG—cingulate gyrus.

In summary, there exists a network of structures including components of the medial temporal lobe, diencephalon, and basal forebrain that mediates the phenomenon of recent memory. It is of considerable interest that a recent PET study of amnesic patients with lesions of diverse etiology found reduced metabolism in a very similar collection of areas—the hippocampus, thalamus, cingulate gyrus, and frontal basal region—implying the existence of a functional connectivity related to memory that fully supports the clinical findings reviewed previously (Fazio et al., 1992). Figure 4.2 offers a more detailed illustration of candidate regions involved in memory functions. The areas depicted will be seen to overlap extensively with a group of structures known as the Papez circuit (Papez, 1937), a network of interconnected cortical and subcortical structures that, in addition to participating in memory functions, has been traditionally associated with emotional behavior. The Papez circuit will be taken up in more detail in Chapter 9.

Another point concerns the interaction between the hippocampus and amygdala. Even though the hippocampus is the essential medial temporal structure for new learning, the amygdala seems to be important in the selection of material that is to be learned. Anatomic evidence indicates that these two structures are strategically positioned to intercept sensory input—visual, auditory, and tactile primarily—so that incoming stimuli can be subjected to an evaluation of their relevance for the survival of the organism (Mesulam, 1990). In other words, a given stimulus is assigned a hedonic value that determines its memorability. If the hedonic value is positive (a pleasurable experience) or negative (a painful experience), the stimulus is likely to be remembered; if, however, the value is neither positive nor negative (the experience is neutral), the stimulus will likely be ignored. The amygdala may function to attach an emotional valence to information reaching the hippocampus and then to determine whether that information is worthy of storage (Chapter 9). In other words, the process whereby the hippocampus either consolidates or discards information reaching the limbic system may depend on the assignment of emotional significance by the amygdala.

Table 4.1 provides a listing of the diseases and injuries that affect the areas in Figure 4.1 and cause amnesia. These diverse etiologies should be assiduously sought and treated promptly to maximize any recovery that might occur. It is important to recall that normal aging and psychiatric disorders can mimic neurologically based amnesia. Aging (Chapter 12) causes a mild retrieval deficit, often most marked for names, that represents an exaggeration of the normal forgetfulness shared by all humans (Devinsky, 1992). In contrast, psychogenic amnesia—in Freud's helpful phrase, "the forgetting of the disagreeable"—usually occurs in young adults and typically features the abrupt onset of inability to recall personal information associated with an emotionally traumatic event; a good general rule is that loss of personal identity strongly implies a psychogenic, not neurologic, origin (Devinsky, 1992). Thorough mental status evaluation, and neuropsychological evaluation in many cases, will usually enable the necessary distinctions to be made.

At a basic level, it is clear that the problem of memory reduces to the question of how synapses change (Squire, 1987). Before leaving this topic, it will be helpful to consider a recent concept that may help explain the neurophysiologic basis of memory formation: long-term potentiation (LTP). The fundamental importance of LTP is in its suggestion that synapses in the brain grow stronger with use. In lower animals, LTP is a promising synaptic model for memory that refers to an enhancement of a

Table 4.1 Etiologies of amnesia

Korsakoff's psychosis
Traumatic brain injury
Herpes simplex encephalitis
Anoxic encephalopathy
Diencephalic tumors
Posterior cerebral artery territory infarction
Transient global amnesia
Early Alzheimer's Disease

postsynaptic response to incoming stimulation that lasts for weeks or even longer. The excitatory neurotransmitters glutamate and aspartate are agonists for the N-methyl-D-aspartate (NMDA) receptor, and NMDA receptor activation with calcium influx appears to play a role in LTP. Recent evidence that the most consistent change in animals undergoing behavioral modification is an increase in the number and/or pattern of synapses suggests that LTP acts by increasing synaptic density in relevant cortical areas (Greenough and Bailey, 1988). The first demonstration of a cellular mechanism for memory consolidation, LTP may be the process whereby the memory structures of the human brain encode information for long-term storage. Because LTP has been demonstrated not only in the hippocampus but also in the neocortex (Teyler and DiScenna, 1987), it may underlie both the formation of new memories and their retention for extended periods. LTP may thus represent the neurophysiologic basis of the physical changes in brain connectivity that establish each individual's unique collection of experiences (Kandel and Hawkins, 1992).

Remote Memory Loss

The catagory of remote memory is included here because it represents the longest storage of experience of which the human mind is capable. An alternate term for "remote memory" is *knowledge*, and the term *fund of information* is also equivalent. Information that is important enough to be selected for storage by the medial temporal system is encoded in the brain for future access. The precise representation of these memories in the brain has been uncertain, but the neocortex certainly acts in some way as the repository for this material. Although it is unlikely that a one-to-one correspondence between a stored memory and a cortical region exists (Squire, 1987), the classic studies of Wilder Penfield—a neurosurgeon who stimulated the exposed brains of awake patients undergoing epilepsy surgery—clearly argue for a major role of the cortex in remote memory localization (Penfield and Jasper, 1954). Animal studies have suggested that millions of widely distributed neurons are involved in the storage of even a single memory (John et al., 1986).

Knowledge of this sort is usually well preserved in neurobehavioral disorders. In AD, for example, memories from years past are typically clear even as amnesia ineluctably precludes the storage of even the simplest new information. A diffuse and redundant cortical representation is probably established as a result of frequent reconsideration of important material. Names of significant people in one's life, for example, are well recalled because of the frequency with which they are employed in daily living. Nevertheless, deficits in remote memory do ultimately occur in AD with the advance of widespread cortical degeneration, at which time other signs of terminal disease—mutism, incontinence, and the vegetative state—are typically evident.

References

Baddeley, A. 1992. Working memory. *Science;* 255: 556–559.

Corkin, S. 1968. Acquisition of motor skill after bilateral medial temporal-lobe excision. *Neuropsychologia;* 6: 255–265.

Corkin, S. 1984. Lasting consequences of bilateral medial temporal lobectomy: clinical course and experimental findings in H.M. *Sem Neurol;* 4: 249–259.

Cummings, J.L., Tomiyasu, U., Reed, S., and Benson, D.F. 1984. Amnesia with hippocampal lesions after cardiopulmonary arrest. *Neurology;* 34: 679–681.

Damasio, A.R., Graff-Radford, N.R., Eslinger, P.J., et al. 1985. Amnesia following basal forebrain lesions. *Arch Neurol;* 42: 263–271.

Devinsky, O. 1992. *Behavioral Neurology. 100 Maxims.* St. Louis, Mosby Year Book.

Fazio, F., Perani, D., Gilardi, M.C., et al. 1992. Metabolic impairment in human amnesia: a PET study of memory networks. *J Cereb Blood Flow Metab;* 12: 353–358.

Frackowiak, R.S.J. 1994. Functional mapping of verbal memory and language. *Trends Neurosci;* 17: 109–115.

Glaser, G.H. 1980. Treatment of intractable temporal lobe-limbic epilepsy (complex partial seizures) by temporal lobectomy. *Ann Neurol;* 8: 455–459.

Goldman-Rakic, P.S. 1992. Working memory and the mind. *Sci Am;* 267(3): 111–117.

Graff-Radford, N.R., Tranel, D., Van Hoesen, G.W., and Brandt, J.P. 1990. Diencephalic amnesia. *Brain;* 113: 1–25.

Greenough, W.T., and Bailey, C.H. 1988. The anatomy of a memory: convergence of results across a diversity of tests. *Trends Neurosci;* 11: 142–147.

Helmstaedter, C., Pohl, C., Hufnagel, A., and Elger, C.E. 1991. Visual learning deficits in nonresected patients with right temporal lobe epilepsy. *Cortex;* 27: 547–555.

Hirst, W. 1982. The amnesic syndrome: descriptions and explorations. *Psychol Bull;* 91: 435–460.

Horel, J.A. 1978. The neuroanatomy of memory. A critique of the hippocampal memory hypothesis. *Brain;* 101: 403–445.

John, E.R., Tang, Y., Brill, A.B., et al. 1986. Double-labeled metabolic maps of memory. *Science;* 233: 1167–1175.

Kandel, E.R., and Hawkins, R.D. 1992. The biological basis of learning and individuality. *Sci Am;* 267(3): 79–86.

Kirshner, H.S. 1986. *Behavioral Neurology. A Practical Approach.* New York, Churchill Livingstone.

Levin, H.S., Benton, A.L. and Grossman, R.G. 1982. *Neurobehavioral Consequences of Closed Head Injury.* New York, Oxford.

Mesulam, M.-M. 1990. Large-scale neurocognitive networks and distributed processing for attention, language, and memory. *Ann Neurol;* 28: 597–613.

Mesulam, M.-M., and Geula, C. 1988. Nucleus basalis (Ch 4) and cortical cholinergic innervation of the human brain: observations based on the distribution of acetylcholinesterase and choline acetyltransferase. *J Comp Neurol;* 275: 216–240.

Milner, B. 1971. Interhemispheric differences in the localization of psychological processes in man. *Br Med Bull;* 27: 272–277.

Milner, B., Corkin, S., and Teuber, H.L. 1968. Further analysis of the hippocampal amnesic syndrome: 14-year follow-up study of H.M. *Neuropsychologia;* 6: 215–234.

Mishkin, M. 1978. Memory in monkeys severely impaired by combined but not by separate removal of amygdala and hippocampus. *Nature;* 273: 297–298.

Morris, M.K., Bowers, D., Chatterjee, A., and Heilman, K.M. 1992. Amnesia following a discrete basal forebrain lesion. *Brain;* 115: 1827–1847.

Papez, J.W. 1937. A proposed mechanism of emotion. *Arch Neurol Psychiatry;* 38: 725–743.

Penfield, W., and Jasper, H. 1954. *Epilepsy and the Functional Anatomy of the Human Brain,* Boston, Little Brown.

Perry, E.K., Tomlinson, B.E., Blessed, G., et al. 1978. Correlation of cholinergic abnormalities with senile plaques and mental test scores in senile dementia. *Br Med J;* 2: 1457–1459.

Petrides, M., Alivisatos, B., Meyer, E., and Evans, A.C. 1993. Functional activation of the human frontal cortex during the performance of verbal working memory tasks. *Proc Natl Acad Sci;* 90: 878–882.

Rezai, K., Andreasen, N.C., Alliger, R., et al. 1993. The neuropsychology of the prefrontal cortex. *Arch Neurol;* 50: 636–642.

Schacter, D.L., Chiu, C.-Y. P., and Ochsner, K.N. 1993. Implicit memory: a selective review. *Ann Rev Neurosci;* 16: 159–182.

Scoville, W.B., and Milner, B. 1957. Loss of recent memory after bilateral hippocampal lesions. *J Neurol Neurosurg Psychiatry;* 20: 11–21.

Shapiro, B.E., Alexander, M.P., Gardner, H., and Mercer, B. 1981. Mechanisms of confabulation. *Neurology;* 31: 1070–1076.

Squire, L.R. 1982. The neuropsychology of human memory. *Ann Rev Neurosci;* 5: 241–273.

Squire, L.R. 1987. *Memory and Brain.* New York, Oxford.

Squire, L.R., and Moore, R.Y. 1979. Dorsal thalamic lesion in a noted case of human memory dysfunction. *Ann Neurol;* 6: 503–506.

Squire, L.R., and Zola-Morgan, S. 1991. The medial temporal lobe memory system. *Science;* 253: 1380–86.

Strub, R.L., and Black, F.W. 1993. *The Mental Status Examination in Neurology.* 3rd ed. Philadelphia, F.A. Davis.

Teyler, T.J., and DiScenna, P. 1987. Long-term potentiation. *Ann Rev Neurosci;* 10: 131–161.

Victor, M., Adams, R.D., and Collins, G.H. 1989. *The Wernicke-Korsakoff Syndrome and Related Neurologic Disorders due to Alcoholism and Malnutrition.* 2nd ed. Philadelphia, F.A. Davis.

Whitehouse, P.J., Price, D.L., Struble, R.G., et al. 1982. Alzheimer disease and senile dementia: loss of neurons in the basal forebrain. *Science;* 215: 1237–1239.

Zola-Morgan, S., and Squire, L.R. 1993. Neuroanatomy of memory. *Ann Rev Neurosci;* 16: 547–563.

Zola-Morgan, S., Squire, L.R., and Amaral, D.G. 1986. Human amnesia and the medial temporal region: enduring memory impairment following a bilateral lesion limited to field CA1 of the hippocampus. *J Neurosci;* 6: 2950–2967.

CHAPTER 5

Language Disorders

Of all the higher functions, the capacity to communicate with language is perhaps the most obvious skill possessed by humankind. Efforts have been made to teach chimpanzees how to communicate using signs, but it has been questioned whether nonhuman primates have the capacity for symbolic language (Savage-Rumbaugh et al., 1980). In any case, human language competence is exceedingly well developed in comparison to that of primates and helps confer an extraordinary mastery of the environment to which no other species can lay claim. It is also clear that language is the most thoroughly understood of all the neurobehavioral domains, primarily because of the elegant study of aphasia that has been the most significant achievement of behavioral neurology. Through the work of some of the most astute clinicians of the nervous system over the past 150 years, the cerebral localization of human language can be rather confidently reviewed (Geschwind, 1970; Damasio, 1992).

As a point of departure, some definitions will be useful. *Language*, for our purposes, will be considered the symbolic system of verbal and written communication between human beings. It is the means by which humans communicate using verbal symbols. All human cultures employ language, and it is the primary means of social discourse among members of the human race. It is, in fact, difficult to imagine life without language—the painful struggles of a severely aphasic patient attempting to speak testify to the central role of language in human existence. A disorder of language due to brain damage is commonly called *aphasia*, but the alternative "dysphasia" is also employed. *Speech* is a more elementary capacity than language, and the term refers to the mechanical act of uttering words using neuromuscular structures responsible for articulation. *Dysarthria*, describing an impairment of speech, may be due to either brain or neuromuscular dysfunction, but it does not in itself imply a language disorder. *Anarthria* is a severe form of dysarthria in which no speech production is possible. Another term that occasionally finds utility is *voice*, the production of sound produced through the vocal apparatus. Voice disorders commonly occur as a result of laryngeal disease, and can be mild, as in *dysphonia*, or severe, as in *aphonia*. *Mutism,* the inability to produce any verbal utterance, can be due to a disorder of language, speech, or voice, and clinical evaluation is required to distinguish between these possibilities.

More difficult to deal with is the notion of thought or cognition. A recurrent philosophical issue revolves around whether thought can be separated from language. It has been argued, for example, that only through language can thought be expressed (Arendt, 1978). The question is not easily answered, but clinical experience suggests that the two are indeed distinct; thinking, for example, may be grossly disturbed in schizophrenic patients (with a "thought disorder") who have intact language (Damasio, 1992). There are also anatomic reasons to suspect that thought and language are distinct; the areas responsible for language are relatively limited, whereas the remainder of the cerebrum, where nonlinguistic functions are carried out, is extensive. The neurobehavioral position is that thought, a complex and multifaceted activity, is often revealed through the symbolic system of language but cannot be regarded as synonymous with language because many other avenues for the operations of thought are available.

With these conceptions in mind, construction of a neuroanatomy of language can begin. As is true of all higher functions, no fully adequate animal model for studying language under controlled experimental conditions exists, and therefore we must turn to the unfortunate but revealing brain lesions that cause aphasia and related disorders. Most often, the event that disturbs language is a *stroke;* the history of aphasia is essentially a chronicle of the linguistic deficits consequent to focal cerebrovascular disease. Aphasia can also accompany brain tumors, infectious processes such as encephalitis, traumatic brain injury, and other pathologies, but the detailed case studies of stroke-related aphasia have led to the most notable advances in the understanding of the cerebral basis of language.

Although descriptions of aphasia have been made in some manner since ancient times, the modern era of aphasiology began in the late nineteenth century with the appearance of two seminal publications (Broca, 1865; Wernicke, 1874). In 1861, the French physician and anthropologist

Paul Broca presented the case of a 51-year-old man named Leborgne who had become speechless with the exception of the word "tan," and who had, as revealed at autopsy, extensive destruction of the left inferior frontal lobe and adjacent areas. Broca later reported other cases further supporting the localization of speech production in the left frontal lobe (Broca, 1865). Thirteen years after Broca's first case presentation, the German neurologist Carl Wernicke published his doctoral thesis, which concluded that impaired language comprehension was associated with destruction of the left superior temporal lobe (Wernicke, 1874). Subsequently, other case descriptions came to light confirming these observations, and as more examples of aphasia were analyzed, a scheme for left hemisphere language representation began to take shape. The contributions of Broca and Wernicke, establishing the primacy of cerebral areas essential for language in the left hemisphere, stand as superb examples of the lesion method, demonstrating how higher functions can be related to brain regions. Other investigations since that time have refined the study of aphasia, and there have been debates regarding details of the aphasia syndromes, but the localizing value of these two early studies has clearly stood the test of time. The method of clinical-anatomic correlation, now made more convenient by modern neuroimaging (Naeser and Hayward, 1978), remains a powerful technique in the understanding of the brain's functioning in health as well as disease.

The literature on aphasia is extensive and often difficult. Many different classification schemes of various aphasias have been proposed, leading unfortunately to much confusion. It is not the purpose here to discuss all the subtleties of aphasia as a syndrome, as others have done so previously (Benson, 1979; Albert et al., 1981), but rather to draw upon the clinical literature as it illuminates general conclusions about the anatomy of language. First, however, it will prove useful to deal with the complex issue of language lateralization.

Cerebral Dominance and Handedness

The most crucial observation made by Broca in 1865 was that language disturbance followed damage to the left but not the right cerebral hemisphere. His work and that of many others since then has made it abundantly clear that, in the great majority of instances, significant aphasia follows lesions of the left hemisphere, and that comparably sized and placed lesions in the right hemisphere do not as a rule cause the syndrome. It has traditionally been taught that the localization of language in the left hemisphere is true for nearly all right-handers (99%) and even the majority (67%) of left-handers (Damasio and Damasio, 1992). The lateralization of language remains the most striking example of a higher function that is confined to one side of a generally symmetrical organ. The reasons for this are not immediately apparent, as other organs such as the lungs and kidneys manifest no such asymmetry. Nevertheless, knowledge that language is generally associated with the left hemisphere has important localizing value for the clinician and the neuroscientist.

The findings of Broca and his successors have led to a notion of *cerebral dominance* for language. The left hemisphere, by implication, has been dubbed the "dominant" one because language is held to be virtually indispensable to human life. Although the concept of dominance is frequently invoked, a certain degree of caution is warranted. Whereas the importance of language is unquestionable, other capacities are equally vital to a full human existence. As will be apparent at several points throughout this book, the right hemisphere participates significantly in many aspects of attention, emotion, visuospatial ability, music, humor, and other abilities without which human life would be immeasurably poorer. Moreover, other functions of undeniable significance, such as memory and complex cognitive skills, are best regarded as bilaterally distributed. Reference to the left hemisphere as the one dominant *for language* is appropriate, but it must be realized that other critical functions are associated with the right hemisphere or with both sides of the cerebrum.

There are, as just indicated, some individuals who are not left dominant for language. The most obvious of this group is people who are not right-handed. As a general rule, about 10% of the population is left-handed or sinistral (Hardyck and Petrinovich, 1977), and of these, perhaps a third have right hemisphere dominance for language (Damasio, 1992). The situation, however, may be more complicated. Other estimates propose that 70% of the population is strongly right-handed or dextral, 10% is strongly left-handed, and 20% is ambidextrous; in this scheme, dextrals are left dominant for language, and sinistrals and ambidextrals have what has been called *anomalous dominance*, meaning that language is bilaterally represented (Geschwind and Behan, 1984). In those with anomalous dominance, aphasia may occur following damage

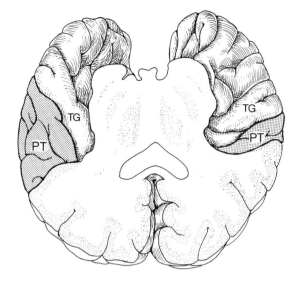

Figure 5.1 Typical left-right asymmetry of the upper temporal lobes; the planum temporale (PT) is larger on the left. TG—transverse gyrus of Heschl.

to either hemisphere but, when present, tends to be milder and to have a better prognosis than a similar syndrome in a dextral. The main clinical point is that variations from strong dextrality suggest the possibility that language can be dominant in the right hemisphere or distributed in both hemispheres. *Crossed aphasia,* the combination of aphasia and a right hemisphere lesion in a right-handed person, occurs but is extremely rare (Brown and Hecaen, 1976; Alexander et al., 1989a).

The percentages given above supporting the idea of anomalous dominance are interesting in view of neuroanatomic data indicating interhemispheric structural differences in the planum temporale, a triangular cortical area on the superior surface of the temporal lobe more or less equivalent to Wernicke's area (Figure 5.1). In a postmortem study of 100 brains, Geschwind and Levitsky (1968) found that the planum temporale was larger on the left in 65% of individuals, on the right in 11%, and equal on each side in the remainder. Asymmetry of the superior temporal lobe has also been shown in newborns (Witelson and Pallie, 1973) and in utero (Chi et al., 1977), indicating that there appears to be a tendency for cerebral lateralization of language very early in development.

The other exception to left hemisphere dominance for language is seen in childhood. Despite the differences in cortical architecture

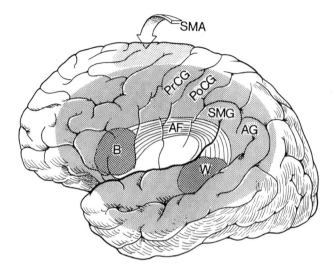

Figure 5.2 Lateral view of the left hemisphere showing areas important for language. B—Broca's area; W—Wernicke's area; AF—arcuate fasciculus; SMA—supplementary motor area; AG—angular gyrus; SMG—supramarginal gyrus; PrCG—precentral gyrus; PoCG —postcentral gyrus.

described above, full lateralization of language does not appear until after childhood. The precise age when this occurs is not clear and may vary depending on many factors, but children under ten years of age seem to have less completely lateralized language functions. Aphasias can certainly occur in children with left hemisphere lesions and often resemble adult syndromes rather closely (Cranberg et al., 1987), but recovery from seemingly devastating lesions can be quite remarkable (Smith and Sugar, 1975). This resiliency in children surely also depends in part on the plasticity of the young brain, a concept that deserves much further study.

Aphasia

The collection of gray and white matter structures around the Sylvian fissure in the human left hemisphere is perhaps the best known region in behavioral neurology. This is known as the perisylvian region, and, together with adjacent areas that also participate, constitutes the cerebral basis of propositional language (Figure 5.2). *Perisylvian aphasias* are the language disorders that result from damage to structures immediately above and below the Sylvian fissure. Reading and writing, as will be seen, also depend upon this anatomic region, although the visual system participates as well.

Prosody, the term referring to the emotional components of language, is mediated by an analogous zone on the right side of the cerebrum (Ross, 1981); this topic will be addressed in Chapter 8.

The part of the cerebrum devoted to the production of language is Broca's area, located in the posterior portion of the left inferior frontal gyrus (Figure 5.2). It is essentially the same territory occupied by Brodmann areas 44 and 45 (see Figure 1.3). Here the semantic components of a sentence or phrase are assembled into a grammatically correct and well-articulated utterance. Lesions of this area are associated with often dramatic difficulties in verbal output, an impairment appropriately referred to as *nonfluency*, or "nonfluent speech." Severe, lasting *Broca's aphasia* is due to damage involving Broca's area and adjacent cortical and subcortical regions (Alexander et al., 1990), whereas a milder "Broca's area aphasia" results from damage to Broca's area exclusively (Mohr et al., 1978). *Aphemia*, a nonaphasic syndrome of transient mutism or dysarthria, has also been described with small lesions of the lower precentral gyrus that spare Broca's area (Schiff et al., 1983). These syndromes are usually due to a stroke in the distribution of the left middle cerebral artery, but nonfluent aphasia from degenerative disease—the syndrome of *primary progressive aphasia*—has also been described (Weintraub et al., 1990). A patient with Broca's aphasia, or any nonfluent aphasia, is not unlike a normal person struggling with a foreign language; speech is sparse, effortful, and grammatically incorrect. In contrast to normal speech production of 100 to 150 words per minute, Broca's aphasia is characterized by word production of less than 50 words per minute. Because of the proximity of Broca's area to the lower portions of the precentral gyrus, weakness or paresis of the contralateral (right) arm and face are usually seen with Broca's aphasia; sensory loss in the same bodily regions is present as well if the postcentral gyrus is involved. Patients with this syndrome have relatively well preserved auditory comprehension; it is the production of language that is primarily affected.

In contrast, the region of the hemisphere most concerned with the understanding of language is situated in the posterior portion of the left superior temporal gyrus (Figure 5.2). This is known as Wernicke's area and corresponds with the posterior part of Brodmann area 22 (see Figure 1.3). Wernicke's area is responsible for processing incoming verbal stimuli into meaningful information. Damage to this region leads to impaired auditory comprehension despite retained fluency of language, a syndrome known as *Wernicke's aphasia* (Geschwind, 1967). As with Broca's aphasia, a left middle cerebral artery stroke is the usual cause of Wernicke's aphasia, but similar fluent aphasias frequently occur as a component of Alzheimer's Disease (Chapter 12; Weintraub et al., 1990). A patient with Wernicke's aphasia has difficulty understanding spoken language, including his own as well as that of others. In contrast, speech production is fluent, although typically rapid and paraphasic. When neologistic speech is severe, the term *jargon aphasia* is sometimes used. No paresis or sensory loss is typically present in patients so afflicted, and the syndrome of Wernicke's aphasia is the conceptual opposite of Broca's aphasia in that language input is affected whereas its output is more preserved.

Broca's and Wernicke's areas are also connected by a band of subcortical white matter known as the arcuate fasciculus (Figure 5.2). This tract has importance in that the act of repetition depends on its integrity. As originally predicted by Wernicke (1874) and later supported by Geschwind (1965), damage to the arcuate fasciculus, typically with associated cortical pathology, results in selective impairment of repetition; there is an interruption of the flow of accurately processed input in Wernicke's area to the intact output zone of Broca's area, and repetition breaks down, often with paraphasic word or letter substitutions. This syndrome is called *conduction aphasia* (Damasio and Damasio, 1980), and affected patients display a curious deficit in repetition that may be quite surprising in the presence of their spared auditory comprehension and verbal fluency.

So far, we have seen the effects of limited focal lesions in the language zone, but there is an unfortunate syndrome involving the entire perisylvian region. When a large infarct destroys the areas previously discussed, which not infrequently occurs, the deficits are additive, and individuals suffer with impaired output, input, and of course repetition. This *global aphasia*, accompanied by hemiplegia of the right side of the body, is one of the more tragic sequelae of central nervous system disease. As can be imagined, the outcome is typically poor. A better prognosis has been seen in global aphasia, however, when separate focal lesions in Broca's and Wernicke's area coexist, a condition known as *global aphasia without hemiparesis* (Tranel et al., 1987).

A final important component of spoken language is naming. The ability to name an object—for example, the collection of pages between two covers the reader is holding known as a book—depends on the assignment of a verbal symbol to an item that is in this case visually perceived. The resultant name that is generated becomes, of course, one of the foundations of language, permitting the development of a lexicon (vocabulary) and the expansion of symbolic representation. The left angular gyrus (Brodmann area 39; see Figure 1.3) is anatomically arranged to receive auditory, visual, and somatosensory information and has been suggested as the region where naming takes place by virtue of cross-modal associations (Geschwind, 1965). Lesions in this area are regularly associated with prominent *anomia,* and the syndrome of *anomic aphasia* is characteristically associated with damage to the left angular gyrus. In actual fact, however, anomia is a universal feature of aphasia and can therefore be caused by lesions that cause any aphasic syndrome. Furthermore, anomia is often encountered in diffuse conditions such as acute confusional state and Alzheimer's Disease in which word-finding difficulty is embedded in the many other deficits present. Despite its poor localizing value in many cases, further study may reveal subtypes of anomia that can be linked more specifically with known language areas.

Thus far the linguistic functions of the perisylvian zone in the left hemisphere have been described. There remains a large expanse of cortex and subjacent white matter that abuts upon this area (Figure 5.2). Although less familiar than the major language areas just discussed, these extrasylvian zones of the brain contribute importantly to normal language, and the study of syndromes related to their destruction is quite instructive. Three more aphasia syndromes have been associated with these regions of the left hemisphere (Table 5.1). These aphasias have all been grouped under the heading of *transcortical aphasias,* and the alternate term "extrasylvian aphasias" is also appropriate.

As a first point, these aphasias all demonstrate sparing of repetition, which is not surprising in view of the fact that the primary circuit mediating auditory input, speech output, and the connections between them is intact. Extrasylvian aphasias are typically due to hypotensive or hypoxic injury in the border zone regions of the hemisphere where terminal anastomoses occur between the middle cerebral and the anterior and posterior cerebral arteries. This anatomic feature accounts for the preservation of the perisylvian region, which is irrigated solely by the middle cerebral artery. *Transcortical motor aphasia* is due to a lesion in the

Table 5.1 Aphasia syndromes and their localization

Aphasia type	Spontaneous speech	Auditory comprehension	Repetition	Naming	Localization (left hemisphere)
Broca's	Nonfluent	Good	Poor	Poor	Broca's area
Wernicke's	Fluent	Poor	Poor	Poor	Wernicke's area
Conduction	Fluent	Good	Poor	Poor	Arcuate fasciculus
Global	Nonfluent	Poor	Poor	Poor	Perisylvian region
Transcortical motor	Nonfluent	Good	Good	Poor	Anterior border zone
Transcortical sensory	Fluent	Poor	Good	Poor	Posterior border zone
Anomic	Fluent	Good	Good	Poor	Angular gyrus
Mixed transcortical	Nonfluent	Poor	Good	Poor	Anterior and posterior border zone

Neurobehavioral Anatomy

anterior extrasylvian region, often involving the supplementary motor area (Brodmann area 6; see Figure 1.3) and characterized by particular difficulty in the initiation of speech (Alexander and Schmitt, 1980; Freedman et al., 1984). *Transcortical sensory aphasia*, marked by difficulty with language comprehension, follows lesions in the posterior extrasylvian region (Brodmann area 37 and parts of 39 and 19; see Figure 1.3) and their deep white matter connections (Kertesz et al., 1982; Alexander et al., 1989a). These two aphasias are analogous to Broca's and Wernicke's aphasias, with the notable exception of spared repetition. Finally, there is the intriguing entity called *mixed transcortical aphasia*, or "isolation of the speech area," in which the entire C-shaped extrasylvian region is damaged and the only remaining skill is repetition (Geschwind et al., 1968). Individuals with this disorder may demonstrate the remarkable phenomenon of *echolalia*, in which the examiner's statements are automatically repeated. Table 5.1 displays the modern classification of these eight major aphasias, including the various deficits by which they are characterized and the affected cerebral areas.

Before leaving the topic of spoken language, the category of *subcortical aphasia* deserves comment. The reported syndromes of aphasia due to subcortical damage have been controversial because the cortex is traditionally seen as responsible for language function, but clearly documented aphasias have been reported from lesions of the left thalamus, basal ganglia, and white matter (Filley and Kelly, 1990). In general, these are relatively mild syndromes that resemble the transcortical aphasias in that repetition is spared. The prognosis is usually favorable. Some have argued that subcortical aphasia is only due to transient metabolic alterations in overlying language cortex (Skyhoj Olsen et al., 1986), but there may be subcortical components of language systems that serve to "activate" the cortex in the production of its linguistic activities. It is too early to be certain of the contributions of the subcortical regions to language, but further case studies will doubtless be useful in this regard.

Alexia

In illiterate individuals, reading and writing are obviously poorly developed. However, in patients who had previously acquired these skills, much has been learned about the cerebral origin of these unspoken linguistic capacities. Two lines of inquiry have established most of our present knowledge of the anatomy of reading: the study of acquired disorders of reading—alexia—and the investigation of developmental dyslexia, a syndrome in which children may never learn to read well despite ample opportunity and general cognitive ability.

Alexia has been classically divided into two distinct varieties: alexia with agraphia and alexia without agraphia (pure alexia). Both syndromes were recognized in the late nineteenth century, and, like many other neurobehavioral syndromes of that era, both have endured through a century of clinical research. These syndromes and a third alexia added more recently will be considered.

The French neurologist Jules Dejerine described alexia with agraphia and pure alexia in two publications one year apart (Dejerine, 1891, 1892). *Alexia with agraphia* is a disorder of both reading and writing that is, in effect, a syndrome of acquired illiteracy. The lesion involves the inferior parietal and posterolateral temporal regions of the left hemisphere, most critically the angular gyrus (Dejerine, 1891), and associated deficits including right homonymous visual field defects, mild fluent aphasia, and components of Gerstmann's syndrome may be present (Figure 5.2). Involvement of the angular gyrus in this syndrome is of interest in view of the likelihood that this gyrus plays a special role in linguistic function. Similar to its role in the process of naming, the angular gyrus probably enables the cross-modal associations between visual and auditory systems by which one learns to read (Geschwind, 1965).

Alexia without agraphia (Dejerine, 1892), on the other hand, serves as an instructive contrast to alexia with agraphia because in this syndrome the angular gyrus is intact. An excellent example of a *disconnection syndrome* (Geschwind, 1965), pure alexia is typically due to lesions in the left occipital lobe and the splenium of the corpus callosum that prevent incoming visual information from reaching the angular gyrus for linguistic interpretation (Figure 5.3). Thus one can observe the remarkable phenomenon of a patient who can write easily but has difficulty reading what has just been written. Right homonymous hemianopia is characteristically present, and color anomia and object agnosia can be seen as well.

Finally, there is a variety of reading disturbance called *frontal alexia*, alternatively known as "anterior alexia" because of its association with Broca's aphasia, or as the "third alexia" (Benson, 1977). Patients with this syndrome have severe nonfluent aphasia and right hemiparesis, and their

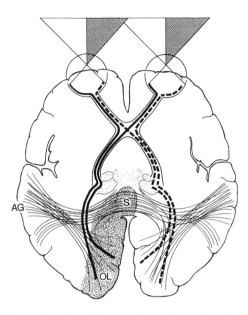

Figure 5.3 Horizontal section of the cerebrum illustrating the lesions in the left occipital lobe and the splenium of the corpus callosum resulting in pure alexia. OL—occipital lobe; S—splenium of the corpus callosum; AG—angular gyrus.

reading impairment is characterized by inability to read letters despite preserved reading of familiar words (literal alexia). In addition, words with high semantic content such as "house" or "car" are read more easily than small functor words such as "the" and "in," so that the reading disturbance parallels the spoken language of patients with Broca's aphasia.

The alexias are an intriguing group of syndromes that offer insights into the complicated processes of reading. For clinical purposes, the most important point is that reading disorders can often be overlooked unless they are specifically sought. Neuroanatomically, it is convenient to envision them as left hemisphere syndromes related to posterior (alexia without agraphia), central (alexia with agraphia), and anterior (frontal alexia) pathology. An understanding of the precise contributions each of these areas makes to the many steps involved in reading awaits further study.

Although not one of the standard categories of alexia, another recently described entity has also helped illuminate how the brain mediates reading. This has been termed *deep dyslexia* (Coltheart et al., 1980) and features the presence of semantic paralexias (e.g., "watch" for "clock"), difficulty reading nonsense words (e.g., "bliv"), and improved performance with highly imagible words such as "automobile." This syndrome has been tentatively linked with damage to left perisylvian lesions, and its characteristics suggest a right hemisphere role in decoding written language (Benson, 1994). To elaborate, a written word that is readily visualized may activate an image in the intact right hemisphere of deep dyslexics that assists in reading, even if an incorrect but related word (semantic paralexia) is produced.

In contrast, another form of dyslexia has long been recognized. *Developmental dyslexia*, or difficulty learning to read despite adequate intelligence and educational opportunity, is a common disorder, estimated to occur in 5 to 10% of school-age children (Benton and Pearl, 1978). More common in boys than girls, dyslexia is an anomaly of left hemisphere development that has both genetic and environmental causes (Pennington, 1991). The specific neuroanatomic substrate of this impairment in reading and spelling is under active investigation, but evidence increasingly suggests that the planum temporale (Figure 5.1) is part of the cerebral network necessary for the normal development of reading. Dyslexic children often show loss of the normal left-right asymmetry in the planum region, so that the plana are symmetric in size (Galaburda et al., 1985). Recent PET studies have also found that dyslexic men have metabolic dysfunction in the left temporoparietal region (Rumsey et al., 1994). Microscopic abnormalities such as neuronal ectopias and architectonic dysplasias in the perisylvian zone of the left hemisphere are also likely to contribute to dyslexia (Galaburda et al., 1985). These data are consistent with results of cognitive research suggesting that dyslexia is essentially a disorder of written language processing, not a visual or spatial processing problem (Pennington, 1991).

Agraphia

Writing, like reading, is a linguistic skill not possessed by all persons who have a command of spoken language. Even in those who are literate, writing is employed less often than spoken language for communication and is therefore less securely represented in the brain. *Agraphia*, the impairment of previously intact writing due to brain damage, can thus be caused by lesions virtually anywhere in the cerebrum. Indeed, the fragility of writing in disorders of the brain is evidenced by the fact that agraphia routinely appears even in diffuse syndromes such as the acute confusional state (Chedru and Geschwind, 1972) and dementia (Appell et al., 1982). This section will consider the various forms in which writing may break down; the curious phenomenon of hypergraphia will be taken up in Chapter 9.

On the basis of this syndrome appearing with a variety of lesions, many classifications of agraphia have been attempted, none of them entirely successful. It seems reasonable, however, to begin with the fact that a number of agraphia syndromes can be ascribed to motor and even nonneurologic disorders, a group aptly named the mechanical agraphias (Benson, 1994). In this category would be writing impairments due to corticospinal dysfunction, basal ganglia disease, cerebellar disturbance, peripheral neuropathy, myopathy, and bone or joint disease. Neurologists are familiar with the clumsy writing resulting from paresis, the *micrographia* of Parkinson's Disease, and the tremulous writing due to cerebellar tremor. These deficits are rather self-evident and do not reflect a cognitive disorder, but they often coexist with neurobehavioral syndromes and cloud the clinical picture (Benson and Cummings, 1985). The localization of writing has not been resolved with any certainty. As might be imagined, most often agraphia accompanies aphasia following left hemisphere lesions. Typically the features of the agraphia tend to parallel the characteristics of the aphasia; as examples, agraphia with nonfluent aphasia shows effortful and sparse written output with agrammatism, whereas agraphia with fluent aphasia discloses easily written output of normal length but with uncertain meaning and paragraphias (Benson and Cummings, 1985). Spatial agraphia with right hemisphere lesions is also known, in which errors are made due to hemineglect and constructional impairments (Ardila and Rosselli, 1993). Agraphia can also be seen in the left hand only of a patient with a lesion of the corpus callosum (Geschwind, 1965).

In view of the multitude of settings in which agraphia can occur, cases of agraphia in the absence of other disorders are of great theoretical interest. Such examples, unfortunately, are uncommon. Rare cases of "pure" agraphia have been reported with lesions of the left superior frontal region (Dubois et al., 1969) and the left superior parietal lobe (Auerbach and Alexander, 1981). The old idea of Exner (1881) that writing is localized in the left premotor area just anterior to the hand region of the precentral gyrus and superior to Broca's area is clearly insufficient because many studies have noted agraphia when this area is intact (Roeltgen, 1993).

Agraphia is also one of a tetrad of findings known as *Gerstmann's syndrome*, the others being acalculia, right-left disorientation, and finger agnosia (Gerstmann, 1940). This aggregate of features was felt to represent a dissolution of the body schema (Gerstmann, 1940). Although the localizing value of this entity has been questioned (Benton, 1961), clinical experience does suggest that this combination of deficits raises the suspicion of a left parietal lesion (Strub and Geschwind, 1974). Fragments of the syndrome—partial Gerstmann's syndrome—can often be found. A large left-side lesion placed in the angular gyrus has been claimed to manifest itself reliably by a variety of deficits: this *angular gyrus syndrome* consists of Gerstmann's syndrome, anomic aphasia, and alexia with agraphia (Benson et al., 1982).

Finally, the problem of *acalculia* deserves some comment. The ability to calculate is again restricted to persons with some educational background, and is therefore a skill quite susceptible to various kinds of brain damage. However, calculation disturbances have been observed in three main settings. Acalculia in aphasia can result from difficulty with reading and writing numbers; with right hemisphere involvement, acalculia can be due to the inability to align or position numbers properly; and in what has been called *anarithmetria*, usually in the context of a left posterior lesion, the conduct of performing arithmetic operations itself is impaired (Boller and Grafman, 1985). Thus acalculia can occur with either right or left hemisphere lesions, but when it occurs in isolation as anarithmetria, the left parietal lobe typically appears to be implicated (Takayama et al., 1994).

References

Albert, M.L., Goodglass, H., Helm, N.A., et al. 1981. *Clinical Aspects of Dysphasia.* Vienna, Springer-Verlag.

Alexander, M.P., and Schmitt, M.A. 1980. The aphasia syndrome of stroke in the left anterior cerebral artery territory. *Arch Neurol;* 37: 97–100.

Alexander, M.P., Fischette, M.R., and Fisher, R.S. 1989. Crossed aphasia can be mirror image or anomalous. Case reports, review and hypothesis. *Brain;* 112: 953–973.

Alexander, M.P., Hiltbrunner, B., and Fischer, R.S. 1989. Distributed anatomy of transcortical sensory aphasia. *Arch Neurol;* 46: 885–892.

Alexander, M.P., Naeser, M.A., and Palumbo, C. 1990. Broca's area aphasias: aphasia after lesions including the frontal operculum. *Neurology;* 40: 353–362.

Appell, J., Kertesz, A., and Fisman, M. 1982. A study of language functioning in Alzheimer's disease. *Brain Lang;* 17: 73–91.

Ardila, A., and Rosselli, M. 1993. Spatial agraphia. *Brain Cognition;* 22: 137–147.

Arendt, H. 1978. *The Life of the Mind.* New York, Harcourt Brace Jovanovich.

Auerbach, S.H., and Alexander, M.P. 1981. Pure agraphia and unilateral optic ataxia associated with a left superior parietal lobule lesion. *J Neurol Neurosurg Psychiatry;* 44: 430–432.

Benson, D.F. 1977. The third alexia. *Arch Neurol;* 34: 327–331.

Benson, D.F. 1979. *Aphasia, Alexia, and Agraphia.* New York, Churchill Livingstone.

Benson, D.F. 1994. *The Neurology of Thinking.* New York, Oxford.

Benson, D.F., and Cummings, J.L. 1985. Agraphia. In: Fredricks, J.A.M. (ed.). *Handbook of Clinical Neurology.* 2nd ed., Vol. 45, *Clinical Neuropsychology,* Amsterdam, Elsevier, pp. 457–472.

Benson, D.F., Cummings, J.L., and Tsai, S.I. 1982. Angular gyrus syndrome simulating Alzheimer's disease. *Arch Neurol;* 39: 616–620.

Benton, A.L. 1961. The fiction of the "Gerstmann" syndrome. *J Neurol Neurosurg Psychiatry;* 24: 176–181.

Benton, A.L., and Pearl, D. 1978. *Dyslexia.* New York, Oxford.

Boller, F., and Grafman, J. 1985. Acalculia. In: Fredricks, J.A.M. (ed.). *Handbook of Clinical Neurology.* 2nd ed., Vol. 45, *Clinical Neuropsychology,* Amsterdam, Elsevier, pp. 473–481.

Broca, P. 1865. Sur la faculté du langage articulé. *Bull Soc Anthrop (Paris);* 6: 337–393.

Brown, J.W., and Hecaen, H. 1976. Lateralization and language representation. *Neurology;* 26: 183–189.

Chedru, F., and Geschwind, N. 1972. Writing disturbances in acute confusional states. *Neuropsychologia;* 10: 343–354.

Chi, J.G., Dooling, E.C., and Gilles, F.H. 1977. Gyral development of the human brain. *Ann Neurol;* 1: 86–93.

Coltheart, M., Patterson, K., and Marshall, J.C. 1980. *Deep Dyslexia.* London, Routledge and Kegan Paul.

Cranberg, L.D., Filley, C.M., Alexander, M.P., and Hart, E.J. 1987. Acquired aphasia in childhood: clinical and CT investigations. *Neurology;* 37: 1165–1172.

Damasio, A.R. 1992. Aphasia. *N Engl J Med;* 326: 531–539.

Damasio, A.R., and Damasio, H. 1992. Brain and language. *Sci Am;* 267(3): 89–95.

Damasio, H., and Damasio, A.R. 1980. The anatomical basis of conduction aphasia. *Brain;* 103: 337–350.

Dejerine, J. 1891. Sur un cas de cécité verbale avec agraphie, suivi d'autopsie. *Mem Soc Biol;* 3: 197–201.

Dejerine, J. 1892. Contribution à l'étude anatomo-pathologique et clinique des différentes variétés de cécité verbale. *Mem Soc Biol;* 4: 61–90.

Dubois, J., Hecaen, H., and Marcie, P. 1969. L'agraphie "pure." *Neuropsychologia;* 7: 271–286.

Exner, S. 1881. *Untersuchungen über die Lokalisation der Funktionen in der Grosshirnrinde des Menschen.* Vienna, Wilhelm Braumüller.

Filley, C.M., and Kelly, J.P. 1990. Neurobehavioral effects of focal subcortical lesions. In: Cummings, J.L. (ed.). *Subcortical Dementia.* New York, Oxford, pp. 59–70.

Freedman, M., Alexander, M.P., and Naeser, M.A. 1984. Anatomic basis of transcortical motor aphasia. *Neurology;* 34: 409–417.

Galaburda, A.M., Sherman, G.F., Rosen, G.D., et al. 1985. Developmental dyslexia: four consecutive patients with cortical anomalies. *Ann Neurol;* 18: 222–233.

Gerstmann, J. 1940. Syndrome of finger agnosia, disorientation for right and left, agraphia and acalculia. *Arch Neurol Psychiatry;* 44: 398–408.

Geschwind, N. 1965. Disconnexion syndromes in animals and man. *Brain;* 88: 237–294, 585–644.

Geschwind, N. 1967. Wernicke's contribution to the study of aphasia. *Cortex;* 3: 449–463.

Geschwind, N. 1970. The organization of language and the brain. *Science;* 170: 940–944.

Geschwind, N., Behan, P.O. 1984. Laterality, hormones, and immunity. In: Geschwind, N., and Galaburda, A.M., (eds.). *Cerebral Dominance. The Biological Foundations.* Cambridge, Harvard University Press, pp. 211–224.

Geschwind, N., and Levitsky, W. 1968. Human brain: left-right asymmetry in temporal speech region. *Science;* 161; 186–187.

Geschwind, N. Quadfasel, F.A., and Segarra, J.M. 1968. Isolation of the speech area. *Neuropsychologia;* 6: 327–340.

Hardyck, C., and Petrinovich, L.F. 1977. Left-handedness. *Psychol Bull;* 84: 385–404.

Kertesz, A., Sheppard, A., and MacKenzie, R. 1982. Localization in transcortical sensory aphasia. *Arch Neurol;* 39: 475–478.

Mohr, J.P., Pessin, M.S., Finkelstein, S., et al. 1978. Broca aphasia: pathologic and clinical. *Neurology;* 28: 311–324.

Naeser, M.A., and Hayward, R.W. 1978. Lesion localization in aphasia with cranial computed tomography and the Boston Diagnostic Aphasia Exam. *Neurology;* 28: 545–551.

Pennington, B.F. 1991. *Diagnosing Learning Disorders. A Neuropsychological Framework.* New York, Guilford.

Roeltgen, D.P. 1993. Agraphia. In: Heilman, K.M., and Valenstein, E. (eds.). *Clinical Neuropsychology.* 3rd ed. New York, Oxford, pp. 63–89.

Ross, E.D. 1981. The aprosodias: functional-anatomic organization of the affective components of language in the right hemisphere. *Arch Neurol;* 38: 561–569.

Rumsey, J.M., Zametkin, A.J., Andrenson, P., et al. 1994. Normal activation of frontotemporal language cortex in dyslexia, as measured with oxygen 15 positron emission tomography. *Arch Neurol;* 51: 27–38.

Savage-Rumbaugh, E.S., Rumbaugh, D.M., and Boysen, S. 1980. Do apes use language? *Am Sci;* 68: 49–61.

Schiff, H.B., Alexander, M.P., Naeser, M.A., and Galaburda, A.M. 1983. Aphemia. Clinical-anatomic correlations. *Arch Neurol;* 40: 720–727.

Skyhoj Olsen, T., Bruhn, T., and Oberg, G.E. 1986. Cortical hypoperfusion as a possible cause of "subcortical aphasia." *Brain;* 109: 393–410.

Smith, A., and Sugar, O. 1975. Development of above-normal language and intelligence 21 years after left hemispherectomy. *Neurology;* 25: 813–818.

Strub, R., and Geschwind, N. 1974. Gerstmann's syndrome without aphasia. *Cortex;* 10: 378–387.

Takayama, Y., Sugishita, M., Akiguchi, I., and Kimura, J. 1994. Isolated acalculia due to left parietal lesion. *Arch Neurol;* 51: 286–291.

Tranel, D., Biller, J., Damasio, H., et al. 1987. Global aphasia without hemiparesis. *Arch Neurol;* 44: 304–308.

Weintraub, S., Rubin, N.P., and Mesulam, M.-M. 1990. Primary progressive aphasia. Longitudinal course, neuropsychological profile, and language features. *Arch Neurol;* 47: 1329–1335.

Wernicke, C. 1874. *Der Aphasische Symptomencomplex.* Breslau, Cohn and Weigert.

Witelson, S.F., and Pallie, W. 1973. Left hemisphere specialization for language in the newborn. Neuroanatomical evidence of asymmetry. *Brain;* 96: 641–646.

CHAPTER 6

Apraxia

Apraxia is an acquired disorder of skilled purposeful movement (Heilman and Rothi, 1993). The term is often used as shorthand for "ideomotor apraxia" (see page 93), its most common variety, but it is best considered as a generic designation for higher motor impairment. Thus apraxia represents a loss of motor skill qualitatively distinct from paresis just as aphasia is distinct from dysarthria. In clinical practice, an apraxic patient must be shown to have a disorder of skilled movement not caused by significant paresis, akinesia, ataxia, sensory loss, inattention, comprehension deficit, or cognitive impairment. Apraxia is commonly encountered with aphasia, but it is not simply an aspect of linguistic dysfunction; the concurrence of the two syndromes is more likely a result of the neuroanatomic proximity of the language and higher motor systems than a manifestation of a common underlying mechanism (Hecaen and Albert, 1978). Like aphasia, however, apraxia is typically caused by ischemic cerebrovascular disease. In essence, apraxia is a syndrome of higher motor dysfunction, in the same way that agnosia (Chapter 7) represents higher sensory impairment.

Some terminological issues need to be dealt with as a first step. Many neurobehavioral syndromes with some component of motor dysfunction have been given the name "apraxia," but it is questionable whether they should be considered apraxias as defined above. *Constructional apraxia* is an alternate term for visuospatial impairment, and *dressing apraxia* denotes difficulty with dressing; both are right hemisphere syndromes (Chapter 8). *Ocular apraxia*, also called "oculomotor apraxia" or "psychic paralysis of gaze," is a component of Balint's syndrome and is described with the visual agnosias (Chapter 7). *Gait apraxia* (Denny-Brown, 1958) describes a disorder of gait seen in diseases affecting the frontal lobes such as normal pressure hydrocephalus (Chapter 12). *Verbal apraxia* is a term sometimes used by speech pathologists to describe impaired speech fluency and dysarthria (Kirshner, 1986). The discussion of apraxia that follows will confine itself to relatively uncontroversial uses of the word.

One of the most challenging syndromes in behavioral neurology, apraxia has presented theoretical problems since it was first recognized in the nineteenth century (Heilman and Rothi, 1993). The seminal papers of Hugo Liepmann in the early 1900s (Liepmann, 1900, 1906, 1908, 1920; Liepmann and Maas, 1907) structured the consideration of apraxia but raised many issues that are far from resolved. One problem has been the bewildering array of definitions of apraxia, engendering much confusion about its true meaning; this conceptual difficulty is illustrated by the fact that the definition advanced above actually describes what apraxia is not, rather than what it is (Heilman and Rothi, 1993). Furthermore, apraxic patients rarely complain of their deficits (Geschwind, 1975), in contrast to the often obvious problems encountered in those with aphasia and other syndromes. For these reasons, apraxia testing is often omitted from the mental status examination, and useful diagnostic and prognostic information is not obtained. In this chapter, apraxia will be considered in the context of the original classification of Liepmann, one that has long endured and serves to organize current thinking on this controversial subject. Table 6.1 lists the varieties of apraxia and their putative neuroanatomic bases.

Table 6.1 Localization of apraxia

Type	Lesion(s)
Limb-kinetic	Contralateral premotor area
Ideomotor	
Buccofacial	Left frontal operculum
Limb	Left perisylvian area or anterior corpus callosum
Axial	Left temporal lobe
Ideational	Left parietal lobe or diffuse involvement

Limb-Kinetic Apraxia

This variety of apraxia is the least frequently diagnosed, reflecting an uncertainty about whether it differs from mild paresis. Also known as "melokinetic apraxia" or "innervatory apraxia," *limb-kinetic apraxia* occurs in patients with limited lesions of the premotor area (the lateral portion of Brodmann area 6; see Figure 1.3) or subjacent white matter, and it is a unilateral disorder opposite to the involved hemisphere (Hier et al., 1987). These patients display a loss of the usual agility, efficiency, and precision of the affected side, most notably in the hand. Thus there may be difficulty with such tasks as picking up a coin from a table and buttoning a shirt. Although gross movements are normal and there is no incoordination, tasks such as pantomime and object manipulation present obstacles. Gestures used for pantomime appear clumsy, and the simple manual act of playing cards poses special difficulties. Limb-kinetic apraxia is a disorder in which only the most demanding motor acts, requiring the most delicately organized cortical circuitry, are precluded. Clinical recognition of this deficit may temper what is otherwise considered a good recovery from a frontal lobe insult.

Limb-kinetic apraxia has been a controversial entity, some authorities maintaining that the syndrome only reflects primary motor dysfunction (Kirshner, 1986; Strub and Black, 1993). Although it is possible that limb-kinetic apraxia reflects corticospinal dysfunction alone, it is noteworthy that lesions in the internal capsule, a subcortical component of the corticospinal tract, may not cause the syndrome (Hier et al., 1987). The premotor lesion may therefore cause a qualitatively distinct form of motor impairment.

Ideomotor Apraxia

Ideomotor apraxia is the most common of the apraxias and has been subjected to the most detailed analysis. The defining feature of this disorder is the failure of a patient to carry out a motor act on verbal command, even though comprehension of the request is preserved, the primary motor system for its execution is intact, and the activity can be easily performed spontaneously (Benson and Geschwind, 1985). Thus there has been presumed to be a separation between the idea of an act and its performance. The syndrome may be evident in the buccofacial (oral), limb, or axial musculature. Patients fail most notably on pantomime tasks; they show less severe impairment in imitation of the examiner or use of an actual object. In contrast to limb-kinetic apraxia, ideomotor apraxia is usually bilateral, and in contrast to ideational apraxia (see page 97), ideomotor apraxia refers to a single action, not a sequential movement.

Ideomotor praxis is tested by directing the patient to perform certain learned movements that require buccofacial, limb, and axial musculature. Examples would be, respectively, "Blow out a match," "Flip a coin," and "Swing a baseball bat." Intransitive gestures can also be observed, such as those elicited by directing a patient to "Cough," "Wave good-bye," and "Stand up." First the examiner asks for the action without demonstrating it; if the patient fails this task, imitation of the examiner's movement can sometimes improve performance. If there is still no success, an occasional patient can improve on a transitive task by actually using the object involved (e.g., blowing out a lighted match). Inability to use the actual object indicates the most severe form of ideomotor apraxia. By advancing through this sequence, the examiner can develop a quite detailed notion of the depth and nature of the apraxic disturbance.

There are several ways that errors in ideomotor praxis can be made. Most unmistakable is simply the failure to generate any response at all. Perseveration on a task performed previously is common (e.g., after successfully blowing out a match, the patient then repeats that procedure when asked to suck on a straw). Sometimes a vocalization is produced instead of the desired action itself (e.g., saying "cough" rather than coughing). Finally, the use of a body part as an object is frequently seen (e.g., using the hand instead of the comb).

Theories concerning ideomotor apraxia have proved to be a major impetus to the notion of cerebral disconnection, first posited by Liepmann and then vigorously defended by Geschwind (Geschwind, 1965). There is now a Liepmann-Geschwind model of ideomotor apraxia that predicts the localization of lesions based on disconnection of critical cerebral areas (Figure 6.1).

The model proposed considers ideomotor apraxia to occur after damage to one or more of three different areas (Absher and Benson, 1993). First, a lesion in the left parietal lobe can cause damage to the arcuate fasciculus, interrupting the flow of information anteriorly and preventing the motor system from receiving the direction to act (Benson et al., 1973). Conduction aphasia is commonly present. Second, a large lesion in the left premotor area can cause the deficit by interfering with the motor execution of the act, usually in association with nonfluent aphasia and right hemiparesis (Geschwind, 1975). When there is hemiparesis, apraxia in the nonparetic left hand is sometimes called *sympathetic*

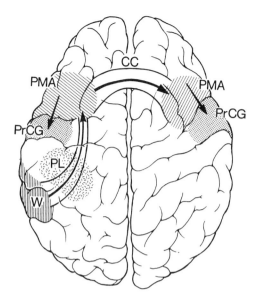

Figure 6.1 Schematic view of brain areas important for ideomotor praxis. W—Wernicke's area; PL—parietal lobe; PMA—premotor area; PrCG—precentral gyrus; CC—corpus callosum. After Geschwind, 1975.

apraxia. Finally, damage to the anterior corpus callosum can lead to ideomotor apraxia that is evident only in the left hand (*callosal apraxia*; Geschwind and Kaplan, 1962); the right hand is unaffected and there is no aphasia in this situation.

The disconnection theory of ideomotor apraxia has not gone unchallenged, however. An issue of considerable controversy in this area centers on the possibility of left hemisphere repositories for movement patterns. These engrams for praxis could be stored in the frontal lobe, where programming for motor execution might take place (Devinsky, 1992). Alternatively, Heilman has made an argument for the existence of "visuokinesthetic engrams" in the parietal lobe (Heilman and Rothi, 1993), pointing out that some apraxic patients can neither perform accurate movements nor recognize them in others and therefore must have lost the internal representation of the movements (Heilman et al., 1982). At this point, the debate between the disconnection and the praxis engram theories cannot be resolved, although it is not inconceivable that all may be correct depending on the patient and the lesion involved.

It should be apparent that ideomotor apraxia can occur with lesions virtually anywhere in the perisylvian language area, and indeed clinical experience bears out this prediction (Alexander et al., 1992). The relatively low frequency of apraxia with right hemisphere lesions (DeRenzi et al., 1980; Alexander et al., 1992) also suggests a dominance of the left hemisphere for learned movements not unlike its dominance for language. Left hemisphere dominance for praxis is also supported by studies of callosal apraxia (Graff-Radford et al., 1987). A notable recent finding has been that buccofacial (oral) apraxia seems to relate particularly to left frontal operculum and paraventricular white matter lesions (Tognola and Vignolo, 1980; Alexander et al., 1992). Limb apraxia, on the other hand, is not currently associated with a specific perisylvian area (Basso et al., 1980, 1987; Kertesz and Ferro, 1984; Alexander et al., 1992). In the case of axial apraxia, perisylvian lesions do not appear to be involved, and the cerebral basis of axial praxis is unresolved; Geschwind (1975) suggested that descending pathways from the left temporal lobe to the pons and cerebellum could be responsible.

A related matter concerns the relationship of praxis to skills, often discussed in the context of procedural memory (Chapter 4). Although the neurologic literature on amnesia rarely intersects with that on apraxia, it may well be that skill learning and the acquisition of praxis are identical phenomena. The anatomic basis of skill learning has remained unclear—except that the medial temporal system is not involved—but there is some evidence that motor structures including the basal ganglia (Martone et al., 1984) and the cerebellum (Sanes et al., 1990) participate in the acquisition of new skills. With practice and repetition, motor skills may be increasingly incorporated into cortical areas and become gradually less dependent on subcortical structures. It is speculative but reasonable to posit that there may be a cortical representation of these motor memories in the left hemisphere and that praxis represents the motor equivalent of remote declarative memory. Ideomotor apraxia in Alzheimer's Disease (Cummings and Benson, 1992), therefore, would imply a loss of learned motor skills that accompanies the decline in other cognitive domains resulting from cortical degeneration.

The importance of ideomotor apraxia lies in its localizing value and in its propensity to interfere with recovery of function in patients with cerebrovascular disease. A secure association of this form of apraxia with focal left hemisphere lesions or, less often, the anterior corpus callosum, has been established, and neuroimaging techniques are likely to refine the anatomy of the syndrome still further. In the rehabilitation of persons with neurologic disease, the deleterious effects of ideomotor apraxia can be quite problematic. Patients with right hemiplegia who must use their left side, for example, may discover that acquisition of motor skills by the left hand is severely limited by sympathetic apraxia. Similarly, nonfluent aphasics with buccofacial apraxia may have difficulty producing speech sounds, thus complicating the existing language problem and impeding the rehabilitative process.

Ideational Apraxia

The final apraxic category initially proposed by Liepmann is *ideational apraxia*, which in his view was the failure to perform a sequential motor act even though each constituent act could be performed in isolation (Liepmann, 1920). Thus patients fail at a complex task because of a faulty overall plan, despite the preservation of individual acts (Lehmkuhl and Poeck, 1981). Ideational apraxia is present, for example, when a patient cannot complete a series of actions such as folding a letter, inserting it in an envelope and sealing it, and applying a postage stamp, despite being able to perform each act by itself. Although damage to the left parietal lobe has been implicated in the genesis of ideational apraxia (Hier et al., 1987; Devinsky, 1992), the localization is unsettled because patients with diffuse cortical involvement from degenerative dementia also display the syndrome (Pick, 1905; Cummings and Benson, 1992). It is possible that parietal involvement in Alzheimer's Disease (Chapter 12) explains the failure to perform sequential acts, but alternatively, this deficit could imply frontal lobe dysfunction because it resembles the executive function deficits seen with bilateral prefrontal damage (Chapter 10).

Unfortunately, other definitions of the term "ideational apraxia" have been advanced, and serious confusion exists in this area (Heilman and Rothi, 1993). The term has been employed to mean a deficit in the manipulation of actual objects, or tool use (DeRenzi et al., 1968), and the loss of knowledge of how to use an object or tool has been emphasized (DeRenzi and Lucchelli, 1988). Others have interpreted this syndrome as a conceptual defect (Ochipa et al., 1989), an interpretation that may reconcile these various viewpoints. None of these formulations of ideational apraxia, however, appears to indicate cerebral pathology with any precision, and its practical utility as a concept is limited.

References

Absher, J.R., and Benson, D.F. 1993. Disconnection syndromes: an overview of Geschwind's contributions. *Neurology;* 43: 862–867.

Alexander, M.P., Baker, E., Naeser, M.A., et al. 1992. Neuropsychological and neuroanatomical dimensions of ideomotor apraxia. *Brain;* 115: 87–107.

Basso, A., Luzzatti, C., and Spinnler, H. 1980. Is ideomotor apraxia the outcome of damage to well-defined regions of the left hemisphere? Neuropsychological study of CAT correlation. *J Neurol Neurosurg Psychiatry;* 43: 118–126.

Basso, A., Capitani, E., Della Sala, S., et al. 1987. Recovery from ideomotor apraxia. A study on acute stroke patients. *Brain;* 110: 747–760.

Benson, D.F., and Geschwind, N. 1985. Aphasia and related disorders: a clinical approach. In: Mesulam, M.-M. *Principles of Behavioral Neurology.* Philadelphia, F.A. Davis, pp. 193–238.

Benson, D.F., Sheremata, W.A., Buchard, R., et al. 1973. Conduction aphasia. *Arch Neurol;* 28: 339–346.

Cummings, J.L., and Benson, D.F. 1992. *Dementia. A Clinical Approach.* 2nd ed. Boston, Butterworth-Heinemann.

Denny-Brown, D.D. 1958. The nature of apraxia. *J Nerv Ment Dis;* 126: 9–33.

DeRenzi, E., and Lucchelli, F. 1988. Ideational apraxia. *Brain;* 111: 1173–1185.

DeRenzi, E., Pieczuro, A., and Vignolo, L.A. 1968. Ideational apraxia: a quantitative study. *Neuropsychologia;* 6: 41–52.

DeRenzi, E., Motti, F., and Nichelli, P. 1980. Imitating gestures: a quantitative approach to ideomotor apraxia. *Arch Neurol;* 37: 6–10.

Devinsky, O. 1992. *Behavioral Neurology. 100 Maxims.* St. Louis, Mosby Year Book.

Geschwind, N. 1965. Disconnexion syndromes in animals and man. *Brain;* 88: 237–294, 585–644.

Geschwind, N. 1975. The apraxias: neural mechanisms of disorders of learned movement. *Am Sci;* 63: 188–195.

Geschwind, N., and Kaplan, E. 1962. A human cerebral deconnection syndrome. *Neurology;* 12: 675–685.

Graff-Radford, N.R., Welsh, K., and Godersky, J. 1987. Callosal apraxia. *Neurology;* 37: 100–105.

Hecaen, H., and Albert, M.L. 1978. *Human Neuropsychology.* New York, John Wiley and Sons.

Heilman, K.M., and Rothi, L.J.G. 1993. Apraxia. In: Heilman, K.M., and Valenstein, E. (eds.). *Clinical Neuropsychology.* 3rd ed. New York, Oxford, pp. 141–163.

Heilman, K.M., Rothi, L.J., and Valenstein, E. 1982. Two forms of ideomotor apraxia. *Neurology;* 32: 342–346.

Hier, D.B., Gorelick, P.B., and Schindler, A.G. 1987. *Topics in Behavioral Neurology and Neuropsychology.* Boston, Butterworths.

Kertesz, A., and Ferro, J.M. 1984. Lesion size and location in ideomotor apraxia. *Brain;* 107: 921–933.

Kirshner, H. 1986. *Behavioral Neurology: A Practical Approach.* New York, Churchill Livingstone.

Lehmkuhl, G., and Poeck, K. 1981. A disturbance in the conceptual organization of actions in patients with ideational apraxia. *Cortex;* 17: 153–158.

Liepmann, H., 1900. Das Krankheitsbild der Apraxie (motorischen Asymbolie auf Grund eines Falles von einseitiger Apraxie). *Monatsschrift für Psychiat Neurol;* 8: 15–44, 102–132, 182–197.

Liepmann, H. 1906. Der weitere Kranksheitverlauf bei den einseitig Apraktischen und der Gehirnbefund auf Grund von Schnittserien. *Monatsschrift für Psychiat Neurol;* 17: 289-311, 217–243.

Liepmann, H. 1908. *Drei Aufsätze aus dem Apraxiegebiet.* Berlin, Karger.

Liepmann, H. 1920. Apraxie. *Ergbn der ges Med;* 1: 516–543.

Liepmann, H., and Maas, O. 1907. Fall von linksseitiger Agraphie und Apraxie bei rechtsseitiger Lähmung. *Z für Psychol Neurol;* 10: 214–217.

Martone, M., Butters, N., Payne, M., et al. 1984. Dissociations between skill learning and verbal recognition in amnesia and dementia. *Arch Neurol;* 41: 965–970.

Ochipa, C., Rothi, L.J.G., and Heilman, K.M. 1989. Ideational apraxia: a deficit in tool selection and use. *Ann Neurol;* 25: 190–193.

Pick, A. 1905. *Studien über Motorische Apraxie und ihr Nahestehende Erscheinungen.* Leipzig, Deuticke.

Sanes, J.N., Dimitrov, B., and Hallett, M. 1990. Motor learning in patients with cerebellar dysfunction. *Brain;* 113: 103–120.

Strub, R.L., and Black, F.W. 1993. *The Mental Status Examination in Neurology.* 3rd ed. Philadelphia, F.A. Davis.

Tognola, G., and Vignolo, L.A. 1980. Brain lesions associated with oral apraxia in stroke patients: a clinico-neuroradiological investigation with the CT scan. *Neuropsychologia;* 18: 257–272.

CHAPTER 7

Agnosia

Agnosia is fundamentally a disorder of recognition. Like aphasia and apraxia, it most often follows a focal or multifocal cerebrovascular event. A patient with agnosia fails to recognize a stimulus even when primary sensory modalities have registered its features adequately. From the Greek word *gnosis,* and meaning "absence of knowledge," the term was first introduced by Sigmund Freud in 1891 in his early monograph on aphasia (Freud, 1891). Since then, no syndrome in behavioral neurology has engendered more debate, confusion, and controversy. It has been asserted, for example, that the number of suggested mechanisms for visual agnosia nearly equals the number of reported cases of the syndrome (Benson and Greenberg, 1969). A consideration of agnosia challenges the student of behavior due to the complexity of patients with various agnosias and the conceptual difficulties inherent in the organization of higher sensory function.

The detection of agnosia in a given individual is rarely straightforward. Patients may not offer specific complaints that suggest agnosia, and findings may be subtle on examination. It will be recalled, in fact, that no specific category for agnosia was included in the mental status examination (Chapter 2), as the syndrome is sufficiently uncommon that cases can be considered on an individual basis. Agnosic deficits may appear, however, in the course of the clinical history taking, as, for example, in the case of reported difficulty recognizing a familiar object or sound. Problems may also be uncovered in the mental status examination, such as comprehension deficit suggesting pure word deafness, and even in the elemental neurologic examination when a person shows impairments in visual or tactile function or in higher sensory processing. Extra time and ingenuity are often required to elicit and interpret the agnosias, but the results of this effort can be informative and clinically useful.

A standard definition of agnosia holds that it involves "a normal percept that has somehow been stripped of its meaning" (Teuber, 1968). Information from the external world is received but not recognized; its previously acquired meaning is no longer attached to it. A key feature of agnosia is that it exists only in a given sensory modality; an object that cannot be identified through one modality can be recognized in another. A visual agnosic, for example, cannot identify a set of keys by sight but can easily do so when allowed to hear them jingle or feel them manually. Similarly, a word-deaf patient cannot understand spoken language but is easily able to read. Thus agnosia is modality specific and represents a disruption of a single input system that associates meaning with sensation. It is apparent in this formulation that agnosia differs from anomia; inability to name an object implies a loss of its word representation and does not differ depending on the sensory system involved, whereas inability to recognize an object implies a loss of access to the encoded meaning that is normally activated through a single sensory modality. Moreover, an anomic patient recognizes the meaning of an object that cannot be named.

In clinical practice, demonstration of agnosia requires the absence of primary sensory loss, acute confusional state, aphasia, and severe dementia, all of which can mimic the syndrome. Because agnosia generally occurs in the context of large hemispheric lesions, this requirement is frequently difficult to meet, and unequivocal cases are rare in the literature. Indeed, vigorous opposition to the concept of agnosia, especially visual agnosia, has been raised by critics who claim that agnosia merely reflects a combination of primary sensory loss and intellectual deterioration (Bay, 1953; Bender and Feldman, 1972). However, recent years have witnessed substantial progress in the identification of agnosias, and a better understanding of the anatomical basis of these intriguing disorders is emerging. Three general categories have been traditionally considered: visual, auditory, and tactile (Bauer, 1993). Table 7.1 summarizes the presumed localization of these various syndromes.

Visual Agnosia

The first point to be considered in this section is the issue of *cortical blindness*. In this syndrome, extensive bilateral destruction of the primary visual cortex in the occipital lobe (Brodmann area 17 [see Figure 1.3], also called the striate cortex or calcarine cortex) or its underlying white matter leads

Table 7.1 Localization of agnosia

Type	Lesion(s)
Visual	
Apperceptive	Bilateral occipital lobe
Associative	Bilateral occipitotemporal region
Object agnosia	Left or bilateral occipitotemporal region
Prosopagnosia	Right or bilateral occipitotemporal region
Central achromatopsia	Bilateral occipitotemporal region
Simultanagnosia	Bilateral occipitoparietal region
Auditory	
Pure word deafness	Left or bilateral temporal lobe
Auditory sound agnosia	Right or bilateral temporal lobe
Tactile	Contralateral parietal lobe

to blindness with preserved pupillary responses and absent optokinetic nystagmus (Symonds and Mackenzie, 1957). The syndrome is often accompanied by denial of blindness, a form of anosognosia known as *Anton's syndrome* (Anton, 1899). Affected patients act as though their vision is intact, and their propensity to collide with walls and furniture may be explained away with confabulations about poor lighting or the inadequacy of their glasses. The origin of this visual anosognosia is not known (Damasio, 1985), but it is possible that an associated right parietal lesion could impair the awareness of disability or that coexistent bilateral medial temporal lesions affecting memory could affect the ability to remember blindness.

Another point to be clarified is the nature of the visual agnosia reported as part of the Klüver-Bucy syndrome, a disorder first produced in monkeys by the ablation of both anterior temporal lobes (Klüver and Bucy, 1939). This syndrome, which is also encountered in several human conditions affecting the temporal lobes (Lilly et al., 1983), includes among its manifestations a disturbance of vision, but the deficit is essentially one of failure to recognize the emotional significance of a visually presented object. For example, monkeys so affected fail to distinguish edible from inedible objects. The alternate term "psychic blindness" (Klüver and Bucy, 1939), then, may be preferable to "visual agnosia," and the disorder may be more appropriately considered a visual-limbic disconnection than a disturbance of higher visual function. Visual agnosia is properly considered a cognitive disorder, whereas the Klüver-Bucy syndrome involves a disturbance of emotional processing. Chapter 9 will take up the Klüver-Bucy syndrome in more detail.

The terminology surrounding the topic of *visual agnosia* and its variants is difficult, and no classification scheme has gained universal acceptance. The problem of determining a taxonomy for the visual agnosias is an important one, for it influences how theories of higher visual function are developed (Farah, 1990). Despite the uncertainty in this field, a basic distinction that enjoys widespread popularity is that proposed by Lissauer between apperceptive and associative varieties (Lissauer, 1890). This division presupposes a two-step process of visual recognition: the synthesis of visual elements into a unified image ("apperception") and the matching of the image with previously encoded visual information ("association"). Although this distinction may not be straightforward in individual cases (DeRenzi and Lucchelli, 1993), Lissauer's terminology will be employed here as an organizing framework.

Apperceptive visual agnosia, the more controversial of the two types, is a failure to recognize objects because of a failure to perceive them. Patients with apperceptive visual agnosia have bilateral occipital lobe lesions and areas of impaired elemental vision, but they fail to recognize objects even in preserved areas of vision. This syndrome differs from cortical blindness by the less extensive occipital destruction that allows normal visual acuity in spared fields, but forms and shapes are not recognized, and affected patients are unable to draw misidentified items or match them to samples (Benson and Greenberg, 1969). The specific deficits beyond these general features have varied greatly in the reported cases (Bauer, 1993).

Associative visual agnosia, less common but more convincing when it is encountered, involves a defect in recognizing a well-perceived visual stimulus. Again there is impairment of visual recognition, but these patients are clearly not blind in a functional sense; unlike apperceptive visual agnosics, they can make drawings of pictures they cannot recognize or name, and they can match drawings and pictures to samples (Rubens and Benson, 1971). In addition, deficits in color naming and pure alexia (Chapter 5) are frequently seen in associative visual agnosia, which led Geschwind to explain the syndrome as a visual-verbal disconnection (Geschwind, 1965). However, there have been autopsy-verified cases of associative visual agnosia with bilateral lesions of the occipitotemporal cortex and subjacent white matter (Benson et al., 1974; Albert et al., 1979), suggesting that destruction of the areas retaining memories for visual objects is an alternative explanation.

Since Lissauer's original apperceptive/associative distinction, other more specific categories of visual agnosia have been examined. Each of these entities—object agnosia, prosopagnosia, central achromatopsia, and simultanagnosia—identifies a breakdown in some aspect of higher visual function. In all these syndromes, primary visual cortices are typically intact whereas some components of the visual association areas are damaged (Table 7.1). The anatomic basis of these disorders is becoming clarified through more numerous case studies and functional imaging techniques, and the study of higher visual function is an area of active research and controversy.

Object agnosia refers specifically to difficulty recognizing objects such as a pencil, chair, or clock. Object recognition has been thought to depend on either left unilateral or bilateral occipitotemporal regions (lingual and fusiform gyri), and infarction in the cortex and underlying white matter of these areas has caused object agnosia (Bauer, 1993). The term *optic aphasia* refers to a milder form of this disorder in which visually presented objects can be recognized but not named and auditory and tactile naming are normal (Bauer, 1993). Recent PET data from normal subjects indicate that object recognition may depend predominantly on left occipitotemporal regions (Sergent et al. 1992). Although the issue of lateralization in this syndrome has not been resolved, the frequent occurrence of right homonymous hemianopsia and alexia with object agnosia argues for a left hemisphere advantage for object recognition.

In contrast, facial recognition may depend on right hemisphere structures more than left. The interesting syndrome of *prosopagnosia* or face agnosia involves selective impairment of the recognition of faces, which may even extend to the ability to recognize one's own face in a mirror (Bauer, 1993). It has been a matter of some controversy whether bilateral lesions are necessary for the development of prosopagnosia. Many cases have been found to have bilateral lesions of the occipitotemporal cortex and white matter (Damasio et al., 1982). Recent observations have indicated, however, that a single right occipitotemporal lesion is sufficient to cause the syndrome (DeRenzi et al., 1994). Although both hemispheres participate in face recognition, the right visual association cortices appear to have an advantage in this capacity (Damasio et al., 1990). PET studies in normal subjects have also been consistent with this notion (Sergent et al. 1992). Thus face and object processing appear to be dissociated so that the right and left hemispheres are functionally specialized for these respective tasks.

Central achromatopsia is a loss of color vision due to occipitotemporal damage (Damasio et al., 1980). When both hemispheres are involved, the achromatopsia is complete, and unilateral lesions can cause quadrantic or hemifield color deficits. Patients complain of a "gray" or "washed-out" look in affected areas of vision. Supportive work from neurophysiological studies of laboratory animals has documented the existence of color-coded neurons in the occipitotemporal regions that are presumably dedicated to central color processing (Damasio, 1985). A different syndrome is *color anomia,* often occurring with pure alexia (Geschwind and Fusillo, 1966), in which color naming but not color recognition is impaired.

Finally, there is the intriguing problem of *simultanagnosia* (simultaneous agnosia), a disorder in which there is failure to synthesize all the elements of a picture or scene even though its constituent components can be recognized in isolation (Wolpert, 1924). Simultanagnosia is in fact one of the three features of *Balint's syndrome* (Balint, 1909), a rare condition caused by bilateral occipitoparietal lesions; the other components are so-called *ocular apraxia* (also referred to as "oculomotor apraxia" or "psychic paralysis of gaze"), an inability to shift gaze voluntarily from a fixation point, and *optic ataxia,* difficulty in pointing to objects in the visual fields due to a disturbance of stereopsis. The usual reported cause of Balint's syndrome has been stroke from hypotension. Recently, cases of simultanagnosia heralding the onset of degenerative dementia have been presented, and in some patients an atypical posterior distribution of changes consistent with Alzheimer's Disease has been found (Graff-Radford et al., 1993). The complete Balint's syndrome has also been described recently in cases of posterior cortical atrophy (Benson et al., 1988). The interesting suggestion has been made that simultanagnosia is a disorder of vigilance in which attentional mechanisms of both posterior hemispheres are disturbed and there is difficulty maintaining conscious experience of visual stimuli—the patient therefore "looks but does not see" (Rizzo and Hurtig, 1987).

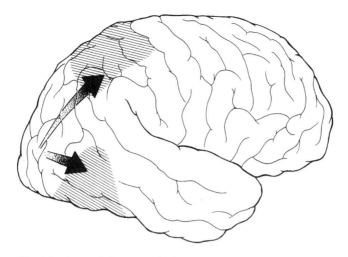

Figure 7.1 Visual association areas in the parietal and temporal lobes, processing spatial and object properties, respectively, of the visual image. After Mishkin, et al., 1993.

The anatomy of higher visual processing has recently become clarified from studies in higher primates and normal humans, and this new information illuminates the visual agnosias in general (Figure 7.1). It now appears as though there are two systems, *ventral* and *dorsal,* that serve to process primary visual information once it has been assembled by the occipital cortex (Mishkin et al., 1983; Haxby et al., 1991). These systems have also been labeled *parvocellular* and *magnocellular,* respectively, corresponding to separate populations of neurons in the lateral geniculate nucleus of the thalamus that provide visual input to the cortical processing areas. The ventral system, involving the temporal lobe (Brodmann area 37; see Figure 1.3), deals with object properties such as shape, form, and color, and the dorsal system, extending into the parietal lobe (Brodmann area 7; see Figure 1.3), with spatial properties such as location, motion, and stereopsis. These two parallel neural streams may also be considered the *what* and the *where* systems, respectively.

In light of this dichotomy, all the variants of visual agnosia that have just been considered can be reconciled. Apperceptive visual agnosia is related to bilateral occipital damage that prevents the adequate perception of visual stimuli. Associative visual agnosia is a term that best serves at present as a generic designation for object and face recognition deficits that follow bilateral occipitotemporal lesions. The ventral system, responsible for object properties, is affected in object agnosia, prosopagnosia, and central achromatopsia, whereas the dorsal system, responsible for spatial properties, is affected in simultanagnosia. After a century of perplexing case reports and cryptic theorizing, this formulation offers a systematic framework for visual agnosia that should usefully guide further study of this fascinating topic.

Before leaving the visual agnosias, brief mention of defects in *visual imagery* should be made. Imagery means "seeing in the mind's eye" and, in contrast to visual hallucinations and dreaming, is a voluntary act. Activation of stored information in the visual system is required for visual imagery, and imagery defects probably reflect damage to visual association areas where knowledge of the external environment is represented. Case studies have disclosed that visual imagery impairments may selectively implicate the ventral and dorsal systems, and these deficits parallel the recognition disorder associated with these regions—that is, loss of object- color imagery is associated with prosopagnosia and achromatopsia due to temporooccipital damage, and loss of visuospatial imagery occurs with visual disorientation from parietooccipital damage (Levine et al., 1985). Although it might be imagined that the right hemisphere excels at visual imagery, the left hemisphere also appears to participate, and the current clinical and experimental evidence favors the view that both hemispheres make important contributions to visual imagery (Kosslyn, 1988; Sergent, 1990).

Auditory Agnosia

Auditory agnosia is analogous to visual agnosia in that bilateral cerebral lesions are often implicated, but in this case the damage centers in the temporal lobes. As in the case of cortical blindness, extensive bilateral involvement results in *cortical deafness;* the damage is in the primary auditory cortices (Heschl's gyri; Brodmann areas 41 and 42 [see Figure 1.3]) or their underlying white matter (Earnest et al., 1977). However, the syndrome of auditory agnosia requires demonstration of a modality-specific impairment in recognition of auditory stimuli. Two forms of auditory agnosia have been described: auditory word agnosia, or pure word deafness, and auditory sound agnosia.

Pure word deafness is a syndrome of impaired recognition of speech sounds. Voices are heard but words do not make sense. In contrast, hearing as tested by pure tone audiometry is intact. Although the syndrome is closely allied to Wernicke's aphasia (Chapter 5), and may indeed evolve from this aphasia in a recovering patient, it is distinguished from aphasia by the preservation of spontaneous speech, reading, and writing (Coslett et al., 1984). Precise delineation of the two syndromes can be difficult, however, because word-deaf patients usually have repetition impairment and may have paraphasic speech. The pathologic anatomy of these cases is thought to involve a disconnection of the primary auditory area on both sides (Heschl's gyri; Brodmann areas 41 and 42 [see Figure 1.3]) from Wernicke's area (Geschwind, 1970), and lesions may be bilateral (Auerbach et al., 1982) or unilateral left temporal (Albert and Bear, 1974). The rarity of pure word deafness relates in part to the discrete location of lesions necessary to disconnect Wernicke's area from auditory input without at the same time destroying it.

Auditory sound agnosia is even less common than pure word deafness. Here the deficit involves recognition of nonverbal sounds, such as bells ringing and dogs barking, in the presence of normal hearing and intact language function. Although the anatomic basis of this syndrome is uncertain, it may be a right hemisphere analog of pure word deafness because reported cases have documented either right side (Spreen et al., 1965) or bilateral (Albert et al., 1972) lesions that interrupt the input of nonverbal sounds to the right hemisphere processing system. Recent studies of patients with unilateral right or left temporoparietal strokes have suggested that the cortical auditory areas of both hemispheres participate in the recognition of nonverbal sounds but that the right side is concerned with sound discrimination and the left side with semantic processing of the sound (Schnider et al., 1994).

Tactile Agnosia

Tactile agnosia is the least well understood of the agnosias, although ironically it is frequently sought in the routine neurologic examination. For practical purposes it is acceptable to equate tactile agnosia with "astereognosis," a "cortical" sensory deficit commonly acknowledged to be of modest localizing value in parietal lobe lesions contralateral to the hand in which the deficit is found (Hecaen and David, 1945). As is true for all the agnosias, acute confusional state, aphasia, and severe dementia must be excluded before a diagnosis of tactile agnosia can be made. Then, if primary somatosensory function—pain, temperature, light touch, vibration, and proprioception—is intact and the patient fails to identify shapes or objects placed in the hand, a contralateral parietal lobe lesion can be suspected.

The neuroanatomic basis of tactile agnosia is unclear. It may be that judgment of such tactile features as size, shape, texture, and weight is a specific sensory function of the postcentral gyrus (Brodmann areas 3, 1, and 2; see Figure 1.3) or that recognition of these properties depends on additional processing in more posterior parietal areas. If both these are possible, then a distinction into apperceptive and associative forms, as in visual agnosia, is conceivable. Studies of tactile recognition have found clinical deficits to correlate with lesions in the hand region of the contralateral postcentral gyrus (Corkin et al., 1970; Roland, 1976), supporting the apperceptive hypothesis, but much uncertainty remains. It should also be mentioned that tactile agnosia may be due to impaired spatial orientation seen in right hemisphere lesions generally (Semmes, 1965) and that occasional cases of left hand tactile agnosia may represent a modality-specific naming deficit due to callosal disconnection (Geschwind and Kaplan, 1962).

References

Albert, M.L., and Bear, D.1974. Time to understand: a case study of word deafness with reference to the role of time in auditory comprehension. *Brain;* 97: 373–384.

Albert, M.L., Soffer, D., Silverberg, R., and Reches, A. 1979. The anatomic basis of visual agnosia. *Neurology;* 29: 876–879.

Albert, M.L., Sparks, R., von Stockert, T., and Sax, D. 1972. A case of auditory agnosia: linguistic and nonlinguistic processing. *Cortex;* 8: 427–443.

Anton, G. 1899. Über die Selbstwahrnehmungen der Herderkrankungen des Gehirns durch den Kranken bei Rindenblindheit und Rindentaubheit. *Arch für Psychiat;* 11: 227–229.

Auerbach, S.H., Allard, T., Naeser, M., et al. 1982. Pure word deafness: analysis of a case with bilateral lesions and a defect at the prephonemic level. *Brain;* 105: 271–300.

Balint, R. 1909. Seelenlähmung des "Schauens," optische Ataxie, räumliche Störung der Aufmerksamkeit. *Monatschr für Psychiat Neurol;* 25: 51–81.

Bauer, R.M. 1993. Agnosia. In: Heilman, K.M., and Valenstein, E. *Clinical Neuropsychology.* 3rd ed. New York, Oxford, pp. 215–278.

Bay, E. 1953. Disturbances of visual perception and their examination. *Brain;* 76: 515–550.

Bender, M.B., and Feldman, M. 1972. The so-called "visual agnosias." *Brain;* 95: 173–176.

Benson, D.F., and Greenberg, J.P. 1969. Visual form agnosia. *Arch Neurol;* 20: 82–89.

Benson, D.F., Davis, R.J., and Snyder, B.D. 1988. Posterior cortical atrophy. *Arch Neurol;* 45: 789–793.

Benson, D.F., Segarra, J., and Albert, M.L. 1974. Visual agnosia–prosopagnosia. A clinico-pathologic correlation. *Arch Neurol;* 30: 307–310.

Corkin, S., Milner, B., and Rasmussen, T. 1970. Somatosensory thresholds: contrasting effects of postcentral-gyrus and posterior parietal lobe excision. *Arch Neurol;* 23: 41–58.

Coslett, H.B., Brashear, H.R., and Heilman, K.M. 1984. Pure word deafness after bilateral primary auditory cortex infarcts. *Neurology;* 34: 347–352.

Damasio, A.R. 1985. Disorders of complex visual processing: agnosias, achromatopsia, Balint's syndrome, and related difficulties of orientation and construction. In: Mesulam, M.-M. *Principles of Behavioral Neurology.* Philadelphia, F.A. Davis, pp. 259–288.

Damasio, A.R., Damasio, H., and Van Hoesen, G.W. 1982. Prosopagnosia: anatomic basis and behavioral mechanisms. *Neurology;* 32: 331–341.

Damasio, A.R., Tranel, D., and Damasio, H. 1990. Face agnosia and the neural substrates of memory. *Ann Rev Neurosci;* 13: 89–109.

Damasio, A.R., Yamada, T., Damasio, H., et al. 1980. Central achromatopsia: behavioral, anatomic, and physiologic aspects. *Neurology;* 30: 1064–1071.

DeRenzi, E., and Lucchelli, F. 1993. The fuzzy boundaries of apperceptive agnosia. *Cortex;* 29: 187–225.

DeRenzi, E., Perani, D., Carlesimo, G.A., et al. 1994. Prosopagnosia can be associated with damage confined to the right hemisphere—an MRI and PET study and review of the literature. *Neuropsychologia;* 32: 893–902.

Earnest, M.P., Monroe, P.A., and Yarnell, P.R. 1977. Cortical deafness: demonstration of the pathologic anatomy by CT scan. *Neurology;* 27: 1172–1175.

Farah, M.J. 1990. *Visual Agnosia.* Cambridge, MIT Press.

Freud, S. 1891. *On Aphasia.* New York, International Universities Press.

Geschwind, N. 1965. Disconnexion syndromes in animals and man. *Brain;* 88: 237–294, 585- 644.

Geschwind, N. 1970. The organization of language and the brain. *Science;* 170: 940–944.

Geschwind, N., and Fusillo, M. 1966. Color-naming deficits in association with alexia. *Arch Neurol;* 15: 137–146.

Geschwind, N., and Kaplan, E. 1962. A human cerebral deconnection syndrome. *Neurology;* 12: 675–685.

Graff-Radford, N.R., Bolling, J.P., Earnest, F., et al. 1993. Simultanagnosia as the initial sign of degenerative dementia. *Mayo Clin Proc;* 68: 955–964.

Haxby, J.V., Grady, C.L., Horwitz, B., et al. 1991. Dissociation of object and spatial visual processing pathways in human extrastriate cortex. *Proc Natl Acad Sci;* 88: 1621–1625.

Hecaen, H., and David, M. 1945. Syndrome pariétal traumatique: asymbolie tactile et hemiasomatognosie paroxystique et douloureuse. *Rev Neurol;* 77: 113–123.

Klüver, H., and Bucy, P.C. 1939. Preliminary analysis of functions of the temporal lobes in monkeys. *Arch Neurol Psychiat;* 42: 979–1000.

Kosslyn, S.M. 1988. Aspects of a cognitive neuroscience of mental imagery. *Science;* 240: 1621–1626.

Levine, D.N., Warach, J., and Farah, M. 1985. Two visual systems in visual imagery: disso-ciation of "what" and "where" in imagery disorders due to bilateral posterior cerebral le-sions. *Neurology;* 35: 1010–1018.

Lilly, R., Cummings, J.L., Benson, D.F., and Frankel, M. 1983. The human Klüver-Bucy syndrome. *Neurology;* 33: 1141–1145.

Lissauer, H. 1890. Ein Fall von Seelenblindheit nebst einem Beitrag zur Theorie derselben. *Arch für Psychiat;* 21: 222–270.

Mishkin, M., Ungerleider, L.G., and Macko, K.A. 1983. Object vision and spatial vision: two cortical pathways. *Trends Neurosci;* 6: 414–417.

Rizzo, M., and Hurtig, R. 1987. Looking but not seeing: attention, perception, and eye movements in simultanagnosia. *Neurology;* 37: 1642–1648.

Roland, P.E. 1976. Astereognosis. Tactile discrimination after localized hemisphere lesions in man. *Arch Neurol;* 33: 543–550.

Rubens, A.B., and Benson, D.F. 1971. Associative visual agnosia. *Arch Neurol;* 24: 305–316.

Schnider, A., Benson, D.F., Alexander, D.N., and Schnider-Klaus, A. 1994. Non-verbal envi-ronmental sound recognition after unilateral hemispheric stroke. *Brain;* 117: 281–287.

Semmes, J. 1965. A non-tactual factor in astereognosis. *Neuropsychologia;* 3: 295–315.

Sergent, J. 1990. The neuropsychology of visual image generation: data, method, and the-ory. *Brain and Cognition;* 13: 98–129.

Sergent, J., Ohta, S., and Macdonald B. 1992. Functional neuroanatomy of face and object processing. *Brain;* 115: 15–36.

Spreen, O., Benton, A.L., and Fincham, R.W. 1965. Auditory agnosia without aphasia. *Arch Neurol;* 13: 84–92.

Symonds, C., and Mackenzie, I. 1957. Bilateral loss of vision from cerebral infarction. *Brain;* 80: 415–455.

Teuber, H.L. 1968. Alteration of perception and memory in man. In: Weiskrantz, L. (ed.). *Analysis of Behavioral Change.* New York, Harper and Row.

Wolpert, I. 1924. Die Simultanagnosie: Störung der Gesamtauffassung. *Z ges Neurol Psychiat;* 93: 397–415.

CHAPTER 8

Right Hemisphere Syndromes

Lesions of the right hemisphere produce some of the most intriguing yet problematic syndromes in behavioral neurology. Despite a substantial amount of information that has appeared recently, these disorders present special difficulties because they typically do not reveal themselves through the usual route of verbal mediation. Right hemisphere disorders, though they may often be disabling in reality, are often inapparent to patient and family and may escape unnoticed in the routine mental status examination unless specifically sought. When they are recognized, these disturbances can be elusive because they implicate more intuitive, nonverbal cognitive systems for which standard verbal accounts may be inadequate. Even the terminology for these syndromes is difficult because linguistic descriptions may not fully capture inherently nonverbal phenomena. It is not by coincidence that the best-developed notions of brain-behavior relationships center on the linguistic system, which is so much more accessible to the examiner. One of the many challenges facing behavioral neurology is the continued development of a satisfactory lexicon and a meaningful taxonomy of right hemisphere functions and their dissolution.

Many of the syndromes discussed in this chapter represent a breakdown in the brain's ability to orient the body within external space and to formulate an adequate behavioral repertoire within it. We live in a three-dimensional world within which we must attend to all relevant information, analyze it, remember important components of it, and generate appropriate motor responses based upon it. None of this can be satisfactorily mediated by the left hemisphere linguistic system, and a large body of evidence does indeed support the idea that the right hemisphere is specialized for these tasks. In light of the major importance of visuospatial integration—and the disabling syndromes that right hemisphere damage often produces—reference to this hemisphere as "minor" is unjustified.

Even though our culture strongly rewards linguistic abilities, many other equally adaptive capacities are mediated by the right hemisphere, which itself can be considered "dominant" for a variety of functions. This chapter will attempt to illustrate the extent to which this hemisphere contributes to the totality of human mental life. Table 8.1 lists the major right hemisphere syndromes. The concluding section, on the emotional aspects of right hemisphere function, will provide a transition to the detailed discussion of emotion in Chapter 9.

Table 8.1 Right hemisphere syndromes

Neglect
Constructional apraxia
Spatial disorientation
Dressing apraxia
Aprosody
Amusia
Emotional disorders

Neglect

The phenomenon of neglect dramatically illustrates the role of the right hemisphere in mediating visuospatial competence. *Neglect* is a breakdown in the ability to report, respond to, or orient to normally received sensory stimuli; when stimuli presented contralateral to the side of a cerebral lesion are so ignored, *hemineglect* is an appropriate term. Although mild forms of hemineglect can sometimes be seen after left hemisphere lesions, the syndrome is much more severe and frequent after right hemisphere damage (Mesulam, 1981; Denes et al., 1982). Patients with hemineglect display a remarkable array of behaviors such as dressing only one side of the body, shaving just one side of the face, and eating food on only one side of a full plate. These deficits are brought out more systematically by double simultaneous testing for sensory extinction, line bisection and line cancellation tasks, and drawing tests such as drawing a clock with the hands at 11:10. It is as though one-half of the world is no longer available to these individuals, even though primary sensation is intact.

The often poor outcome of right hemisphere patients with hemineglect (Denes et al., 1982; Heilman et al., 1993) testifies to the importance of the right hemisphere in overall adaptation. A hemianopia, for example, might seem to deprive a patient of half the visual world, whereas in fact most people learn to adapt by simply turning the head as an adjustment; neglect patients, on the other hand, lack the capacity to appreciate the part of the world they are missing, and full vision is of little use in this situation. Patients with hemineglect are therefore at higher risk driving a motor vehicle, for example, than are hemianopic individuals.

Other striking deficits can be observed in patients with neglect. One problem is *anosodiaphoria* (Critchley, 1953), which refers to unconcern about left hemiparesis or hemiplegia even as it is acknowledged by the patient. More serious is actual unawareness of left hemiplegia, a deficit known as *anosognosia* (Babinski, 1914). A severely impaired patient may express firm *denial* of the deficit, even to the point of believing that the affected limbs belong to someone else.

Still another deficit allied with neglect is *motor impersistence.* This is a failure to persist at a variety of willed acts such as eye closure, arm extension, and tongue protrusion. Typically seen in left hemiparetic patients with neglect (Hier et al., 1983; Kertesz et al., 1985), impersistence indicates a vigilance deficit that may imply right frontal dysfunction. Again it is apparent that recovery from a right hemisphere lesion might be difficult indeed.

The anatomy of neglect has been worked out in some detail (Figure 8.1). It seems clear that the right hemisphere is much more involved in visuospatial surveillance than the left (Heilman and Van Den Abell, 1980), and it has been nominated as the hemisphere dominant for attention (Weintraub and Mesulam, 1987). Neglect seems to be particularly strongly correlated with destruction of the right parietal lobe (Hier et al., 1983). It appears that the left hemisphere does attend to the right hemispace, and therefore right hemineglect can be a feature of acute left hemisphere lesions, but the right hemisphere attends to *both* sides. Thus an acute right hemisphere lesion can result in impressive left hemineglect because there is little ability of the left hemisphere to compensate as can the right hemisphere in the opposite situation (Figure 8.1).

These considerations lead to a review of the cerebral basis of attention, with which neglect is intimately connected. As we saw in Chapter 2, attention can be divided into categories of selective, sustained, and directed. Selective and sustained inattention can be thought of as causing neglect of both sides, and directed inattention is essentially synonymous with hemineglect. Although the acute confusional state is usually due to a

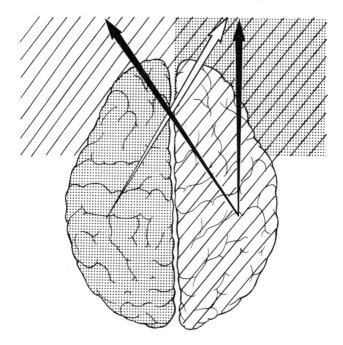

Figure 8.1 Schematic diagram of right hemisphere dominance for attention. Whereas the left hemisphere can only attend to the right side of extrapersonal space, the right hemisphere can attend to both sides. After Weintraub and Mesulam, 1987.

widespread disturbance of the diffuse attentional system, it can also result from right parietal damage (Mesulam et al., 1976), and a frequent chronic sequel of such lesions is hemineglect. A network of frontal, parietal, and limbic structures in the right hemisphere mediating attention to the left hemispace has been postulated on the basis of observations of neglect patients with damage to all these regions (Mesulam, 1981). These areas all appear to mediate specific aspects of directed attention: the frontal component, consisting of prefrontal cortex and the frontal eye field (Brodmann area 8; see Figure 1.3), subserves motor exploration and visual scanning; the parietal component, including posterior and inferior parietal cortex, subserves sensory awareness; and the limbic component, the cingulate gyrus, subserves motivational relevance (Mesulam, 1981).

Constructional Apraxia

The term *constructional apraxia,* although criticized for being applied to a syndrome that is not a true apraxia (Geschwind, 1975), is widely used to refer to impairment in the production of drawings. Alternative terms—none entirely satisfactory—include "constructional impairment," "visuospatial impairment," and "apractagnosia." Leaving aside the debate on whether this deficit qualifies as a true apraxia, the more standard usage will be used and the cerebral lesions most often responsible for impairments of this sort will be described. Right hemisphere lesions typically produce clinically significant syndromes, but left side lesions also cause constructional disturbances that are qualitatively distinct from the deficits that follow right side injury.

It has been known for several decades that patients who struggle the most with producing two- and three-dimensional drawings are considerably more likely to have a right than a left hemisphere lesion. In particular, the right parietal lobe has been suggested as most closely associated with constructional apraxia (Piercy et al., 1960). Errors on drawings typically made by these patients may include left hemineglect (as reviewed earlier), loss of perspective, impairment of the overall contour, a tendency to work from right to left (instead of the reverse), and the phenomenon of "closing in," in which the copy is placed too close to or even on top of the original drawing (Hecaen and Albert, 1978; Kaplan, 1983). In contrast, patients with left hemisphere lesions, even though they may have less marked or lasting impairment, also show constructional apraxia; their problems include simplification, perseveration, and loss of internal detail (Hecaen and Albert, 1978; Kaplan, 1983).

Spatial Disorientation

Individuals with lesions of the posterior right hemisphere often display a loss of familiarity with their environment. Obvious difficulties resulting from *spatial disorientation* may be evident when a patient is found to be unable to give directions on how to get home from the hospital or gets lost trying to find the nurses' station. Deficits detected on map completion tasks can alert the clinician to the possibility of a right hemisphere lesion. Fisher (1982) has described seven such cases and speculated that an acute insult to the right parietooccipital region was responsible. These cases are particularly noteworthy in view of the recent evidence from functional imaging studies implicating the parietal lobes in the analysis of spatial properties of visual stimuli (Chapter 7); the right parietal component of this dorsal system may be essential in the maintenance of orientation for place. When combined with bifrontal pathology, spatial disorientation can lead to a delusional belief that an individual's locale has been duplicated and therefore exists simultaneously in two places: the syndrome of *reduplicative paramnesia* (Filley and Jarvis, 1987). Similar pathology can also lead to another reduplicative condition called the *Capgras syndrome*, in which patients have the delusional belief that familiar people have been replaced by imposters (Alexander et al., 1979).

A closely related problem is the inability to recognize familiar environments, a syndrome that has been termed *environmental agnosia* (Landis et al., 1986). In contrast to the parietal lesion necessary for spatial disorientation, a temporooccipital lesion is required for this syndrome (Landis et al., 1986), in keeping with the *what* versus *where* distinction developed in Chapter 7 (see page 107) regarding the visual processing system. A loss of knowledge regarding the locations of familiar sites probably reflects either (1) reduced access to cortical areas encoding this information (a disconnection between the perceived material and stored knowledge about it) or (2) the actual obliteration of the encoded information. In the first case, it would be appropriate to consider the syndrome a specific agnosia, and in the second, the term amnesia would be more precise. In a thorough study, Landis et al. (1986) present a strong case for loss of topographic familiarity representing an environmental agnosia, noting that some patients can produce maps of their environment from memory even though they cannot recognize the setting when faced with the actual physical landscape.

Dressing Apraxia

Again the use of the word "apraxia" is debatable, but *dressing apraxia* is widely known as a specific impairment in dressing that may be plainly apparent clinically. When presented with the task of putting on a garment, especially with a sleeve turned inside out or other additional impediment, a patient so affected will have trouble recognizing top and bottom, back and front, and so on. The deficit involves elements both of neglect and spatial disorientation (Brain, 1941). Care should be taken not to mistake the motor disorder of hemiparesis or parkinsonism for dressing apraxia. In keeping with the importance of right parietal regions in spatial orientation, the location of lesions causing this impairment is usually the right parietal lobe (Hier et al., 1983). Difficulty with activities of daily living can clearly result from dressing apraxia.

Aprosody

Prosody refers to the emotional or affective components of propositional language. A simple sentence such as "I went to the movies" may take on distinctly different meanings depending on whether the declaration is inflected by the speaker with elation, dejection, or surprise. Prosody confers this affective coloration on the grammatical and semantic elements of language by the phenomena of melody, pauses, intonation, stresses, and accents. Clinical studies of patients with destructive lesions of the right hemisphere have demonstrated that, whereas aphasia is absent, difficulties in producing (Ross and Mesulam, 1979) and comprehending (Heilman et al., 1975) affective language are commonly seen, and the syndrome of *aprosody* can then be diagnosed. In contrast to the left hemisphere's dominance for propositional language, therefore, these considerations lead to the notion that the right hemisphere is dominant for the affective components of language (Ross and Mesulam, 1979).

Related to prosody is *gesture* or "body language," which provides another avenue for a speaker to communicate beyond the restraints of propositional language. In contrast to volitional movements intended to express symbols known as pantomime, impairment of which is linked to aphasia and left hemisphere damage, gesture is a right hemisphere function and its impairment is often associated with aprosody (Ross, 1984). Taken together, prosody and gesture serve to embellish propositional language with emotional coloration that significantly expands the speaker's communicative power.

Detailed clinical studies of prosody and gesture have been pursued (Ross, 1981). There appears to be a right hemisphere system for the mediation of prosody (Figure 8.2) that is a mirror image of the left hemisphere propositional language system reviewed in Chapter 5 (Figure 5.2). Focal lesions in this circuit often result in clinically detectable aprosodic deficits that bear close similarity to the analogous syndrome that follows a similarly placed lesion of the left hemisphere (Table 8.2). Hence there are clinical examples of such entities as motor, sensory, global, and transcortical aprosodias that can be clinically tested and diagnosed (Ross, 1981). Although the detection of these aprosody syndromes can be clinically challenging, aprosodic language is often a useful neurobehavioral sign of right hemisphere pathology. In theoretical terms, the study of aprosody has offered important insights regarding the means by which emotional dimensions serve to enrich propositional language (Ross, 1985).

Table 8.2 Aprosody syndromes and their localization

Aprosody type	Spontaneous prosody	Prosodic comprehension	Prosodic repetition	Comprehension of emotional gesturing	Localization (right hemisphere)
Motor	Poor	Good	Poor	Good	Inferior frontal gyrus
Sensory	Good	Poor	Poor	Poor	Superior temporal gyrus
Conduction*	Good	Good	Poor	Good	Inferior parietal lobe
Global	Poor	Poor	Poor	Poor	Perisylvian region
Transcortical motor	Poor	Good	Good	Good	Anterior border zone
Transcortical sensory	Good	Poor	Good	Poor	Posterior border zone
Anomic*	Good	Good	Good	Poor	Angular gyrus
Mixed transcortical	Poor	Poor	Good	Poor	Anterior and posterior border zone

* Hypothesized but not yet observed.

Source: E.D. Ross. 1985. Modulation of affect and nonverbal communication by the right hemisphere. In: Mesulam, M.-M. *Principles of Behavioral Neurology.* Philadelphia, F.A. Davis, pp. 239–257. Used with permission.

Neurobehavioral Anatomy

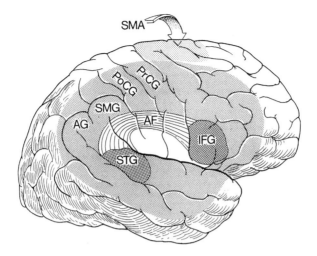

Figure 8.2 Lateral view of the right hemisphere showing areas important for prosody. IFG—inferior frontal gyrus; STG—superior temporal gyrus; AF—arcuate fasciculus; SMA— supplementary motor area; AG—angular gyrus; SMG— supramarginal gyrus; PrCG—precentral gyrus; PoCG—postcentral gyrus.

Amusia

The loss of melodic speech that occurs with aprosody after right hemisphere lesions is one of many suggestions that music may in some way be associated with the right hemisphere. However, the topic of musical representation in the brain is an extremely complex one, and inclusion of *amusia* on the list of right hemisphere syndromes risks oversimplification. The many elements required for the successful performance or appreciation of music—pitch, duration, timbre, volume, tempo, melody, harmony, rhythm, and so on—are extremely diverse and do not allow ready localization. Moreover, because musical competence is relatively uncommon in the general population, very few well studied cases of amusia are available. Nevertheless, the traditional view that music is primarily a right hemisphere function (Milner, 1962) is accurate enough as a rough approximation to justify its discussion here.

One of the most striking demonstrations of right hemisphere participation in music is the unexpected production of intact singing in a musically competent individual with a left hemisphere lesion and nonfluent aphasia. Often as surprising to the patient as to the examiner, such an output clearly suggests the unimpaired musical capacity of the right hemisphere. Studies using unilateral intracarotid barbiturate injection to inactivate the hemisphere temporarily (the Wada test or "reversible hemispherectomy") have verified this observation by finding that right carotid injection impairs singing ability much more than left (Gordon and Bogen, 1974). This capacity may even be exploited by speech pathologists to help nonfluent aphasics intone speech in an effort to improve their verbal output (Sparks et al., 1974).

Even though it has been held that most people appear to be right hemisphere dominant for music, the representation of this highly complex activity is bihemispheric, depending in part on the aspect of music being considered (Gates and Bradshaw, 1977). For example, rhythm, which is closely linked to language, is more a function of the left hemisphere, whereas melody is more associated with the right hemisphere (Polk and Kertesz, 1993). Both hemispheres undoubtedly participate by means of intricate patterns of interaction, and functional imaging studies are beginning to disclose widespread neurobehavioral networks dedicated to musical function (Sergent, 1993). Studies performed with highly skilled musicians have suggested the interesting possibility of left hemisphere mediation of music in these individuals, whereas persons with no musical instruction may process music more with the right hemisphere (Bever and Chiarello, 1974).

A distinction between syndromes affecting musical execution— *expressive amusia*—and those affecting musical perception— *receptive amusia*—may be useful. It has been suggested that musical execution depends on the right hemisphere, whereas musical perception is a right hemisphere function in naive listeners but a left hemisphere function in those who are musically sophisticated (Damasio and Damasio, 1977). A shift of musical dominance may thus take place from right to left as musical sophistication increases (Damasio and Damasio, 1977). Brust (1980), however, has cautioned against premature speculation on the hemispheric lateralization of music, as amusias have been seen in persons with or without simultaneous aphasia and with left or right hemisphere damage. The multifaceted nature of music leads to the conclusion that it must certainly have a very complex and multifocal cerebral representation.

In clinical practice, amusia is rather infrequent but has been reported a number of times after right hemisphere lesions in skilled musicians (McFarland and Fortin, 1982). An excellent recent example is a case study describing expressive and receptive amusia and aprosody in a woman with well-documented right frontal and temporal degeneration (Confavreux et al., 1992). In practical terms, amusia is generally more likely with right than left hemisphere lesions. More specific localization of musical function within certain lobes of the hemispheres cannot as yet be attempted.

Emotional Disorders

Until recently, the subject of *emotion* has been largely avoided by neurologists; psychiatry and psychology have been primarily charged with the task of addressing this imposing topic. One important reason for this omission is that emotional disorders were long thought to have little or nothing to do with the structure and function of the brain. Only lately has this assumption been seriously reconsidered, and indeed empirical evidence relating brain disease with emotional disorder has appeared. For example, substantial new information has been recently presented on schizophrenia that increasingly implicates brain dysfunction. In addition, behavioral neurology has produced many descriptions of emotional changes with structural brain disease, and these provide fascinating insights into the cerebral organization of emotional functions. Some of these syndromes will be discussed in Chapter 9, but now the perplexing and often disabling disorders in emotional adjustment that can follow damage to right hemisphere structures will be considered.

As mentioned earlier, syndromes of the right hemisphere are difficult to describe because of the essentially nonverbal nature of the deficits. Yet patients with right hemisphere destruction manifest changes in emotion and personality that are as clinically significant as they are elusive to capture descriptively (Price and Mesulam, 1985). These changes are manifest in the realms of affect, language, and interpersonal relations, and our understanding is still very limited. Much of this complexity, however, can be put into context by a brief consideration of the neurology of emotion.

There is no question that the limbic system (Chapter 9) plays a critical role in the primary emotions of the organism, ensuring such essential requirements of survival as feeding, aggression, flight, and reproduction. Instinctual drives result from the activity of the limbic system, which in humans has showed only modest enlargement in comparison to that of higher primates (Eccles, 1989). The enormous expansion of the neocortex in humans, however, has enabled the operation of a much more elaborate behavioral repertoire (Eccles, 1989), which is evident in the emotional as well as the cognitive realm. It is likely that the specifically human emotions—affection, resentment, pride, guilt, pity, envy, and the like—require a considerable degree of neocortical participation. Damasio (1994) has drawn a useful distinction between the "primary" emotions, subserved by limbic structures and the "secondary" emotions that depend more on neocortical regions. Thus humans share many features of emotional behavior with lower animals but in addition display unique behaviors that result from the interplay between the limbic system and the extensive neocortical regions that regulate it.

The distribution and extent of the neocortical systems subserving emotions are largely unknown. Clearly the neocortex mediates a variety of modulatory influences upon the limbic system that render human emotional behavior far more complex than the predictable stimulus-bound behavior of a lower animal in which the limbic system is anatomically more prominent. The frontal lobes provide a crucial element of neocortical control, and these areas can be viewed as essential to drive regulation (Chapter 10). In addition, the right hemisphere exerts a complementary although more subtle influence on limbic activity, enabling a richer and more variegated interpersonal life by means of such attributes as prosody (see page 119), affect, and socialization. Although the important role of the right hemisphere in emotional life has ample documentation (Joseph, 1988), the potential contributions of the left hemisphere have not been ignored, and a lively debate has centered on the cerebral laterality of emotion.

Much has been written over the years about the lateralization of higher functions in the brain, and substantial effort has been devoted to the exploration of differences in the capacities of the left and right hemispheres (Springer and Deutsch, 1989). Contrasts such as analytic-synthetic, logical-intuitive, and rational-emotional have been touted as defining traits, often with a paucity of supporting data. It is no surprise that a brisk controversy on the lateralization of emotion has developed. Two major theories on this contentious topic are current (Figure 8.3).

One idea is that the left hemisphere is primarily concerned with positive emotions and the right with negative emotions (Sackheim et al., 1982). Thus happiness, for example, is mediated by the left side and sadness by the right. In contrast to this hemispheric *valence hypothesis*, the *right hemisphere hypothesis* holds that all higher emotion is mediated by

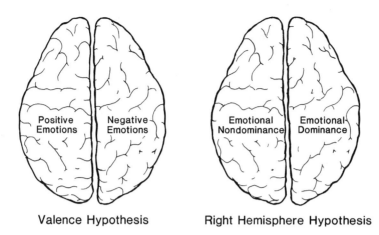

| Valence Hypothesis | Right Hemisphere Hypothesis |

Figure 8.3 Two hypotheses concerning the hemispheric lateralization of emotion.

the right hemisphere (Bear, 1983). In this scheme, right hemisphere dominance for emotion is postulated. Evidence from humans with left and right hemisphere lesions has been offered in support of both theories, and the issue is unresolved; the following paragraphs will simply describe some key studies that are clinically helpful.

It has been known for half a century that aphasic patients with left frontal lesions can exhibit a *catastrophic reaction* of profound depression and agitation (Goldstein, 1948). Although this dramatic condition might reflect disruption of left hemisphere systems subserving positive emotions, it may simply represent a reaction to the devastating loss of linguistic competence in nonfluent aphasia. More recently, however, a consistent body of data has supported the association of left frontal cerebrovascular lesions and depression, even with lesions too far anterior to cause significant aphasia (Robinson et al., 1984). These lesions may be either cortical or subcortical, and affected patients can be helped with tricyclic antidepressants (Starkstein and Robinson, 1990); destruction of ascending catecholaminergic tracts may be responsible for this poststroke depression. Other evidence supporting the valence hypothesis has been presented. In a report summarizing the consistent results of three studies, Sackheim et al. (1982) found that (1) pathologic laughter was associated with right hemisphere and crying with left hemisphere damage, (2) right hemispherectomy led to a euphoric mood change, and (3) epileptic foci causing gelastic (laughing) epilepsy were predominantly on the left side.

Evidence favoring the right hemisphere hypothesis has also been adduced. One of the more notable attempts to describe emotional behavior in neurologic patients is a now-classic study in which patients with left hemisphere lesions characteristically displayed the catastrophic reaction of Goldstein, whereas the typical response of right hemisphere damaged patients was one of "indifference" (Gainotti, 1972). Gainotti interpreted these findings by suggesting that the right hemisphere was more important for the mediation of emotional behavior. Many patients with right side lesions do indeed show a remarkable passivity in the face of severe hemiplegia or other deficit. As discussed earlier, this lack of concern is related to the problems of anosodiaphoria, anosognosia, and denial. Another line of inquiry showing results consistent with the notion of right hemisphere dominance for emotion is in the area of temporolimbic epilepsy; "emotive" personality traits such as emotionality, elation, and sadness were correlated with right side foci and "ideative" traits such as a sense of personal destiny, philosophical interests, and humorlessness with left side foci (Chapter 9; Bear and Fedio, 1977). In another context, a large study of soldiers with unilateral penetrating head injuries found an association of affective disorders with right hemisphere and intellectual disorders with left hemisphere injuries (Lishman, 1968). Finally, there are intriguing data from many studies indicating a robust tendency for unilateral hysterical conversion symptoms to occur more often on the left side of the body than on the right (Stern, 1977; Galin et al., 1977; Ley, 1980).

It is probable that the cerebral laterality of emotion will not soon be established without question, but recent evidence from normal subjects has supported the right hemisphere hypothesis. Using a technique to lateralize visual input to the left or right hemifield, Wittling and Roschmann (1993) showed films with positive and negative emotional valence to young adult volunteers and found that either variety produced a stronger subjective response when presented to the right hemisphere than when presented to to the left. These data suggest that both positive and negative feelings are mediated by the right hemisphere.

Other studies have attempted to examine aspects of interpersonal life that require a considerable degree of emotional competence. One such domain is humor, and it has been found that patients with right hemisphere lesions demonstrate difficulty with appropriate responses to humorous material presented to them (Gardner et al., 1975). The ability to comprehend metaphor, the recognition of similarity between seemingly dissimilar terms, is also impaired in right hemisphere patients, who tend to interpret metaphors literally as often as figuratively (Winner and Gardner, 1977). In a related investigation, Brownell et al. (1984) noted that such patients have problems appreciating the connotative meaning of words—their allusions and implications—but retain an understanding of their literal, denotative aspects. These deficits indicate that the right hemisphere plays an important role in the nuances of interpersonal relationships. Right hemisphere patients may fail to comprehend the subtle shades of meaning conveyed in conversation by humor, metaphor, and connotation, and thus their appreciation of emotional language may be perturbed as a result (Brownell et al., 1984).

Finally, some intriguing speculations have been based on data that suggest dreams can be eliminated after damage to the right posterior hemisphere (Humphrey and Zangwill, 1951). If dreams represent the "royal road to a knowledge of the unconscious activities of the mind" (Freud, 1900), then perhaps the right hemisphere may be the substrate for the unconscious and the psychoanalytic concept of primary process thinking (Galin, 1974). However, dreaming may not be solely a right hemisphere phenomenon. Other investigators have suggested that whereas the visual aspect of dreams does implicate the right hemisphere, the narrative quality of dreams—which can persist in the absence of visual imagery—may implicate left hemisphere structures (Kerr and Foulkes, 1981). Dreams may therefore result from the activation of widespread neurobehavioral networks in both hemispheres. This notion is consistent with evidence favoring bihemispheric participation in visual imagery (Chapter 7).

As a general rule, despite Freud's early interests in neurology and neuroanatomy, the relevance of Freudian theory to behavioral neurology is tenuous at best. Attractive as it may seem to many in clinical neuroscience, it is not possible with existing knowledge to relate psychoanalytic concepts to brain structure and function. Nevertheless, the importance of the right hemisphere in many emotional operations suggests that further elucidation of right hemisphere function will likely be assisted by the insights of psychiatrists, psychologists, and others who are experienced in the observation, analysis, and treatment of emotional disorders. A collaboration between neurobiologists and mental health professionals will nowhere bear more fruit than in the study of the poorly understood human right hemisphere.

References

Alexander, M.P., Stuss, D.T., and Benson, D.F. 1979. Capgras syndrome: a reduplicative phenomenon. *Neurology;* 29: 334–339.

Babinski, J. 1914. Contribution à l'étude des troubles mentaux dans l'hémiplégie organique cérébrale (anosognosie). *Rev Neurol;* 27: 845–847.

Bear, D.M. 1983. Hemispheric specialization and the neurology of emotion. *Arch Neurol;* 40: 195–202.

Bear, D.M., and Fedio, P. 1977. Quantitative analysis of interictal behavior in temporal lobe epilepsy. *Arch Neurol;* 34: 454–467.

Bever, T.G., and Chiarello, R.J. 1974. Cerebral dominance in musicians and non-musicians. *Science;* 185: 537–539.

Brain, W.R. 1941. Visual disorientation with special reference to lesions of the right cerebral hemisphere. *Brain;* 64: 244–272.

Brownell, H.H., Potter, H.H., and Michelow, D. 1984. Sensitivity to denotation and connotation in brain-damaged patients: a double dissociation? *Brain Lang;* 22: 253–265.

Brust, J.C.M. 1980. Music and language. Musical alexia and agraphia. *Brain;* 103: 367–392.

Confavreux, C., Croisile, B., Garassus, P., et al. 1992. Progressive amusia and aprosody. *Arch Neurol;* 49: 971–976.

Critchley, M. 1953. *The Parietal Lobes.* London, Edward Arnold.

Damasio, A.R. 1994. *Descartes' Error. Emotion, Reason, and the Human Brain.* New York, Grosset/Putnam.

Damasio, A.R., and Damasio, H. 1977. Musical faculty and cerebral dominance. In: Critchley, M., and Henson, R.A. (eds.). *Music and the Brain.* London, William Heinemann, pp. 141–155.

Denes, G., Semenza, C., Stoppa, E., and Lis, A. 1982. Unilateral spatial neglect and recovery from hemiplegia. *Brain;* 105: 543–552.

Eccles, J.C. 1989. *Evolution of the Brain: Creation of the Self.* London, Routledge.

Filley, C.M., and Jarvis, P.E. 1987. Delayed reduplicative paramnesia. *Neurology;* 37: 701–703.

Fisher, C.M. 1982. Disorientation for place. *Arch Neurol;* 39: 33–36.

Freud, S. 1900. *The Interpretation of Dreams.* Translated and edited by Strachey, J. New York, Avon.

Gainotti, G. 1972. Emotional behavior and hemispheric side of lesion. *Cortex;* 8: 41–55.

Galin, D. 1974. Implications for psychiatry of left and right cerebral specialization. A neurophysiological context for unconscious processes. *Arch Gen Psychiatry;* 31: 572–583.

Galin, D., Diamond, R., and Braff, D. 1977. Lateralization of conversion symptoms: more frequent on the left. *Am J Psychiatry;* 134: 578–580.

Gardner, H., Ling, P.K., Flamm, L., and Silverman, J. 1975. Comprehension and appreciation of humorous material following brain damage. *Brain;* 98: 399–412.

Gates, A., and Bradshaw, J.L. 1977. The role of the cerebral hemispheres in music. *Brain Lang;* 4: 403–431.

Geschwind, N. 1975. The apraxias: neural mechanisms of disorders of learned movement. *Am Sci;* 63: 188–195.

Goldstein, K. 1948. *Language and Language Disturbances.* New York, Grune and Stratton.

Gordon, H.W., and Bogen, J.E. 1974. Hemispheric lateralization of singing after intracarotid sodium amylobarbitone. *J Neurol Neurosurg Psychiatry;* 37: 727–738.

Hecaen, H., and Albert, M.L. 1978. *Human Neuropsychology.* New York, Wiley-Interscience.

Heilman, K.M., and Van Den Abell, T. 1980. Right hemisphere dominance for attention: the mechanism underlying hemispheric asymmetries of inattention (neglect). *Neurology;* 30: 327–330.

Heilman, K.M., Scholes, R., and Watson, R.T. 1975. Auditory affective agnosia. Disturbed comprehension of affective speech. *J Neurol Neurosurg Psychiatry;* 38: 69–72.

Heilman, K.M., Watson, R.T., and Valenstein, E. 1993. Neglect and related disorders. In: Heilman, K.M., and Valenstein, E. (eds.). *Clinical Neuropsychology.* 3rd ed. New York, Oxford, pp. 279–336.

Hier, D.B., Mondlock, J., and Caplan, L.R. 1983. Behavioral abnormalities after right hemisphere stroke. *Neurology;* 33: 337–344.

Humphrey, M.E., and Zangwill, O.E. 1951. Cessation of dreaming after brain injury. *J Neurol Neurosurg Psychiatry;* 14: 322–325.

Joseph, R. 1988. The right cerebral hemisphere: emotion, music, visual-spatial skills, body-image, dreams, and awareness. *J Clin Psychol;* 44: 630–673.

Kaplan, E. 1983. Process and achievement revisited. In: Wapner, S., and Kaplan, B. (eds.) *Toward a Holistic Developmental Psychology.* Hillsdale, New Jersey, Lawrence Erlbaum, pp. 143–156.

Kerr, N.H., and Foulkes, D. 1981. Right hemisphere mediation of dream visualization: a case study. *Cortex;* 17: 603–610.

Kertesz, A., Nicholson, I., Cancilliere, A., et al. 1985. Motor impersistence: a right hemisphere syndrome. *Neurology;* 35: 662–666.

Landis, T., Cummings, J.L., Benson, D.F., and Palmer, E.P. 1986. Loss of topographic familiarity. An environmental agnosia. *Arch Neurol;* 43: 132–136.

Ley, R.G. 1980. An archival examination of an asymmetry of hysterical conversion symptoms. *J Clin Neuropsychol;* 2: 61–70.

Lishman, W.A. 1968. Brain damage in relation to psychiatric disability after head injury. *Br J Psychiatry;* 114: 373–410.

McFarland, H.R., and Fortin, D. 1982. Amusia due to right temporoparietal infarct. *Arch Neurol;* 39: 725–727.

Mesulam, M.-M. 1981. A cortical network for directed attention and unilateral neglect. *Ann Neurol;* 10: 309–325.

Mesulam, M.-M., Waxman, S.G., Geschwind, N., and Sabin, T.D. 1976. Acute confusional states with right middle cerebral artery infarctions. *J Neurol Neurosurg Psychiatry;* 39: 84–89.

Milner, B. 1962. Laterality effects in audition. In: Mountcastle, V.B. (ed.). *Interhemispheric Relations and Cerebral Dominance.* Baltimore, Johns Hopkins University Press.

Piercy, M., Hecaen, H., and de Ajuriaguerra, J. 1960. Constructional apraxia associated with unilateral cerebral lesions—left and right sided cases compared. *Brain;* 83: 225–242.

Polk, M., and Kertesz, A. 1993. Music and language in degenerative disease of the brain. *Brain and Cognition;* 22: 98–117.

Price, B.H., and Mesulam, M.-M. 1985. Psychiatric manifestations of right hemisphere infarctions. *J Nerv Ment Dis;* 173: 610–614.

Robinson, R.G., Kubos, K.L., Starr, L.B., et al. 1984. Mood disorders in stroke patients. Importance of location of lesion. *Brain;* 107: 81–93.

Ross, E.D.1981. The aprosodias: functional-anatomic organization of the affective components of language in the right hemisphere. *Arch Neurol;* 38: 561–569.

Ross, E.D. 1984. Right hemisphere's role in language, affective behavior, and emotion. *Trends Neurosci;* 7: 342–346.

Ross, E.D. 1985. Modulation of affect and nonverbal communication by the right hemisphere. In: Mesulam, M.-M. *Principles of Behavioral Neurology.* Philadelphia, F.A. Davis, pp. 239–257.

Ross, E.D., and Mesulam, M.-M. 1979. Dominant language functions of the right hemisphere? Prosody and emotional gesturing. *Arch Neurol;* 36: 144–148.

Sackheim, H.A., Greenberg, M.S., Weiman, A.L., et al. 1982. Hemispheric asymmetry in the expression of positive and negative emotions. Neurologic evidence. *Arch Neurol;* 39: 210–218.

Sergent, J. 1993. Music, the brain and Ravel. *Trends Neurosci;* 16: 168–172.

Sparks, R., Helm, N., and Albert, M. 1974. Aphasia rehabilitation resulting from melodic intonation therapy. *Cortex;* 10: 303–316.

Springer, S., and Deutsch, G. 1989. *Left Brain, Right Brain.* 3rd edition. New York, W.H. Freeman.

Starkstein, S., and Robinson, R.G. 1990. Depression following cerebrovascular lesions. *Sem Neurol;* 10: 247–253.

Stern, D. 1977. Handedness and the lateral distribution of conversion reactions. *J Nerv Ment Dis;* 164: 122–128.

Weintraub, S., and Mesulam, M.-M. 1987. Right cerebral dominance in spatial attention. *Arch Neurol;* 44: 621–625.

Winner, E., and Gardner, H. 1977. The comprehension of metaphor in brain-damaged patients. *Brain;* 100: 717–729.

Wittling, W., and Roschmann, R. 1993. Emotion-related hemisphere asymmetry: subjective emotional responses to laterally presented films. *Cortex;* 29: 431–448.

CHAPTER 9

Temporal Lobe Syndromes

It has been informally remarked that the Sylvian fissure separates neurology (above) from psychiatry (below). Although any distinction between neurology and psychiatry may ultimately prove artificial (Chapter 1), it is true that a wide spectrum of emotional states, normal and otherwise, has been linked with the temporal lobe and the limbic system to which it is intimately related. These complex regions therefore outline a unique avenue for exploration of emotional phenomena mediated by the brain. Although cognitive domains including memory (Chapter 4) and language (Chapter 5) are closely linked with the temporal lobe, it will be the main purpose here to concentrate on temporal lobe epilepsy or, more precisely, *temporolimbic epilepsy* (TLE), as this common illness has long been postulated to produce a plethora of emotional disturbances.

This book is largely concerned with cognition, the operations of which are simpler to define and measure than those of emotion. The neuroanatomy of cognition is, similarly, less complex than that of emotion. Chapter 8 considered emotion in the context of right hemisphere disorders, and theories regarding the cerebral lateralization of emotion were reviewed. Chapter 10 will examine emotion (and cognition) in the setting of frontal lobe function. There remain, however, what have been called the "primary" emotions: pleasure, pain, desire, anger, ecstasy, fear, and the like (Ross et al., 1994). These powerful and basic feelings now direct our attention to the temporal lobes and their important connections to the limbic system.

The Limbic System

The term "limbic" derives from the Latin word for "border" (*limbus*), and it was Paul Broca who first introduced the idea of a limbic lobe (Broca, 1878). He pointed out that a ring of cortical gyri around the upper brain

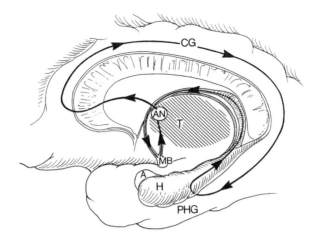

Figure 9.1 The Papez circuit. H—hippocampus; A—amygdala; PHG—parahippocampal gyrus; CG—cingulate gyrus; AN—anterior nucleus of thalamus; MB—mammillary body; T—thalamus.

stem—the cingulate gyrus, parahippocampal gyrus, and hippocampus—was characterized by phylogenetically primitive cortex. In lower animals, these areas are largely concerned with olfaction, but this sensory modality is relatively unimportant in humans; the *limbic system* has taken on other roles in our species.

In 1937, James Papez published an influential paper on the putative anatomic basis of emotion (Papez, 1937). Papez proposed that an interconnected circuit of limbic structures—the hippocampus, fornix, mammillary body, mammillothalamic tract, anterior thalamic nucleus, cingulate gyrus, and parahippocampal gyrus—mediates both the experience and expression of emotion (Figure 9.1). This *Papez circuit* has come to be regarded as playing a critical role in the primary emotions that form the basis of instincts or drives—feeding, aggression, flight, and sexual reproduction. The experience of these emotions was postulated as occurring in the cingulate gyrus, and their expression as organized through the hypothalamus. Despite criticism of the limbic system concept because of its uncertain boundaries (Brodal, 1981), more than 50 years of study have largely supported Papez' ideas. At the very least, the concept of the Papez circuit has anchored extensive research efforts concerned with the cerebral basis of both emotion and memory.

In 1949, Paul MacLean extended Papez' concept to include additional areas important to the phenomena of emotion: the amygdala, the septum and adjacent basal forebrain, the nucleus accumbens in the striatum, and the orbitofrontal cortex (MacLean, 1949). The work of MacLean gave further support to the assignment of emotional functions to the limbic system, although the exact role of many limbic structures is far from clear.

For our purposes, five major structures and their connections will serve as the most critical limbic components: the hippocampus and septal region, which have major roles in memory (Chapter 4), and the amygdala, cingulate gyrus, and hypothalamus, which are prominently involved in emotion. Of particular importance with regard to this chapter are the hippocampus and amygdala, closely linked structures that serve as primary regions mediating memory and emotion, respectively.

The amygdala is a highly complex nucleus adjacent to the hippocampus that has recently been envisioned as an evaluator of the emotional significance of stimuli entering the central nervous system (LeDoux, 1987). Receiving both interoceptive (e.g., hunger, thirst) and exteroceptive (e.g., vision, audition, somatic sensation) information, the amygdala functions to determine the biological relevance of sensory data reaching the brain. Thus the amygdala is immediately interposed between the arrival of information and its further processing. It is thought that this evaluation by the amygdala occurs in a nonconscious fashion so that "emotional memories" may be the conscious products of unconscious activity (LeDoux, 1994). The implications of such unconscious learning are great; some of the most vexing problems in psychiatry—including anxiety and panic attacks—probably involve a learned pattern of fear that occurs without conscious awareness and can be very difficult to reverse (LeDoux, 1994).

The proximity of the hippocampus to the amygdala is not merely an anatomic coincidence; the same information that reaches the amygdala is also presented to the hippocampus, so that there is the possibility of storing the material for future use. Thus the commonplace observation that memories of highly charged emotional experiences will be more easily formed and less readily dislodged than memories with little emotional significance is not surprising. Figure 9.2 illustrates the convergence of major sensory streams through the temporal pole and into the limbic system, where incoming information undergoes rapid processing that enables a prompt and appropriate response by the individual.

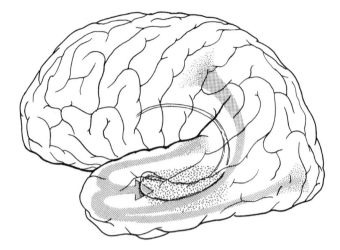

Figure 9.2 Schematic view of the connections between major sensory systems and the limbic system. An irritative lesion in the medial temporal lobe may functionally alter these connections. After Ross, et al., 1994

Let us consider the implications of this arrangement. Successful existence depends on the organism reacting appropriately to environmental contingencies. On a fundamental level, evaluation of the importance of sensory information is clearly indispensable. In the case of a visual stimulus, for example, the information may be trivial (a stranger passing by on the street) or urgent (a rapidly approaching truck). The amygdala, assessing these possibilities, has several options for further action. First, there may be no further processing at all, as the stimulus is a neutral one requiring no action. Second, there may be the admittance of the stimulus into conscious awareness, a process that contributes to the experience of emotion. In a general way, this experience constitutes one component of mood. Although not clearly dependent on the cingulate gyrus alone as Papez thought, the experience of emotion very likely involves cortical areas related to the limbic system (Halgren et al., 1978; Gloor et al., 1982). Efferents from the amygdala to various cortical regions are doubtless involved in this process. Third, there is the option of emotional expression, which may be displayed by an immediate reaction to the information received—i.e., jumping out of the way of the truck.

Behavior such as this constitutes part of what we know as affect and involves known amygdala connections to motor systems (Damasio and

Van Hoesen, 1983) and the autonomic (Bard, 1928) and endocrine (Scharrer and Scharrer, 1954) effectors mediated through the hypothalamus. In this regard, there is further intriguing evidence supporting an immunoregulatory function of the hypothalamus (Brooks et al., 1982), which may help explain a variety of psychosomatic diseases (MacLean, 1949). Finally, the information evaluated by the amygdala may be transferred by its connections to the hippocampus for storage in memory; thus, for example, one might quickly learn that a particular street is a potentially dangerous place because of the frequent presence of fast-moving vehicles. Just as the hippocampus is the crucial area for allowing the storage of information within the brain, the amygdala is the primary region for assessing whether information when first encountered requires such storage.

The anatomic complexity of the limbic system is not insignificant, and, with the exception of the hippocampus (Chapter 4), isolated lesions of limbic structures are uncommon. Because the contribution of various areas to emotional behavior is uncertain, it is best to consider the limbic system as a functional unit. There is clinical and theoretical utility in viewing this network as critical to primary emotions and therefore to entities such as instincts, drives, pain, pleasure, fear, anger, and motivation. A complete portrait of the human neurobehavioral repertoire must include the limbic system as it performs its fundamental emotional functions and interacts with cerebral areas more concerned with cognition.

Temporolimbic Epilepsy

The temporal lobes have intimate anatomic relationships with the limbic system and, as we have seen, are closely involved with emotional behavior. The detailed anatomy of the combined temporolimbic system is intricate, but the interrelated topography of the temporal lobes and deeper limbic structures helps explain why patients with temporal lobe lesions often manifest disorders that come to the attention of psychiatrists as readily as to neurologists. As discussed above, a key anatomic feature is that all major sensory systems—vision, audition, and somatic sensation—are projected to the anterior temporal lobes and thence to the amygdala and hippocampus (Figure 9.2). This funneling of sensory input into emotionally relevant parts of the brain has implications for temporolimbic epilepsy (TLE), the major disease that has been examined in this regard. Not only is TLE a very common type of seizure disorder and thus accessible to detailed study, but it represents a specific cerebral lesion whose neurobehavioral manifestations can be readily examined (Waxman and Geschwind, 1975).

The topic of epilepsy introduces a different conceptual approach to brain-behavior relationships than that exploited heretofore in this book. The majority of syndromes in behavioral neurology begin with a destructive lesion or pathologic process in a given cerebral region or set of structures that then permits the observation and analysis of deficits that may occur. In contrast to the "negative" signs and symptoms produced by, for example, a stroke, epilepsy results in "positive" features as a result of its characteristically irritative nature. Thus an entirely novel set of phenomena can inform thinking about the representation of behavior in the brain. Deficits can now be related to the abnormal excitability of tissue as well as to the absence of normal excitability.

A *seizure* is a clinical event caused by a paroxysmal and excessive discharge of cortical neurons. The term *epilepsy*, or alternatively *seizure disorder*, refers to a condition of recurrent, unprovoked seizures. Standard classifications divide seizure disorders into two broad categories: *generalized*, meaning that the entire brain is affected in a widespread fashion, and *partial*, implying the existence of a localized area of irritability from which the seizure originates. Partial seizures are further divided into *simple partial seizures* and *complex partial seizures*, the difference being that consciousness is preserved in the former but impaired or lost in the latter. Complex partial seizures most often result from an irritable focus in one of the temporal lobes. Because epileptic foci causing complex partial seizures can be found outside the temporal lobes, however, the popular term "temporal lobe epilepsy" is not synonymous with complex partial epilepsy. Similarly, the older term "psychomotor epilepsy" cannot be equated with complex partial seizures and has in fact fallen from common use.

From the viewpoint of behavioral neurology, the use of the term TLE serves to focus attention on the anatomic inseparability of the temporal lobes and the limbic system, a feature that has major neurobehavioral implications (Spiers et al., 1985). Moreover, the designation TLE is of more than theoretical importance; it has been estimated that, given the likelihood that the illness is underreported, the prevalence of TLE in the general population may be as high as 1% (Spiers et al., 1985).

It will be useful to consider briefly the phenomenology of TLE. An important point to keep in mind is that TLE patients can have behavioral changes of three general types: ictal, postictal, and interictal. These categories respectively describe the period during a seizure, immediately following a seizure, and between seizures. *Ictal* phenomena include a variety of alterations in the motor, sensory, autonomic, cognitive, and emotional realms. A complete listing of these clinical features is beyond the scope of this book, but some of the more notable include focal jerking of the limbs and complex automatisms, focal numbness or discomfort, and an unpleasant "rising" sensation in the abdomen. Cognitive experiences include illusions such as micropsia, macropsia, and metamorphopsia and hallucinations in any sensory modality, frequently olfactory or gustatory (Currie et al., 1971). In addition, there are often cognitive alterations such as the "dreamy state" first described by Hughlings-Jackson over a century ago (Hughlings-Jackson, 1888–1889), which may be accompanied by illusions of familiarity (*déjà vu*—already seen; *déjà vécu*—already experienced) or unfamiliarity (*jamais vu*—never seen; *jamais vécu*—never experienced) (Bancaud et al., 1994). Finally, emotional experiences are well described, the most common of which is a combination of fear and depression (Williams, 1956). However, rare cases of ictal euphoria have been reported, and it has been suggested that Fyodor Dostoyevsky may have experienced this emotion and described it through the character of Prince Myshkin in *The Idiot* (Alajouanine, 1963). *Postictal* alterations are simply those of a lethargic acute confusional state (Chapter 3), and are typically transient. *Interictal* changes, however, are those that can be observed during the great majority of the patient's life when seizures are not occurring. These proposed changes in personality and behavior are controversial but intriguing.

The history of epilepsy has unfortunately been blemished by a stigma attached to the illness, so much so, for example, that demonic possession was once believed to be its cause. Even today there is a negative connotation to epilepsy that many other diseases do not share. It is in this setting that attributions of behavioral changes in patients with TLE must be viewed. There is an understandable tendency for many clinicians to minimize or even deny the alterations that may be present, because it is thought that epileptics already have problems enough without undesirable character traits being attributed to them. Nevertheless, many observers have noted a variety of changes in TLE patients that seem to be rather characteristic.

Schizophreniform Psychosis

One line of inquiry concerns what has been called *schizophreniform psychosis* or schizophrenia-like psychosis (Slater and Beard, 1963). The possibility that psychosis might result from the psychological effects of a chronic and unpredictable illness should be borne in mind, but studies have consistently supported an association between psychosis and TLE but not other seizure types (Perez and Trimble, 1980; Ramani and Gumnit, 1982). In this syndrome, patients with TLE were found to develop an interictal delusional and paranoid psychosis with auditory hallucinations some 14 years after their seizures began (Slater and Beard, 1963). They were thought not to have schizophrenia because there was a curious preservation of affect, for which the modifier "schizophreniform" has therefore been chosen, and because a significant family history of schizophrenia and premorbid schizoid traits in the TLE patients were absent. Further study has suggested that this psychosis may eventually occur in 7% of TLE patients (Trimble, 1992) and is more likely in those with a left temporal focus (Flor-Henry, 1969). The mechanism has been hypothesized to be a *sensory-limbic misconnection* induced by an abnormal area of irritable cortex in the temporal lobe (Spiers et al., 1985). Hence a neutral sensory experience becomes associated with an incongruent feeling state; for example, an innocent stranger seen incidentally might be interpreted as threatening to a TLE patient, and the result would be clinically significant paranoia. Seizure control does not, unfortunately, improve this problem, implying that chronic subictal irritability is sufficient to maintain the syndrome. Neuroleptic medications, ordinarily not used in patients with seizure disorders, may at times be required for the treatment of psychosis. Most recently, evidence has been presented that psychosis in TLE does not differ significantly from typical schizophrenia, supporting the notion that the latter illness may also be a disorder of the temporolimbic system (Mendez et al., 1993).

These considerations lead to a discussion of schizophrenia itself, the disabling disorder of unknown etiology that typically begins in young adulthood and frequently results in chronic mental dysfunction. Although not traditionally considered a neurologic disease, *schizophrenia* is currently being reevaluated in light of increasing evidence that brain dysfunction is of central importance. The response of schizophrenic patients to neuroleptic drugs that act by blockade of dopamine receptors

(Carlsson, 1988) has long suggested that the illness involves more than psychodynamic factors, but the emphasis on psychopharmacology has until recently taken precedence over the investigation of potential structural abnormalities. An early clue to the possibility of brain pathology was the insight that many neurological illnesses, including TLE, may be associated with psychosis resembling schizophrenia (Davison and Bagley, 1969). If neurologic disease can cause psychosis, it was reasoned, then schizophrenia itself may have a neurologic basis. This hypothesis, compelling as it is, has been difficult to substantiate in the past because of the notoriously elusive neuropathology of schizophrenia.

The debate over the details—and even the existence—of neuropathological features of schizophrenia has not been completely settled even after a century of investigation, particularly at the microscopic level. It does appear, however, that brain weight is on average decreased in schizophrenic subjects and that this tissue loss involves gray and not white matter (Roberts, 1991). This observation is consistent with numerous imaging studies using CT and MRI that document brain atrophy in many schizophrenics as reflected in lateral and third ventricular enlargement (Hyde and Weinberger, 1990). Although the basis for this loss of volume is not entirely clear, the temporal lobes appear to be the most implicated. Volumetric studies of postmortem schizophrenic brains have found reductions in the hippocampus, amygdala, and parahippocampal gyrus in comparison to controls (Bogerts, 1985). MRI studies have also noted this selective temporolimbic involvement in schizophrenia; Suddath, et al. (1989) found reductions in hippocampus and amygdala volume. Furthermore, volume loss in the left medial temporal region has been specifically found in schizophrenics (Shenton et al., 1992), and PET studies have found increased metabolism in this same region (Friston et al., 1992). The findings implicating left temporal dysfunction in schizophrenia are particularly intriguing in light of the suggestion of Flor-Henry (1969) that this region may be important in the psychosis of TLE.

There is also evidence for frontal lobe dysfunction, although of a different sort. Here there appears to be a functional rather than structural disturbance. Functional imaging studies have consistently documented bifrontal decreases in metabolic activity, a pattern called "hypofrontality" in schizophrenics, especially when they are given tasks that emphasize prefrontal function (Weinberger and Berman, 1988). Considerable evidence now supports the idea of reduced metabolic activity in the prefrontal cortex (Carpenter and Buchanan, 1994).

Weinberger (1986) has theorized persuasively that the temporal and frontal loci of gray matter dysfunction can explain the essential abnormalities of schizophrenic behavior. Pertinent to this argument is the influential distinction that has been made between the "positive" clinical features of schizophrenia—delusions, hallucinations, and thought disorder—and the "negative" features—apathy, amotivation, and social withdrawal (Crow, 1980). Positive characteristics are seen as related to limbic dysfunction and the likelihood of mesolimbic dopaminergic overactivity; negative manifestations are viewed as due to prefrontal dysfunction, possibly associated with a deficiency of dopamine (Weinberger, 1986). Both neurobehavioral profiles are postulated to be late sequelae of a neurodevelopmental lesion, still undefined, the effects of which become manifest when maturity is reached (Weinberger, 1986).

The relationship of the TLE schizophreniform psychosis to schizophrenia itself becomes clearer in this light. In both conditions there is a putative dysfunction of temporolimbic systems—albeit by different processes—that leads to psychiatric phenomena. If this theory proves to be correct, then perhaps the phenomena are not psychiatric at all, but rather neurologic (Chapter 1). It is intriguing to speculate that the preservation of affect that characterizes schizophreniform psychosis may be due to the *absence* of frontal pathology in TLE, a situation that unfortunately does not obtain in many schizophrenics. Neuropsychological studies comparing schizophrenics and TLE patients with left and right side foci have disclosed that schizophrenics have attentional deficits suggesting frontal dysfunction that are not seen in either TLE group (Gold et al., 1994). The negative features of schizophrenia do indeed bear a close similarity to those of dorsolateral frontal lobe dysfunction (Chapter 10).

Temporolimbic Epilepsy Personality

Another important area of study in TLE—one that has engendered a great deal of controversy—is the idea of a so-called "temporal lobe personality." It is a common experience in the care of persons with TLE, for example, that patient contacts can be prolonged, intense, and affectively charged, a feature referred to as viscosity. This tendency has also been referred to informally but descriptively as "stickiness." The personality alterations many have noted in TLE have been considered to be an inter-ictal disturbance that, like the schizophreniform psychosis, can follow the onset of seizures, and a wide variety of personality traits have been sug-gested to be potential sequelae of the chronic effects of a seizure disorder secondary to a temporal lobe epileptic focus. For a century or more, case reports have described these changes in anecdotal and subjective fashion, and indeed the imprecision of the personality features remains one of the major criticisms of the theory. Moreover, as with schizophreniform psy-chosis, the influence of psychologic factors cannot be ignored. However, in the past two decades more systematic study has been undertaken, and a growing research literature has illuminated this difficult issue to a consid-erable extent.

In 1975, Waxman and Geschwind proposed the existence of an inter-ictal behavioral syndrome in many TLE patients characterized primarily by changes in sexual behavior, religiosity, and hypergraphia (Waxman and Geschwind, 1975). A deepening of emotions manifesting in an intensifi-cation of interpersonal contact was considered central to this syndrome. *Hypergraphia,* the tendency to excessive and compulsive writing, may reveal the same ponderous attention to detail and humorless sobriety that characterize the individual's verbal ouput. Although such a formulation may be seen as calling undue attention to questionable personality changes in persons afflicted with a chronic disease, it is important to point out that Waxman and Geschwind commented that these traits were not necessarily maladaptive and that their observations identified a behavioral *change* rather than a behavioral *disorder* (Waxman and Geschwind, 1975). Pursuing this line of inquiry, Bear and Fedio (1977) undertook a litera-ture review and determined that 18 different personality traits (Table 9.1) could be linked with TLE; they then studied a large group of TLE patients in comparison to normal and neurological control subjects and found that all 18 traits were more prevalent in the TLE group (Bear and Fedio, 1977). These traits were evident both on patients' self-report and the reports of close observers. In clinical practice, detection of all these personality alterations in the same patient is unusual, but finding a cluster of them in one person is not; as in other medical syndromes, individual variability in clinical expression is the rule rather than the exception. Although this controversial syndrome can hardly be said to have achieved universal acceptance, its appellation as the *Geschwind syndrome* has recently been advanced (Benson, 1994).

Table 9.1 Personality traits associated with temporolimbic epilepsy[*]

Inventory trait	Reported clinical observations
Emotionality	Deepening of all emotions; sustained intense affect
Elation, euphoria	Grandiosity, exhilarated mood; diagnosis of manic-depressive disease
Sadness	Discouragement, tearfulness, self-deprecation; diagnosis of depression, suicide attempts
Anger	Increased temper, irritability
Aggression	Overt hostility, rage attacks, violent crimes, murder
Altered sexual interest	Loss of libido, hyposexualism; fetishism, transvestism, exhibitionism, hypersexual episodes
Guilt	Tendency to self-scrutiny and self-recrimination
Hypermoralism	Attention to rules, with inability to distinguish significant from minor infractions; desire to punish offenders
Obsessionalism	Ritualism; orderliness; compulsive attention to detail
Circumstantiality	Loquacious, pedantic; overly detailed, peripheral
Viscosity	Stickiness; tendency to repetition
Sense of personal destiny	Events given highly charged, personalized significance; divine guidance ascribed to many features of patient's life
Hypergraphia	Keeping extensive diaries, detailed notes; writing autobiography or novel
Religiosity	Holding deep religious beliefs, often idiosyncratic; multiple conversions, mystical states
Philosophical interest	Nascent metaphysical or moral speculations; cosmological theories
Dependence	Cosmic helplessness, "at hands of fate"; protestations of helplessness
Humorlessness	Overgeneralized, ponderous expressions of concern; humor lacking or idiosyncratic
Paranoia	Suspiciousness, overinterpretation of motives and events; diagnosis of paranoid schizophrenia

[*] Source: P.A. Spiers, D.L. Schomer, H.W. Blume, and M.-M. Mesulam. 1985. Temporolimbic epilepsy and behavior. In: M.-M. Mesulam. *Principles of Behavioral Neurology.* Philadelphia, F.A. Davis, pp. 289–326. Used with permission.

The mechanism of the syndrome has not been firmly elucidated, but it has been postulated to be a *sensory-limbic hyperconnection*, whereby sensory experience is suffused with excessive emotional coloration because of the increased electrical activity in the temporal lobe that enhances the anatomic and physiologic connection between sensory input and limbic processing (Figure 9.2; Bear, 1979). Ordinary events, therefore, become endowed with extraordinary meaning. A TLE patient, therefore, might interpret a routine life event as a sign of divine guidance, and indeed there are descriptions of sudden religious conversions in these patients, sometimes repeatedly occurring in the same patient (Waxman and Geschwind, 1975). As in schizophreniform psychosis, good seizure control does not appear to modify these features. Presumably, subictal irritability is capable of inducing such hyperconnectivity, and it has been suggested but not proven that the phenomenon of kindling (Goddard, 1983) may be responsible.

The idea of sensory-limbic hyperconnection gains some additional credence in light of a well-known condition first described in primates and known as the *Klüver-Bucy syndrome* (Klüver and Bucy, 1939). These investigators ablated the anterior temporal lobes in male rhesus monkeys and observed a constellation of five changes: hypersexuality, placidity, oral tendencies, visual agnosia or "psychic blindness," and hypermetamorphosis (mandatory environmental exploration). The syndrome has also been described in humans; Pick's Disease, in which anterior temporal lobe degeneration can be severe, often shows elements of the syndrome or the entire array of clinical features (Cummings and Duchen, 1981). It will be seen that these changes constitute a conceptual opposite to the traits of TLE patients, who have functionally just the opposite lesion—a temporal lobe irritable focus that hyperconnects rather than disconnects the sensory and limbic systems (Bear, 1979). Hypersexuality in the Klüver-Bucy syndrome, for example, finds its antithesis in the hyposexuality of TLE patients, and placidity is the opposite of emotional intensity. Still, the mechanism whereby a cortical focus of irritability generates abnormalities of information transmission between different areas of the brain remains uncertain. It is also unclear why some patients appear to develop psychosis whereas others manifest personality change and still others show no significant alterations at all. Advances in the electrographic localization of epileptic areas and in the cellular mechanisms of epileptogenesis will doubtless shed light on these issues.

Other intriguing suggestions have been made in this area. Hermann et al. (1982), using the Minnesota Multiphasic Personality Inventory (MMPI), found more psychopathology in TLE patients with ictal fear than in those without fear and in another group with generalized epilepsy. Epidemiologic studies, although not uniform in methodology, generally suggest that TLE patients are at high risk for psychiatric disorders (Trimble, 1983). Finally, the syndrome of multiple personality has been tentatively linked to TLE (Mesulam, 1981). Although much work lies ahead, the association of temporolimbic epileptogenic lesions and emotional disorder is quite suggestive of a causal relationship.

A particularly troublesome issue is the relationship of TLE to *aggression*. Violence with the intent to harm or destroy, of course, is a major societal problem, and a deeper understanding of its origins would be immensely helpful. Aggression, like any behavior, has an anatomy, and both biologic and sociologic factors contribute to violent behavior. However, the premature identification of any neurologic population, such as those with TLE, as more prone to aggression would unjustly stigmatize the members of that population. As a general rule, in epilepsy of any type, directed violence *during* seizures is vanishingly rare (Delgado-Escueta et al., 1981). In TLE, violent automatisms can rarely occur as part of a seizure (Ashford et al., 1980), and postictal aggression has also been described (Rodin, 1973). Interictal aggression in TLE, however, is more controversial. Case reports of increased interictal aggression in TLE patients have been presented, and animal experiments have shown increased aggression following induction of temporal lobe seizure foci (Devinsky and Vazquez, 1993). A number of studies, however, have not found an increase in aggression when TLE patients are compared to those with other types of epilepsy (Hermann and Whitman, 1984). Studies of neurosurgical patients have nevertheless noted a high incidence of aggressiveness in TLE patients (Serafetinides, 1965), and it has been found that temporal lobectomy for seizure control helps reduce this behavior (Falconer, 1973). In summary, it would appear that whereas aggression is clearly determined by many factors (Pincus and Lewis, 1991), some patients with TLE may develop an increased likelihood of interictal aggression. The resolution of this difficult issue must await well-controlled clinical studies (Stevens and Hermann, 1981).

The existence of the behavioral syndromes in TLE reviewed in this chapter has been strongly questioned, and it is true that both the schizophreniform psychosis and the temporolimbic epilepsy personality suffer from vague definitions and unproven pathogenetic theories. A judgmental attitude toward patients with TLE who may be found to have undesirable behavioral traits is of course inappropriate. Rather, the study of these behavioral changes must ultimately seek, as in any medical setting, to help patients in need through the knowledge gained. Moreover, not all potential changes are necessarily undesirable; positive attributes including artistic creativity and philosophic insight may also prove to be associated with TLE (Devinsky and Vazquez, 1993). What is most intriguing about this often acrimonious debate from a neurobehavioral viewpoint is the possibility of disturbances in sensory-limbic connectivity, speculations that have been and remain amenable to rigorous scientific study. The understanding of brain-behavior relationships demands no less than a willingness to consider and evaluate theoretical behavioral changes due to cerebral disease; TLE is one of the most fertile research areas in this quest.

References

Alajouanine, T. 1963. Dostoiewski's epilepsy. *Brain;* 86: 209–218.

Ashford, J.W., Schulz, S.C., and Walsh, G.O. 1980. Violent automatism in a partial complex seizure. *Arch Neurol;* 37: 120–122.

Bancaud, J., Brunet-Bourgin, F., Chauvel, P., and Halgren, E. 1994. Anatomical origin of *déjà vu* and vivid "memories" in human temporal lobe epilepsy. *Brain;* 117: 71–90.

Bard, P. 1928. A diencephalic mechanism for the expression of rage with special reference to the sympathetic nervous system. *Am J Physiol;* 84: 490–515.

Bear, D.M. 1979. Temporal lobe epilepsy—a syndrome of sensory-limbic hyperconnection. *Cortex;* 15: 357–384.

Bear, D.M., and Fedio, P. 1977. Quantitative analysis of interictal behavior in temporal lobe epilepsy. *Arch Neurol;* 34: 454–467.

Benson, D.F. 1994. *The Neurology of Thinking.* New York, Oxford.

Bogerts, B., Meertz, E., and Schonfeldt-Bausch, R. 1985. Basal ganglia and limbic system pathology in schizophrenia: a morphometric study of brain volume and shrinkage. *Arch Gen Psychiatry;* 42: 784–791.

Broca, P. 1878. Anatomie comparée de circonvolutions cérébrales. Le grand lobe limbique et la scissure limbique dans le série des mammifères. *Rev Anthropol;* 1: 385–498.

Brodal, A. 1981. *Neurological Anatomy.* 3rd ed. New York, Oxford.

Brooks, W.H., Cross, R.J., Roszman, T.L., and Markesbery, W.R. 1982. Neuroimmunomodulation: neural anatomical basis for impairment and facilitation. *Ann Neurol;* 12: 56–61.

Carlsson, A. 1988. The current status of the dopamine hypothesis of schizophrenia. *Neuropsychopharmacology;* 1: 79–86.

Carpenter, W.T., and Buchanan, R.W. 1994. Schizophrenia. *N Engl J Med;* 330: 681–690.

Crow, T.J. 1980. Molecular pathology of schizophrenia: more than one disease process? *Br Med J;* 280: 66–68.

Cummings, J.L., and Duchen, L.W. 1981. Klüver-Bucy syndrome in Pick disease; clinical and pathologic correlations. *Neurology;* 31: 1415–1422.

Currie, S., Heathfield, K.W.G., Henson, R.A., and Scott, D.F. 1971. Clinical course and prognosis of temporal lobe epilepsy. *Brain;* 94: 173–190.

Damasio, A.R., and Van Hoesen, G.W. 1983. Emotional disturbances associated with focal lesions of the limbic frontal lobe. In: Heilman, K.M., and Satz, P. (eds.). *Neuropsychology of Human Emotion.* New York, Guilford, pp. 85–110.

Davison, K., and Bagley, C.R. 1969. Schizophrenia-like psychoses associated with organic disorders of the central nervous system: a review of the literature. In: Herrington, R.N. (ed.). *Current Problems in Neuropsychiatry. Br J Psychiatry;* Special Publication No. 4, pp. 113–184.

Delgado-Escueta, A.V., Mattson, R.H., King, L., et al. 1981. The nature of aggression during epileptic seizures. *N Engl J Med;* 305: 711–716.

Devinsky, O., and Vazquez, B. 1993. Behavioral changes associated with epilepsy. *Neurol Clin;* 11: 127–149.

Falconer, M.A. 1973. Reversibility by temporal-lobe resection of the behavioral abnormalities of temporal-lobe epilepsy. *N Engl J Med;* 289: 451–455.

Flor-Henry, P. 1969. Psychosis and temporal lobe epilepsy. A controlled investigation. *Epilepsia;* 10: 363–395.

Friston, K.J., Liddle, P.F., Frith, C.D., et al. 1992. The left temporal region and schizophrenia. A PET study. *Brain;* 115: 367–382.

Gloor, P., Olivier, A., Quesney, L.F., et al. 1982. The role of the limbic system in experiential phenomena of temporal lobe epilepsy. *Ann Neurol;* 12: 129–144.

Goddard, G.V. 1983. The kindling model of epilepsy. *Trends Neurosci;* 6: 275–279.

Gold, J.M., Hermann, B.P., Randolph, C., et al. 1994. Schizophrenia and temporal lobe epilepsy. A neuropsychological analysis. *Arch Gen Psychiatry;* 51: 265–272.

Halgren, E., Walter, R.D., Cherlow, A.G., and Crandall, P.H. 1978. Mental phenomena evoked by electrical stimulation of the human hippocampal formation and amygdala. *Brain;* 101: 83–117.

Hermann, B.P., and Whitman, S. 1984. Behavioral and personality correlates of epilepsy: a review, methodologic critique, and conceptual model. *Psychol Bull;* 95: 451–497.

Hermann, B.P., Dikmen, S., Schwartz, M.S., and Karnes, W.E. 1982. Interictal psychopathology in patients with ictal fear: a quantitative investigation. *Neurology;* 32: 7–11.

Hughlings-Jackson, J. 1888–1889. On a particular variety of epilepsy ("intellectual aura"), one case with symptoms of organic brain disease. *Brain;* 11: 179–207.

Hyde, T.M., and Weinberger, D.R. 1990. The brain in schizophrenia. *Sem Neurol;* 10: 276–286.

Klüver, H., and Bucy, P.C. 1939. Preliminary analysis of functions of the temporal lobes in monkeys. *Arch Neurol Psychiatry;* 42: 979–1000.

LeDoux, J.E. 1987. Emotion. In: Mountcastle, V.B., Plum, F., and Geiser, S.R. (eds.). *Handbook of Physiology.* Section 1. The Nervous System. Bethesda, American Physiological Society, pp. 419–459.

LeDoux, J.E. 1994. Emotion, memory and the brain. *Sci Am;* 270(6): 50–57.

MacLean, P.D. 1949. Psychosomatic disease and the "visceral brain." Recent developments bearing on the Papez theory of emotion. *Psychosomatic Med;* 11: 338–353.

Mendez, M.F., Grau, R., Doss, R.C., and Taylor, J.L. 1993. Schizophrenia in epilepsy: seizure and psychosis variables. *Neurology;* 43: 1073–1077.

Mesulam, M.-M. 1981. Dissociative states with abnormal temporal lobe EEG. *Arch Neurol;* 38: 176–181.

Papez, J.W. 1937. A proposed mechanism of emotion. *Arch Neurol Psychiatry;* 38: 725–743.

Perez, M.M., and Trimble, M.R. 1980. Epileptic psychosis—diagnostic comparison with process schizophrenia. *Brit J Psychiatry;* 137: 245–249.

Pincus, J.H., and Lewis, D.O. 1991. Episodic violence. *Sem Neurol;* 11: 146–154.

Ramani, V., and Gumnit, R.J. 1982. Intensive monitoring of interictal psychosis in epilepsy. *Ann Neurol;* 11: 613–622.

Roberts, G.W. 1991. Schizophrenia: a neuropathological perspective. *Br J Psychiatry;* 158: 8–17.

Rodin, E.A. 1973. Psychomotor epilepsy and aggressive behavior. *Arch Gen Psychiatry;* 28: 210–213.

Ross, E.D., Homan, R.W., and Buck, R. 1994. Differential hemispheric lateralization of primary and social emotions. *Neuropsychiatry Neuropsychol Behav Neurol;* 7: 1–19.

Scharrer, E., and Scharrer, B. 1954. Hormones produced by neurosecretory cells. *Recent Prog Hormone Res;* 10: 183–232.

Serafetinides, E.A. 1965. Aggressiveness in temporal lobe epileptics and its relation to cerebral dysfunction and environmental factors. *Epilepsia;* 6: 33–42.

Shenton, M.E., Kikinis, R., Jolesz, F.A., et al. 1992. Abnormalities of the left temporal lobe and thought disorder in schizophrenia: a quantitative magnetic resonance imaging study. *N Engl J Med;* 327: 604–612.

Slater, E., and Beard, A.W. 1963. The schizophrenia-like psychoses of epilepsy. *Br J Psychiatry;* 109: 95–150.

Spiers, P.A., Schomer, D.L., Blume, H.W., and Mesulam, M.-M. 1985. Temporolimbic epilepsy and behavior. In: Mesulam, M.-M. *Principles of Behavioral Neurology.* Philadelphia, F.A. Davis, pp. 289–326.

Stevens, J.R., and Hermann, B.P. 1981. Temporal lobe epilepsy, psychopathology, and violence: the state of the evidence. *Neurology;* 31: 1127–1132.

Suddath, R.L., Casanova, M.F., Goldberg, T.E., et al. 1989. Temporal lobe pathology in schizophrenia: a quantitative magnetic resonance imaging study. *Am J Psychiatry;* 146: 464–472.

Trimble, M.R. 1983. Personality disturbances in epilepsy. *Neurology;* 33: 1332–1334.

Trimble, M.R. 1992. The schizophrenia-like psychosis of epilepsy. *Neuropsychiatry Neuropsychol Behav Neurol;* 5: 103–107.

Waxman, S.G., and Geschwind, N. 1975. The interictal behavior syndrome of temporal lobe epilepsy. *Arch Gen Psychiatry;* 32: 1580–1586.

Weinberger, D.R. 1986. The pathogenesis of schizophrenia: a neurodevelopmental theory. In: Nasrallah, H.A., and Weinberger, D.R. (eds.). *Handbook of Schizophrenia, Vol. 1: The Neurology of Schizophrenia.* New York, Elsevier, pp. 397–406.

Weinberger, D.R., and Berman, K.F. 1988. Speculation on the meaning of cerebral metabolic hypofrontality in schizophrenia. *Schizophr Bull;* 14: 157–168.

Williams, D. 1956. The structure of emotions reflected in epileptic experiences. *Brain;* 79: 29–67.

CHAPTER 10

Frontal Lobe Syndromes

The frontal lobes have long fascinated, and perplexed, students of human behavior. One obvious reason for this is their impressive size, occupying more than a third of the brain's cortical surface (Damasio and Anderson, 1993). Moreover, they are the most phylogenetically recent areas of the brain, and no other animal possesses frontal lobes of such size. It seems unavoidable that the frontal lobes are responsible for particularly human capacities, and the period of human evolution has been considered the "age of the frontal lobe" (Tilney, 1928). Yet the precise functions of the frontal lobes remain elusive in many respects. Intimately involved with the highest levels of cognitive and emotional processing, they clearly play a major role in personality, and the maintenance of comportment (Mesulam, 1986) is an essential function. The extensive anatomical connectivity with other regions of the brain (Luria, 1980; Damasio and Anderson, 1993), however, implies that the frontal lobes participate in all the brain's activities, ranging from the simplest to the most complex of behaviors. This powerful organizational influence implies the critical notion of control, and it is instructive to envision the frontal lobes acting as the conductor of the symphony being played by the rest of the brain.

Anatomically located in a position that mirrors their functional importance, the frontal lobes are the most anterior regions of the human brain. Laterally, they occupy all the area anterior to the Rolandic fissure and superior to the Sylvian fissure, and medially, they extend forward from an imaginary line between the top of the Rolandic fissure and the corpus callosum (see Figures 1.1 and 1.2). Numerous parcellations of the frontal lobes have been proposed by anatomists (Stuss and Benson, 1986), but many agree that four functionally distinct regions can be delineated. First, there is the primary motor cortex, Brodmann area 4 (see Figure 1.3), well known to neurologists because of its primary responsibility for contralateral body movements. Second, the premotor area, Brodmann area 6 (see Figure 1.3), lies just anterior to the motor cortex and is concerned with the initiation of movement; the medial extension of area 6 is known as the supplementary motor area and this region on the left plays an important role in the initiation of speech (Chapter 5). Third, Broca's area, corresponding to Brodmann areas 44 and 45 on the left (see Figure 1.3), has a clearly established affiliation with language fluency (Chapter 5), and its analogous zone on the right side is thought to subserve language prosody and emotional gesture (Chapter 8). Finally, the remainder of the frontal lobe, Brodmann areas 8 through 12, 24, 25, 32, 33, 46, and 47 (see Figure 1.3), are designated collectively as the prefrontal cortex. It is in this large and diverse area that the highest functions of the frontal lobes are represented and in which lesions can produce the various neurobehavioral syndromes considered in this chapter.

As in the case of temporolimbic disorders (Chapter 9), clinicians have long noted that frontal lobe lesions may alter personality (Stuss and Benson, 1986). The concept of *personality* presents difficulties in definition, but we will consider it the characteristic repertoire of behavioral responses that an individual uses to meet environmental contingencies. Closely related concepts are character and temperament. An individual's personality is determined by a combination of genetic endowment and environmental learning, all of which are expressed in the structure and function of the brain. Personality is established primarily in the childhood and adolescent years, and, despite the capacity for limited modification later on, the mature adult maintains a stable and lasting personality. A clear and unintended personality change in an adult, therefore, has important neurologic implications, such as the possibility of a frontal lobe meningioma, the onset of Pick's Disease, or traumatic brain injury. Moreover, personality change in frontal lobe disease or injury offers many opportunities for understanding brain-behavior relationships.

A change in comportment often heralds the onset of frontal lobe involvement and characterizes many aspects of the behavior that is so produced (Mesulam, 1985). *Comportment* is a useful concept referring to the patterns by which a person interacts with others, and this interaction may be disturbed by a breakdown in either cognitive or emotional competence. Because the frontal lobes are linked with both cognitive (neocortical) and emotional (limbic) regions, patients may present with features suggesting

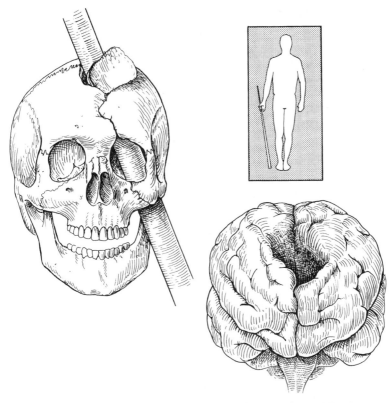

Figure 10.1   The skull, brain, and tamping rod of Phineas Gage. After Damasio, et al., 1994.

cognitive decline—slow thinking, poor judgment, and diminished curiosity—or emotional disorder—inappropriate behavior, social withdrawal, and irritability; often a combination of deficits determines the presentation. The remarkable range of alterations that can occur testifies to the wide spectrum of mental domains in which the frontal lobes participate.

Many good accounts of personality change after frontal lobe injury have been presented, but the most famous is the extraordinary case of Phineas Gage, a 25-year-old railroad company foreman who sustained a remarkable bifrontal lesion in 1848 (Harlow, 1868). While supervising construction of the Rutland and Burlington Railroad across Vermont, Gage was working with a 29-kilogram iron tamping rod in the process of laying an explosive, and during an accidental discharge, the 109-centimeter-long, 3-centimeter-thick rod was propelled at great velocity upward through his face, skull, and brain (Figure 10.1; Macmillan, 1986). The tamping rod exited the skull, flew into the sky, and landed about 30 meters away, where it was later found. Remarkably, Gage recovered after being momentarily stunned and lived for many years after the injury. With the exception of the loss of his left eye, he appeared to have no physical deficits, and neurologically he had neither aphasia nor paresis. It was during these years, however, that a dramatic change in personality and comportment was documented (Harlow, 1868). Prior to his accident, Gage had been a responsible, intelligent, and industrious man with a bright future, but after his injury he was observed to become irreverent, profane, and unreliable. He never again showed the promise of his early years and was clearly "no longer Gage" (Harlow, 1868). No autopsy was conducted upon his death at age 36, but his body was later exhumed so that the skull could be recovered; both the skull and the tamping iron are on display at the Warren Anatomical Medical Museum at Harvard University. Recently, elegant computerized reconstruction of the likely trajectory of the tamping rod, based on careful measurements of the damaged skull, have made it clear that the injury involved the right as well as the left frontal lobe and that the orbitofrontal cortices were most severely affected (Figure 10.1; Damasio et al., 1994). These lesions were therefore the source of the striking behavioral change, as many similar cases of frontal lobe damage since that time have confirmed (Damasio et al., 1994). Like Broca's Leborgne and the amnesic H.M., Phineas Gage demonstrates how the lesion method of behavioral neurology can exploit even a single case to illustrate with singular clarity the relationship of brain and behavior.

The clinical neurologic literature since the time of Phineas Gage has amply confirmed that bilateral frontal lesions are usually necessary for the production of significant neurobehavioral alterations (Cummings, 1985; Mesulam, 1986). Traumatic brain injury, cerebral infarction, neoplasms such as meningioma and butterfly glioma, Pick's Disease, neurosyphilis, multiple sclerosis, and prefrontal leukotomy are all well known to cause behavioral disturbances because of damage to both frontal lobes. Unilateral lesions of any etiology are more difficult to identify, probably because of the ability of an intact frontal lobe to compensate for dysfunction in a damaged one. Nevertheless, careful attention to alterations in personality and comportment can uncover many frontal lobe lesions before the onset of most or all routine neurologic symptoms and signs. Although the frontal lobes have been viewed as neurologically "silent" in the sense that they can harbor large lesions without such features as paresis or aphasia appearing, a neurobehavioral approach can substantially assist in the detection of many frontal lesions. The brain is only "silent" when we lack the skills to listen to it; further study of the frontal lobes will surely lead to refinements in diagnosis based on a deeper knowledge of their unique contributions.

The most characteristic features of the change in personality seen with frontal lobe pathology are impulsive disinhibition and apathetic indifference. Patients can manifest a passive and unmotivated demeanor that unpredictably escalates into euphoric, irritable behavior (Blumer and Benson, 1975). Yet this profile fails to embrace many other features that patients can demonstrate. It has been pointed out that the anatomic complexity of the frontal lobes and the clinical diversity of frontal lobe dysfunction do not permit a simple delineation of a single frontal lobe syndrome (Damasio and Anderson, 1993). Three major syndromes based on areas of primary involvement (Figure 10.2) will be considered: an *orbitofrontal syndrome*, with disinhibition; a *dorsolateral syndrome*, with executive function deficits; and a *medial frontal syndrome*, with apathy (Cummings, 1993). In practice, elements of these three often coexist because frontal pathology often attains considerable size before the patient comes to clinical attention.

Orbitofrontal Syndrome

The preeminent feature of the orbitofrontal syndrome is *disinhibition* (Jarvie, 1954). Patients with bilateral orbitofrontal lesions engage in inappropriate social and sexual activities that demonstrate an erosion of the usual restraints by which interpersonal adult life is regulated. Affect may become irritable, labile, euphoric, or unduly jocular. The terms *moria*, meaning an excited affect resembling hypomania, and *witzelsucht*, the telling of inappropriately caustic or facetious jokes, are both relevant to this syndrome (Hecaen and Albert, 1975). There is often impaired judgment and insight, such that decisions are made without regard for their consequences (Eslinger and Damasio, 1985). The case of Phineas Gage reviewed earlier clearly exemplifies this syndrome (Harlow, 1868; Damasio et al., 1994). Another key feature is distractibility, a deficit prohibiting sustained effort on sequential tasks that would allow their completion. Despite these problematic deficits, it is notable that neuropsychological impairment may be undetectable (Eslinger an Damasio, 1985). Although olfactory function

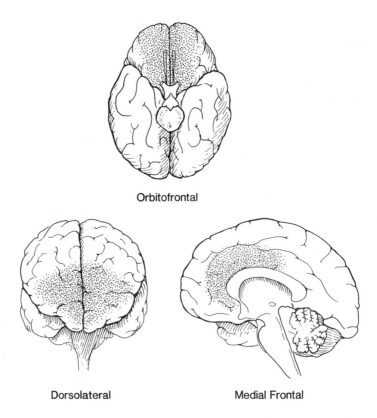

Orbitofrontal

Dorsolateral

Medial Frontal

Figure 10.2 Regions of the frontal lobes affected in orbitofrontal, dorsolateral, and medial frontal syndromes.

may be affected in this syndrome because of damage to the olfactory nerves at the base of the frontal lobes, elemental neurologic findings may also be minimal in such cases, and careful attention to behavioral features is particularly important. Bilateral injury to Brodmann areas 11, 12, and 25 is typically found (see Figures 1.3 and 10.2).

The term *acquired sociopathy* has been proposed in the context of this often troublesome syndrome (Eslinger and Damasio, 1985). The relationship of the orbitofrontal syndrome to antisocial personality disorder (American Psychiatric Association, 1994) is apparent. There are also similarities to the intermittent explosive disorder (American Psychiatric Association, 1994) and the episodic dyscontrol syndrome (Elliott, 1992), although with these disorders, there is a sense of remorse or guilt for the disinhibited behavior that is not present in sociopathy. Lesions of the orbitofrontal regions seem to disturb not only the regulation of limbic

Neurobehavioral Anatomy

drives but also the individual's insight into this deficit. It is possible, therefore, that responsibility for one's actions depends upon the integrity of the orbitofrontal cortex and that the disturbing lack of remorse typifying the antisocial personality may reflect dysfunction in this region. In contrast, individuals with intact frontal lobes who have behavioral disinhibition on the basis of the interictal syndrome of TLE appear to have a preserved if not excessive sense of guilt (Chapter 9). A necessary condition for appropriate behavior, then, is the maintenance of a delicate balance between limbic drives and frontal control that integrates the fulfillment of basic needs into the context of responsible action.

Dorsolateral Syndrome

In this syndrome, *executive function deficits* are paramount, implying that the patient is deficient in the planning, monitoring, and flexibility of behavior. A marked disturbance in the ability to solve problems requiring foresight, goal selection, resistance to interference, use of feedback, and sustained effort is typical. The patient appears inattentive and undermotivated and may make errors on tasks assessing vigilance (Chapter 2). *Perseveration* may be seen (Sandson and Albert, 1987), either during the interview or in the course of the examination; failure at an alternating motor sequence task (Chapter 2) can graphically disclose this tendency. *Stimulus-bound behavior* may be encountered, as in the case of a patient who incorrectly draws the hands on a clock at the 10 and the 11 after being asked to indicate the time 11:10. A related phenomenon is *echopraxia*, the involuntary imitation of the examiner's gestures, which suggests a loss of the internal monitoring of motor behavior (Luria, 1973). Associated communication deficits may also be found. First, linguistic impairments related to left side lesions can occur, including *diminished verbal fluency* as measured by word list generation tasks (Benton, 1968) and transcortical motor aphasia (Chapter 5). Alternatively, if the lesion is in the right dorsolateral area, transcortical motor aprosody (Chapter 8) can be expected. Damage to Brodmann areas 8, 9, 10, 46, and 47 can be found bilaterally in those who have prominent executive function deficits (see Figures 1.3 and 10.2).

In contrast to the orbitofrontal syndrome, neuropsychological deficits are often encountered, but detection of these impairments requires close attention by the neuropsychologist to the process by which a task is approached; a careless and sloppy approach to a standardized test, for example, can indicate prefrontal dysfunction as much as does the actual score generated (Stuss and Benson, 1986). One measure that has been particularly helpful in the detection of left frontal lesions is the Wisconsin Card Sorting Test, which is designed to assess abstract reasoning and the ability to shift mental set while avoiding perseveration (Drewe, 1974). Right frontal lesions are very difficult to identify neuropsychologically, although design fluency tasks—tests probing the facility with which drawings are produced—tend to be maximally impaired with right side lesions (Jones-Gotman and Milner, 1977). Overall, the dorsolateral syndrome is somewhat more identifiable by formal testing than is the orbitofrontal syndrome, and affected patients tend to have a more clearly recognizable "cognitive" disorder. The primary problem, however, is not in the individual's cognitive capacities, but rather in the programming of those functions. The syndrome is characterized by difficulty planning novel cognitive activity and carrying out sequential tasks (Luria, 1980). Although cognitive abilities such as memory, language, and visuospatial skills are themselves intact, patients with dorsolateral lesions lack executive control and therefore cannot properly use these skills; in the perceptive words of Luria, "knowledge is divorced from action" (Luria, 1973).

Medial Frontal Syndrome

In the medial frontal syndrome, *apathy* is the major characteristic. Affected patients are poorly motivated and show limited spontaneous movement, gesture, and speech. The word *abulia* refers to a more severe form of apathy. In the most extreme example, immediately following acute bilateral lesions in the medial frontal areas, *akinetic mutism* appears, characterized by a severe disturbance of motor activity and speech (Ross and Stewart, 1981). In akinetic mutism, which can also follow bilateral damage to the midbrain and diencephalon, wakefulness and self-awareness are preserved, but the initiation of behavior is much reduced or absent. Transcortical motor aphasia occurs with involvement of the left supplementary motor area (Masdeu et al., 1978), and the characteristic difficulty in initiating speech is the linguistic manifestation of the general difficulty with movement seen in this syndrome. Lower extremity paresis and gait disturbance can be seen if the lesion extends to the high precentral gyrus. Sphincteric disturbances are common with bilateral medial frontal damage (Andrew and Nathan, 1964), and patients with this *frontal lobe incontinence* are characteristically indifferent to the loss of bladder and bowel control. Responsible lesions may be in the anterior cingulate gyri (Neilsen and Jacobs, 1951; Barris and Schuman, 1953). Brodmann areas 24, 32, and 33 are implicated in this syndrome (see Figures 1.3 and 10.2).

The loss of spontaneity and initiative encompassed by this syndrome has led to the provocative but tenuous speculation that the anterior cingulate region may have special importance in the familiar philosophic concept of free will (Damasio, 1994; Crick, 1994). Patients with the medial frontal syndrome seem to lack the drive to engage in cognitive and emotional life even though the structures subserving this engagement are themselves intact. Thus they behave as though they have a diminished or absent will to act. It is, of course, hazardous to assign a notion such as free will to a single area of the brain, and it is doubtful that there exists a discrete "center of the will." However, the inert and passive demeanor of patients with medial frontal lesions does suggest that a vital component of voluntary and willful action has been compromised.

Table 10.1 displays the major clinical features of the frontal lobe syndromes discussed in the preceding sections. As is true for all the syndromes considered in this book, correlations of behavioral phenomena with neuroanatomic structures will undoubtedly be refined by the accumulation of further data.

Functions of the Frontal Lobes

The singular development of the human frontal lobes, particularly the prefrontal regions, strongly implies that they make a unique and critical contribution to mental life. Yet the precise description of this role is exceedingly difficult, and the "riddle of frontal lobe function" (Teuber, 1964) remains largely unsolved. The frontal lobes participate in all the higher functions considered in this book, operating in little-understood ways to supervise the entire repertoire of human behavior. The key to understanding the highest cerebral functions clearly lies within the expanses of the frontal lobes, but this investigatory task is only just beginning.

It might be imagined that *intelligence* is a higher function that would logically be localized in the frontal lobes, but, as we have seen, standard neuropsychological assessments of intelligence—most notably using the intelligence quotient (IQ)—may be quite normal in patients

Table 10.1 Clinical features of frontal lobe syndromes[*]

Orbitofrontal
Disinhibition
Inappropriate affect
Impaired judgment and insight
Distractibility

Dorsolateral
Executive function deficits
Perseveration
Stimulus-bound behavior
Diminished verbal fluency

Medial frontal
Apathy
Mutism or transcortical motor aphasia
Lower extremity paresis
Incontinence

[*] Adapted from J.L. Cummings. 1993. Frontal-subcortical circuits and human behavior. *Arch Neurol;* 50: 873–880. Copyright 1993, American Medical Association. Used with permission.

with significant frontal lobe involvement (Eslinger and Damasio, 1985). Intelligence, of course, is a very difficult concept to define, and Gould (1981) has vigorously criticized the use of the IQ as a single metric to describe an individual's intellectual capacity. Gardner (1983) has presented an attractive alternative with his theory of multiple intelligences that expands the notion to include a variety of abilities not adequately evaluated by paper-and-pencil tests. Nevertheless, the IQ, as calculated from the popular Wechsler Adult Intelligence Scale—Revised (Wechsler, 1981), remains a widely used neuropsychological tool, and some understanding of its neurobehavioral interpretation is helpful.

As a general rule, the IQ reflects the function of the brain as a whole, which is in turn dependent on a myriad of genetic and environmental factors influencing neuronal number, synaptic density, myelin integrity, and neurotransmitter metabolism. Recent in vivo MRI studies have suggested that brain size, when corrected for body size, may indeed correlate with IQ (Willerman et al., 1991; Andreasen et al., 1993). Others have maintained that abstract verbal and visuospatial reasoning—key components of intelligence—are associated with postrolandic cortical areas

(Strub and Black, 1988). Functional imaging studies have supported this claim; verbal IQ subtest scores, which to a large extent reflect language competence, are associated with metabolic activity in the left temporoparietal region, and performance IQ subtest scores, which mainly depend on visuospatial ability, are associated with right posterior parietal metabolism (Chase et al., 1984). Thus, even though the IQ as a neuropsychological measure does require the participation of many areas, the main relevant cerebral affiliations may be posterior to the frontal lobes. The implication for clinicians is that neither IQ nor any other single test reliably identifies frontal lobe lesions (Stuss and Benson, 1986). For theorists of frontal lobe function, these considerations imply that some capacity allied with but superordinate to intelligence lies within these cerebral regions; PET studies have indicated that prefrontal areas are activated uniformly during "thinking" tasks that each simultaneously involve different posterior cortical regions (Roland and Friberg, 1985). The frontal lobes seem to have more to do with how a person *uses* intelligence than with intelligence itself.

It is obvious that, in many cases, we simply lack the appropriate instruments with which to measure satisfactorily the controlling functions of the frontal lobes. Many impairments only become apparent in demanding real-life encounters when the individual's capacity to integrate complex information and inhibit inappropriate behaviors is more heavily taxed (Zangwill, 1966). Under structured conditions, patients with frontal lobe lesions often respond well to the organization provided by the setting—the physician's office, the neuropsychology laboratory—and may appear by all criteria quite normal. It is in the everyday world that deficits manifest themselves (Shallice and Burgess, 1991); the internal organization provided by the frontal lobes is diminished, and the delicate regulation of cognition and emotions is upset. This aspect of frontal lobe dysfunction further emphasizes the importance of data obtained by a careful clinical history and interview.

Several attempts have been made to capture the essence of frontal lobe function. These theories are similar in many respects, and their diversity may only reflect the richness of frontal lobe operations and the different perspectives of the observers. Luria, the influential Russian neuropsychologist, emphasized the hierarchical organization of the brain, at the top of which stand the frontal lobes, which act to regulate "cortical tone" (Luria, 1973). Attentional processes figure prominently in this scheme, helping to program and direct mental action. Lhermitte has depicted a loss of autonomy in patients with frontal lobe lesions who exhibited inappropriate "imitation" of the examiner's behavior and "utilization" of nearby environmental objects (Lhermitte et al., 1986). This "environmental dependency syndrome" reflects, in Lhermitte's view, a failure to maintain internal control and an excessive dependence on the external environment (Lhermitte, 1986). Fuster (1989) asserted that the frontal lobes provide for the temporal structuring of behavior, integrating actions in light of past experience and future plans. Control of interfering stimuli through inhibitory protection is central to his theory. Stuss and Benson (1986) pointed out that the frontal lobes act to regulate all the brain's higher functions. In their view, the frontal lobes mediate self-consciousness and bridge the gap between brain and mind. These and other theories all have merit, and each contributes to the detailed but incomplete picture. Further study will doubtless clarify the unique supervisory contributions of the frontal lobes, and perhaps a single unifying function will emerge as more knowledge is gained.

Perhaps the most practical way to envision frontal function is in the context of the neuroanatomic connections of the frontal lobes with sensory, motor, and limbic systems (Nauta, 1971). Interposed between stimulus and response, which in lower animals are governed by brain stem or limbic structures (MacLean, 1990), the frontal lobes provide for flexible, autonomous, and goal-directed behavior that considers both past experience and future objectives. In the absence of normally functioning frontal lobes, the ephemeral quality of "humanness" is somehow perturbed, despite the preservation of many cognitive and emotional domains that are primarily localized elsewhere in the brain. For the clinician responsible for individuals with frontal lobe disorders, a familiarity with theories of frontal function will prove invaluable in the diagnosis and treatment of patients whose deficits may be as difficult to objectify as they are devastating to effective mental life.

References

American Psychiatric Association. 1994. *Diagnostic and Statistical Manual of Mental Disorders*, 4th ed. Washington, D.C., American Psychiatric Association.

Andreasen, N.C., Flaum, M., Swayze, V., et al. 1993. Intelligence and brain structure in normal individuals. *Am J Psychiatry;* 150: 130–134.

Andrew, J., and Nathan, P.W. 1964. Lesions of the anterior frontal lobes and disturbances of micturition and defaecation. *Brain;* 87: 233–262.

Barris, R.W., and Schuman, H.R. 1953. Bilateral anterior cingulate gyrus lesions. *Neurology;* 3: 44–52.

Benton, A.L. 1968. Differential effects in frontal lobe disease. *Neuropsychologia;* 6: 53–60.

Blumer, D., and Benson, D.F. 1975. Personality changes with frontal and temporal lobe lesions. In: Benson D.F., and Blumer, D. (eds.). *Psychiatric Aspects of Neurologic Disease.* Vol. 1. New York, Grune and Stratton, pp. 151–169.

Chase, T.N., Fedio, P., Foster, N.L., et al. 1984. Wechsler adult intelligence scale performance. Cortical localization by fluorodeoxyglucose F 18-positron emission tomography. *Arch Neurol;* 41: 1244–1247.

Crick, F. 1994. *The Astonishing Hypothesis. The Scientific Search for the Soul.* New York, Charles Scribner's Sons.

Cummings, J.L. 1985. *Clinical Neuropsychiatry.* Orlando, Grune and Stratton.

Cummings, J.L. 1993. Frontal-subcortical circuits and human behavior. *Arch Neurol;* 50: 873–880.

Damasio, A.R. 1994. *Descartes' Error. Emotion, Reason, and the Human Brain.* New York, Grosset/Putnam.

Damasio, A.R, and Anderson, S.W. 1993. The frontal lobes. In: Heilman, K.M., and Valenstein, E. (eds.). *Clinical Neuropsychology.* 3rd ed. New York, Oxford, pp. 409–460.

Damasio, H., Grabowski, T., Frank, R., et al. 1994. The return of Phineas Gage: clues about the brain from the skull of a famous patient. *Science;* 264: 1102–1105.

Drewe, E.A. 1974. The effect of type and area of brain lesion on Wisconsin Card Sorting Test performance. *Cortex;* 10: 159–170.

Elliott, F.A., 1992. Violence. The neurologic contribution: an overview. *Arch Neurol;* 49: 595–603.

Eslinger, P.J., and Damasio, A.R. 1985. Severe disturbance of higher cognition after bilateral frontal lobe ablation: patient EVR. *Neurology;* 35: 1731–1741.

Fuster, J.M. 1989. *The Prefrontal Cortex.* 2nd ed. New York, Raven.

Gardner, H. 1983. *Frames of Mind. The Theory of Multiple Intelligences.* New York, Basic Books.

Gould, S.J. 1981. *The Mismeasure of Man.* New York, W.W. Norton.

Harlow, J.M. 1868. Recovery from the passage of an iron bar through the head. *Mass Med Soc Publ;* 2: 327–346.

Hecaen, H., and Albert, M.L. 1975. Disorders of mental functioning related to frontal lobe pathology. In: Benson, D.F., and Blumer, D. (eds.). *Psychiatric Aspects of Neurologic Disease.* Vol. 1. New York, Grune and Stratton, pp. 137–149.

Jarvie, H.F. 1954. Frontal wounds causing disinhibition. *J Neurol Neurosurg Psychiatry;* 17: 14–32.

Jones-Gotman, M., and Milner, B. 1977. Design fluency: the invention of nonsense drawings after focal cortical lesions. *Neuropsychologia;* 15: 653–674.

Lhermitte, F. 1986. Human autonomy and the frontal lobes. Part II: Patient behavior in complex and social situations: The "environmental dependency syndrome." *Ann Neurol;* 19: 335–343.

Lhermitte, F., Pillon, B., and Serdaru, M. 1986. Human autonomy and the frontal lobes. Part I: Imitation and utilization behavior: a neuropsychological study of 75 patients. *Ann Neurol;* 19: 326–334.

Luria, A.R. 1973. *The Working Brain.* New York, Basic Books.

Luria, A.R. 1980. *Higher Cortical Functions in Man.* New York, Consultants Bureau.

MacLean, P.D. 1990. *The Triune Brain in Evolution.* New York, Plenum.

Macmillan, M.B. 1986. A wonderful journey through skull and brains: the travels of Mr. Gage's tamping iron. *Brain and Cognition;* 5: 67–107.

Masdeu, J.C., Schoene, W.C., and Funkenstein, H. 1978. Aphasia following infarction of the left supplementary motor area. *Neurology;* 28: 1220–1223.

Mesulam, M.-M. 1985. Patterns in behavioral neuroanatomy: association areas, limbic system, and hemispheric specialization. In: Mesulam, M.-M. *Principles of Behavioral Neurology.* Philadelphia, F.A. Davis, pp. 1–70.

Mesulam, M.-M. 1986. Frontal cortex and behavior. *Ann Neurol;* 19: 320–325.

Nauta, W.J.H. 1971. The problem of the frontal lobe: a reinterpretation. *J Psychiat Res;* 8: 167–187.

Neilsen, J.M., and Jacobs, L.L. 1951. Bilateral lesions of the anterior cingulate gyri. *Bull LA Neurol Soc;* 16: 231–234.

Roland, P., and Friberg, L. 1985. Localization of cortical areas activated by thinking. *J Neurophysiol;* 53: 1219–1243.

Ross, E.D., and Stewart, R.M. 1981. Akinetic mutism from hypothalamic damage: successful treatment with dopamine agonists. *Neurology;* 31: 1435–1439.

Sandson, J., and Albert, M.L. 1987. Perseveration in behavioral neurology. *Neurology;* 37: 1736–1741.

Shallice, T., and Burgess, P.W. 1991. Deficits in strategy application following frontal lobe damage in man. *Brain;* 114: 727–741.

Strub, R.L., and Black, F.W. 1988. *Neurobehavioral Disorders. A Clinical Approach.* Philadelphia, F.A.Davis.

Stuss, D.T., and Benson, D.F. 1986. *The Frontal Lobes.* New York, Raven Press.

Teuber, H.-L. 1964. The riddle of frontal lobe function in man. In: Warren, J.W., and Akert, K. (eds.). *The Frontal Granular Cortex and Behavior.* New York, McGraw-Hill, pp. 410–444.

Tilney, F. 1928. *The Brain, From Ape to Man.* New York, Hoeber.

Wechsler, D. 1981. *Manual for the Wechsler Intelligence Scale-Revised (WAIS-R).* New York, Psychological Corporation.

Willerman, L., Schultz, R., Rutledge, J.N., and Bigler, E.D. 1991. *In vivo* brain size and intelligence. *Intelligence;* 15: 223–228.

Zangwill, O. 1966. Psychological deficits associated with frontal lobe lesions. *Int J Neurol;* 5: 395–402.

CHAPTER 11

Traumatic Brain Injury

Injury to the brain is an obvious but curiously underemphasized source of neurobehavioral disability. Although incidence and prevalence figures for *traumatic brain injury* (TBI) are not known with certainty, it is widely cited that TBI cases requiring hospitalization in the United States occur at a rate of 200 per 100,000 each year (Kalsbeek et al., 1980) or roughly half a million new TBI cases every year. Of these admissions, 10% have TBI severe enough to require hospitalization of 20 or more days (Kalsbeek et al., 1980), and severe TBI with survival may thus have an incidence of 20 per 100,000 (Alexander, 1982). Many more TBI victims, of course, do not require hospital admission but still experience clinical problems. Motor vehicle accidents, often involving unrestrained or unhelmeted drivers and alcohol abuse, make up the single largest cause of TBI (Kalsbeek et al., 1980), but falls and sports injuries account for many cases as well. Young males aged 15 through 24 constitute the highest risk group (Kalsbeek et al., 1980), and, because many survivors live the greater proportion of their lives after being injured, TBI ranks as one of the most prevalent neurologic disorders (Alexander, 1982).

Whereas it is true that many individuals with TBI recover uneventfully, survivors are often left with significant and lasting impairments. Most tragic of all are those who remain vegetative and never regain consciousness. Other TBI survivors, with severe and irreversible dementia, present major problems in social and occupational adjustment. Still other individuals, less obviously impaired because of milder injuries, may be misdiagnosed with psychiatric disorders or not recognized at all. Given the magnitude of its cognitive and emotional effects, TBI justifies its recent description as a "silent epidemic" (Goldstein, 1990).

Closed head injury is the standard term for cranial injury that does not involve a penetrating wound, as would a gunshot injury in time of war.

Notwithstanding the important facial, skull, neck, and systemic injuries that can occur and preoccupy acute care management, this chapter will consider the acute and chronic consequences of closed head injury that are specifically due to TBI. Death can of course occur immediately on impact, or during the period before the patient reaches medical attention, and a fatal outcome can also develop later on because of irreversible elevations in intracranial pressure that can occur, particularly in young adults (Kelly et al., 1991). In those who survive TBI, however, the most disabling long-term consequences are behavioral. A good physical recovery often belies a poor cognitive and especially emotional outcome. The neurobehavioral sequelae of TBI are protean, ranging from isolated syndromes due to focal contusions to severe dementia or persistent vegetative state (PVS) (Jennett and Plum, 1972) after massive blunt head trauma. In addition, the problem of concussion and its aftermath presents major obstacles to many individuals.

TBI is considered at this point because its clinical diversity provides an appropriate conceptual transition between the focal syndromes reviewed in the last several chapters and the widespread dysfunction represented by dementia, the subject of the concluding chapter. The discussion will follow what has become the customary practice of dividing TBI lesions into focal and diffuse (Auerbach, 1989). Details of acute medical, neurologic, and neurosurgical management can be found elsewhere (Cooper, 1993).

Focal Lesions

The best known focal lesion in TBI is the *contusion,* or bruise of the cortical surface. As the skull is deformed or fractured at the moment of impact, the underlying cortex is damaged, and the injury may also involve subjacent white matter. Typically there is focal hemorrhage and edema along with the neuronal loss and demyelination. Contusions can occur anywhere in the hemispheres but are most likely in the orbitofrontal, frontopolar, and anterior temporal regions, where the brain is thrust forcefully against bony prominences in the anterior and middle cranial fossae (Courville, 1937). Figure 11.1 illustrates the distribution of contusions that are likely to result from TBI.

Contusions are thought to be found classically either in a region directly underlying the site of an external blow (the *coup lesion*) or on the

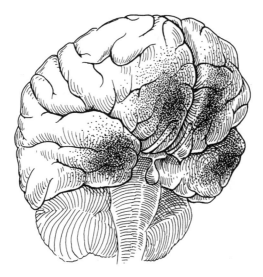

Figure 11.1 Regions of the frontal and temporal lobes most often damaged by contusions in traumatic brain injury.

other side of the brain (the *contrecoup lesion*). Coup lesions are due to direct contact with the inner surface of the skull, but contrecoup lesions are due to horizontal movement of the brain in an immobile skull that produces a cavitation effect in a region roughly opposite the point of impact. Multiple contusions frequently coexist, and it is generally the case that prognosis worsens as the number of contusions increases.

By virtue of their propensity to damage frontal and temporal lobes, contusions are strongly associated with disorders of comportment, impulse control, language, and memory (Blumer and Benson, 1975; Alexander, 1982). Much of the care of severely brain-injured persons revolves around these issues, which are also due in large measure to the diffuse effects of TBI that are frequently present. Because contusions are usually bilateral (Adams et al., 1980), a single neurobehavioral syndrome is seldom encountered.

Other frequent focal lesions are those due to various types of *intracranial hemorrhage*. The most important of these for our purposes is *intracerebral hemorrhage*, often in the thalamus or basal ganglia, which can cause parenchymal destruction related to shearing injury of small deep blood vessels (Adams et al., 1986). This kind of hemorrhage implies a poor prognosis, and survivors can show residual aphasia, neglect, or other syndromes. Subdural and epidural hematomas are also common and are due to bleeding from damaged vessels outside the brain itself but within the skull; *subdural hematoma* results from injury to bridging veins in the subdural space and *epidural hematoma* typically follows rupture of the middle meningeal artery from an overlying skull fracture. Although common and life threatening in TBI, these extraparenchymal hematomas are rather unlikely to eventuate in chronic neurobehavioral sequelae if there is no underlying contusion and they are treated successfully (Levin, 1992). Similarly, *subarachnoid hemorrhage*, which is common in TBI, usually leaves no sequelae if appropriately treated.

Finally, there are two focal lesions that occur in the context of brain herniation, itself a poor prognostic sign because of the potential for destruction of vital centers in the lower brain stem. *Posterior cerebral artery occlusion* resulting from downward herniation of the brain can lead to visual defects such as hemianopia and alexia because of damage to the medial occipital lobe, and, if the occlusion is bilateral, cortical blindness or visual agnosia can result (Alexander, 1982). Small so-called *Duret hemorrhages* in the midline of the brain stem, usually multiple, are due to compression of small arteries and veins in the course of rostral-caudal herniation, and they contribute to stupor and coma (Alexander, 1982).

Diffuse Lesions

The destructive effects of focal lesions associated with TBI are often severe, but even more disabling are the sequelae of diffuse lesions. A wide spectrum of syndromes can follow diffuse trauma to the brain, ranging from concussion with self-limited attentional and mood disorders to irreversible dementia and PVS. The most common cause of PVS is in fact TBI, and next in importance is hypoxic-ischemic injury (see page 170), which can often be associated with a traumatic injury (Multi-Society Task Force on PVS, 1994). PVS alone raises many difficult medical and ethical issues, but it is only one of the many chronic disorders associated with diffuse TBI lesions.

Many patients with TBI are seen when clinical or radiologic evidence of brain swelling is present. Paradoxically, this alarming acute effect is frequently transient and without aftermath. Although it would seem that brain swelling, with its attendant risk of herniation, would be a frequent source of neurobehavioral dysfunction in TBI, there is usually little residual effect if treatment is prompt and effective. *Brain swelling* is a nonspecific term for increased brain volume due to an increase in water content, which in TBI can be caused by vasogenic edema (Fishman, 1975), cytotoxic edema associated with hypoxic-ischemic injury (Fishman, 1975), or cerebrovascular congestion (Kelly et al., 1991). Swelling of the brain by itself does not cause injury, and if herniation is avoided, no chronic sequelae of the transiently increased brain volume are evident (Bruce et al., 1981; Auerbach, 1989). When herniation does occur, of course, the outcome may be catastrophic. In terms of chronic neurobehavioral sequelae, however, other lesions are very significant.

The diffuse lesions that occur in the chronic phase after TBI have been the subject of some controversy over the past several decades, but recently a consensus has been reached that the entity of *diffuse axonal injury* (DAI) is the most frequent and clinically relevant pathologic finding in blunt TBI. Interestingly, penetrating TBI is infrequently associated with DAI because this kind of wound usually involves focal damage without widespread injury. First described in 1956 as "diffuse degeneration of the cerebral white matter" (Strich, 1956), the presence of axonal and white matter damage following TBI has been documented by numerous clinical observations and experimental studies in primates (Adams et al., 1982; Gennarelli et al., 1982). These lesions are widespread, involving the brain stem, corpus callosum, and hemispheric white matter, and are related to shearing injury of the white matter consequent to acceleration and deceleration (Gennarelli et al., 1982). In particular, DAI is more likely to be caused by rotational (angular) forces, such as those that occur during motor vehicle accidents, than by translational (linear) forces (Adams et al., 1982). DAI may also be caused by acceleration-deceleration injury without any impact to the head at all (Gennarelli et al., 1982). Figure 11.2 presents a schematic view of a brain damaged by DAI.

The *duration of unconsciousness* after TBI is an important clinical datum that has been correlated with outcome (Gilchrist and Wilkinson, 1979). TBI causing loss of consciousness does so immediately upon impact, and DAI involving the dorsolateral midbrain and pons is responsible for posttraumatic coma (Adams et al., 1982; Gennarelli et al., 1982). The midbrain is particularly vulnerable to rotational injury, and the ascending reticular activating system (ARAS) in the brain stem that mediates arousal is thereby disrupted. As might be expected, the degree of brain

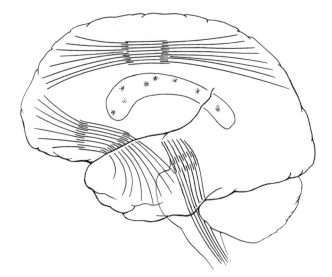

Figure 11.2 Disruption of white matter in the brain stem, cerebral hemispheres, and corpus callosum due to diffuse axonal injury.

stem damage from DAI reflects the severity of the injury, and the longer the period of coma, the poorer the outcome. In contrast, mild degrees of DAI with less brain stem damage result in a better outcome (Levin et al., 1988). DAI can also severely disrupt the hemispheric white matter, and in cases of PVS that follow TBI, the hemispheres exhibit more severe DAI than does the brain stem (Multi-Society Task Force on PVS, 1994). Thus DAI is present in TBI cases representing a wide range of severity and is consistently associated with neurobehavioral manifestations.

Even more important in terms of predicting outcome is a phase of recovery known as *posttraumatic amnesia* (PTA), the period after the recovery of consciousness before a patient regains the ability to acquire new learning. In contrast to the duration of unconsciousness, which is frequently unavailable or uncertain, the length of PTA can be a very useful index because it is often observable within a medical setting and can therefore be accurately determined. Careful studies of TBI patients have revealed that the longer the duration of PTA, the greater the degree of cognitive disability (Brooks et al., 1980). The neuropathologic basis of PTA is uncertain, but DAI in temporal and limbic systems mediating memory function seems likely.

In severe TBI, the most disruptive changes that attend the chronic recovery state are in the realm of personality (Bleiberg et al., 1989). Disinhibition, apathy, and a deterioration in comportment may all occur, and their severity generally correlates with the duration of coma (Levin and Grossman, 1978). These features are reminiscent of deficits seen with frontal lobe involvement (Chapter 10), and it is of interest to consider the pathologic basis of these alterations. Although frontal lobe contusions would be one apparent mechanism leading to the development of frontal lobe behavioral features, DAI may in fact be responsible more often. In the chronic phase following TBI, ventricular enlargement associated with DAI results in a poor neurobehavioral outcome (Filley et al., 1987), implying that frontal-limbic white matter connections have been disrupted. We shall discuss the importance of cerebral white matter more extensively in Chapter 12.

In recent years, the problem of mild head injury has received increased attention as a source of considerable suffering and disability. Difficulties with defining this entity, as well as the equally obscure term "minor head injury," have clouded this area, but it is clear that significant neurobehavioral disability can follow seemingly trivial head injuries (Rimel et al., 1981). A more precise term is "concussion," which has traditionally been defined as the loss of consciousness resulting from a blow to the head (Geisler and Greenberg, 1990). However, it is clear that TBI can occur without loss of consciousness, and may be manifest by confusion or amnesia alone (Fisher, 1966; Kelly et al., 1991). These observations suggest that the deep midline arousal structures (the ARAS; Chapter 3) can be unaffected and at the same time more superficial brain regions can be damaged. This notion is supported by data obtained from experimental animals indicating that TBI affects the most peripheral cerebral regions before it damages the brain stem (Ommaya and Gennarelli, 1974). It therefore appears that a more appropriate definition of *concussion* is "a traumatically induced alteration in mental status" (Kelly et al., 1991, p. 2868). With the use of this definition, "concussion" serves well as a single term encompassing all degrees of mild head injury and provides a solid basis for further clinical and theoretical considerations regarding TBI.

It has classically been taught that concussion is reversible, in that no long-term sequelae of any kind result. Unfortunately, the *postconcussion syndrome* (PCS) has recently become well known as a frequent cause of persistent headache, dizziness, insomnia, inattention, memory disturbance, and depression. Although many individuals do experience a rapid and complete recovery, the PCS is often very troublesome for weeks or months after the injury. The origin of this syndrome has been debated, and undoubtedly psychogenic and litigation issues often contribute to the symptoms. However, as in severe TBI, it appears that the most consistent lesion in concussion is DAI. Because few persons die with recent concussions, autopsied cases are rare, but available postmortem human observations (Oppenheimer, 1968) and animal studies (Ommaya and Gennarelli, 1974; Povlishock et al., 1983) indicate that DAI is the underlying lesion. In parallel with this common neuropathology is the qualitative clinical similarity of concussion and severe TBI; in both syndromes, disruption of the deep brain stem and hemispheric white matter tracts creates persistent problems in arousal, attention, concentration, and mood. DAI is the common denominator of TBI, and the degree of injury determines the severity but not the essential quality of the clinical picture.

Another major category of diffuse lesion is *hypoxic-ischemic injury* (Alexander, 1982). Many TBI cases are complicated by systemic injury leading to hypoxia or hypotension. These insults may occur in up to 90% of severe TBI and may have primary effects on particularly oxygen-dependent areas such as the hippocampus, basal ganglia, and cerebral cortex (Graham et al., 1978). Watershed areas of the cortex are especially vulnerable to hypotensive events. In general, superimposed hypoxic-ischemic injury worsens the prognosis of TBI and often contributes to severe dementia or PVS (Graham et al., 1983). Diffuse laminar necrosis of the cerebral cortex is the usual pathology associated with severe hypoxic-ischemic injury (Multi-Society Task Force on PVS, 1994).

Table 11.1 shows the neurobehavioral sequelae of the lesions that can occur in TBI. Typically a combination of insults leads to a complex clinical picture. An appreciation of the diversity of pathology in TBI is fundamental for appropriate patient care.

The final category of diffuse lesions in TBI is the syndrome of *dementia pugilistica*, a term first introduced in the 1930s (Millspaugh, 1937) as an alternative to the colorful but derisive "punch drunk" encephalopathy (Martland, 1928). This is a dementing illness in boxers characterized by dementia, ataxia, and parkinsonism (Martland, 1928). Neuropsychological deficits have been clearly documented in both active (Drew et al.,

Table 11.1 Neurobehavioral effects of TBI lesions

	Lesion	Site(s)	Sequelae
Focal	Contusion	Frontal lobes Temporal lobes	Disinhibition, apathy, amnesia, aphasia
	Intracerebral hemorrhage	Thalamus Basal ganglia	Initial coma; residual aphasia, hemineglect
	Posterior cerebral artery occlusion	Occipital lobe	Hemianopia, blindness, alexia, visual agnosia
	Duret hemorrhages	Brain stem	Progressive stupor and coma
Diffuse	Diffuse axonal injury	Brain stem Cerebrum Corpus callosum	Initial coma, amnesia; residual PVS, inattention, personality change
	Hypoxic-ischemic injury	Hippocampus Neocortex	Amnesia, dementia, PVS
	Dementia pugilistica	Neocortex, cerebellum, substantia nigra	Dementia, ataxia, parkinsonism

1986) and retired (Casson et al., 1984) boxers, implying that brain injury occurs early in a fighter's career. The severity of cognitive impairment appears to be related to the duration of the pugilist's career and the number of blows received, and progression of dementia even after the cessation of boxing has been observed (Unterharnscheidt, 1970). Computerized tomography (CT) scans often reveal brain atrophy in boxers, and a cavum septum pellucidum—a fluid-filled cavity within the membrane separating the lateral ventricles called the septum pellucidum—is sometimes seen as well (Casson et al., 1982). Electroencephalograms are often abnormal, showing diffuse slow activity (Casson et al., 1984).

Neuropathological studies have shown diffuse atrophy, neurofibrillary tangles in the cortex without neuritic plaques, cerebellar scarring, and depigmentation of the substantia nigra (Corsellis et al., 1973). These changes account well for the clinical features of dementia, ataxia, and parkinsonism. The presence of neurofibrillary tangles has led to speculation regarding the possibility of TBI being a risk factor for Alzheimer's Disease (AD), and there is epidemiologic evidence that such an association may exist (Mayeux et al., 1993). However, the absence of neuritic plaques in dementia pugilistica differs distinctly from the pathology of AD, and the consistent constellation of neuropathological findings favors the view that dementia pugilistica is a disease specifically related to repeated TBI in the boxing ring (Corsellis et al., 1973). DAI is probably also present in dementia pugilistica but has been more difficult to demonstrate (Corsellis et al., 1973).

It is thus inescapable that permanent damage to the brain occurs regularly in boxing, which should not be surprising considering that the only objective of the contest is the production of unconsciousness. A knockout, of course, means nothing less than a blow of sufficient force to produce transient coma, and lasting brain injury is known to result even from repetitive blows that do not involve loss of consciousness (Lampert and Hardman, 1984). It is of interest that neither the boxer's skill as a pugilist (Casson et al., 1984) nor the introduction of medical supervision and safety measures (Drew et al., 1986) appear to prevent the onset of cognitive decline. This "noble art of self-defense" therefore represents the deliberate and sanctioned infliction of injury to the brain—injury that society otherwise assiduously strives to prevent.

References

Adams, J.H., Scott, G., Parker, L.S., et al. 1980. The contusion index: a quantitative approach to cerebral contusions in head injury. *Neuropathol Appl Neurobiol;* 6: 319–324.

Adams, J.H., Graham, D.I., Murray, L.S., and Scott, G. 1982. Diffuse axonal injury due to nonmissile head injury: an analysis of 45 cases. *Ann Neurol;* 12: 557–563.

Adams, J.H., Doyle, D., Graham, D.I., et al. 1986. Deep intracerebral (basal ganglia) hematomas in fatal non-missile head injury in man. *J Neurol Neurosurg Psychiatry;* 49: 1039–1043.

Alexander, M.P. 1982. Traumatic brain injury. In: Benson D.F., Blumer, D. (eds.). *Psychiatric Aspects of Neurologic Disease.* Vol. 2. New York, Grune and Stratton, pp. 219–248.

Auerbach, S.H. 1989. The pathophysiology of traumatic brain injury. In: Horn, L.J., and Cope, D.N. (eds.). *Traumatic Brain Injury.* Philadelphia, Hanley and Belfus, pp. 1–11.

Bleiberg, J., Cope, D.N., and Spector, J. 1989. Cognitive assessment and therapy in traumatic brain injury. In: Horn, L.J., and Cope, D.N. (eds.). *Traumatic Brain Injury.* Philadelphia, Hanley and Belfus, pp. 95–121.

Blumer, D., and Benson, D.F. 1975. Personality changes with frontal and temporal lobe lesions. In: Benson, D.F., and Blumer, D. (eds.). *Psychiatric Aspects of Neurologic Disease.* Vol. 1. New York, Grune and Stratton, pp. 151–169.

Brooks, D.N., Aughton, M.E., Bond, M.R., et al. 1980. Cognitive sequelae in relationship to early indices of severity of brain damage after severe blunt head injury. *J Neurol Neurosurg Psychiatry;* 43: 529–534.

Bruce, D.A., Alavi, A., Bilaniuk, L., et al. 1981. Diffuse cerebral swelling following head injuries in children: the syndrome of "malignant brain edema." *J Neurosurg;* 54: 170–178.

Casson, I.R., Sham, R., Campbell, E.A., et al. 1982. Neurological and CT evaluation of knocked-out boxers. *J Neurol Neurosurg Psychiatry;* 45: 170–174.

Casson, I.R., Siegel, O., Sham, R., et al. 1984. Brain damage in modern boxers. *J Am Med Assoc;* 251: 2663–2667.

Cooper, P.R. (ed.) 1993. *Head Injury.* 3rd edition. Baltimore, Williams and Wilkins.

Corsellis, J.A.N., Bruton, C.J., and Freeman-Browne, D. 1973. The aftermath of boxing. *Psychol Med;* 3: 270–303.

Courville, C.B. 1937. *Pathology of the Central Nervous System.* Mountain View, Calif., Pacific.

Drew, R.H., Templer, D.I., Schuyler, B.A., et al. 1986. Neuropsychological deficits in active licensed professional boxers. *J Clin Psychol;* 42: 520–525.

Filley, C.M., Cranberg, L.D., Alexander, M.P., and Hart, E.J. 1987. Neurobehavioral outcome after closed head injury in childhood and adolescence. *Arch Neurol;* 44: 194–198.

Fisher, C.M. 1966. Concussion amnesia. *Neurology;* 16: 826–830.

Fishman, R.A. 1975. Brain edema. *N Engl J Med;* 293: 706–711.

Geisler, F.H., and Greenberg, J. 1990. Management of the acute head-injury patient. In: Salcman, M. (ed.). *Neurologic Emergencies,* 2nd ed. New York, Raven, pp. 135–165.

Gennarelli, T.A., Thibault, L.E., Adams, J.H., et al. 1982. Diffuse axonal injury and traumatic coma in the primate. *Ann Neurol;* 12: 564–574.

Gilchrist, E., and Wilkinson, M. 1979. Some factors determining prognosis in young people with severe head injuries. *Arch Neurol;* 36: 355–359.

Goldstein, M. Traumatic brain injury: a silent epidemic. *Ann Neurol* 1990; 27: 327.

Graham, D.I., Adams, J.H., and Doyle, D. 1978. Ischemic brain damage in fatal nonmissile head injuries. *J Neurol Sci;* 39: 213–234.

Graham, D.I., McClellan, D., Adams, J.H., et al. 1983. The neuropathology of severe disability after head injury. *Acta Neurochir* (suppl); 32: 65–67.

Jennett, B., and Plum, F. 1972. The persistent vegetative state after brain damage: a syndrome in search of a name. *Lancet;* 1: 734–737.

Kalsbeek, W.D., McLaurin, R.L., Harris, B.S.H., and Miller, J.D. 1980. The national head and spinal cord injury survey: major findings. *J Neurosurg;* 53: S19-S31.

Kelly, J.P., Nichols, J.S., Filley, C.M., et al. 1991. Concussion in sports. Guidelines for the prevention of catastrophic outcome. *J Am Med Assoc;* 266: 2867–2869.

Lampert, P.W., and Hardman, J.M.1984. Morphological changes in brains of boxers. *J Am Med Assoc;* 251: 2676–2679.

Levin, H.S. 1992. Neurobehavioral recovery. *J Neurotrauma;* 9: S359–S373.

Levin, H.S., and Grossman, R.G. 1978. Behavioral sequelae of closed head injury. *Arch Neurol;* 35: 720–727.

Levin, H.S., Williams, D., Crofford, M.J., et al. 1988. Relationship of depth of brain lesions to consciousness and outcome after closed head injury. *J Neurosurg;* 69: 861–866.

Martland, H.S. 1928. Punch drunk. *J Am Med Assoc;* 91: 1103–1107.

Mayeux, R., Ottman, R., Tang, M.-X., et al. 1993. Genetic susceptibility and head injury as risk factors for Alzheimer's Disease among community-dwelling elderly persons and their first-degree relatives. *Ann Neurol;* 33: 494–501.

Millspaugh, J.A. 1937. Dementia pugilistica (punch drunk). *U S Nav Med Bull;* 35: 297–303.

Multi-Society Task Force on PVS. 1994. Medical aspects of the persistent vegetative state. *N Engl J Med;* 330: 1499–1508, 1572–1579.

Ommaya, A.K., and Gennarelli, T.A. 1974. Cerebral concussion and traumatic unconsciousness. *Brain;* 97: 633–654.

Oppenheimer, D.R. 1968. Microscopic lesions in the brain following head injury. *J Neurol Neurosurg Psychiatry;* 31: 299–306.

Povlishock, J.T., Becker, D.P., Cheng, C.L.Y., and Vaughan, G.W. 1983. Axonal changes in minor head injury. *J Neuropathol Exp Neurol;* 42: 225–242.

Rimel, R.W., Giordani, B., Barth, J.T., et al. 1981. Disability caused by minor head injury. *Neurosurgery;* 9: 221–228.

Strich, S.J. 1956. Diffuse degeneration of the cerebral white matter in severe dementia following head injury. *J Neurol Neurosurg Psychiatry;* 19: 163–185.

Unterharnscheidt, F. 1970. About boxing: review of historical and medical aspects. *Texas Rep Biol Med;* 28: 421–495.

CHAPTER 12

Dementia

The first several chapters of this book were primarily devoted to neurobe-havioral syndromes that can be related to focal disruption of cerebral areas concerned with the representation of cognition and emotion. The discussion then turned to traumatic brain injury, a problem that, because of its diverse manifestations, produces both focal and diffuse syndromes. To conclude this volume, it is now appropriate to turn to another syndrome, one that clearly represents widespread brain dysfunction: the increasingly prevalent condition known as dementia. In contrast to the disorders of arousal and attention, dementia features no alterations in level of consciousness or attention. In contrast to focal neurobehavioral syndromes, dementia is usually characterized by multifocal damage to cerebral areas, and, though typical focal syndromes routinely appear as components of dementia, a combination of syndromes adding up to constitute the clinical picture is required for the diagnosis. By far the most common of the neurobehavioral syndromes, dementia assumes special importance because of the prospect of these strongly age-related and mostly irreversible conditions increasing in prevalence as the population of the industrialized world ages (Katzman, 1976).

Perhaps the most frequent complaint heard by behavioral neurologists is that of memory loss. Although many individuals voice this concern, the apprehension about failing memory—real or imagined—is especially evident in the elderly. The ominous and well-publicized problem of dementia impels many older adults to worry about lapses in memory, which frequently are quite within the normal range of functioning for their age group (Cullum et al., 1990). However, the distinction between *benign senescent forgetfulness* (Kral, 1962)—also called "age-associated memory impairment" (Crook et al., 1986)—and early amnesia is often very difficult. A good general rule is that memory impairment sufficient to interfere with usual activities is significant, whereas annoying lapses that can be circumvented by compensatory strategies are not. Neuropsychological testing is often helpful in this setting. If no clear answer can still be provided by testing, reassurance and followup are indicated; dementing illness is usually progressive and will reveal itself in time if it is present. Depression, of course, must also be considered at this early stage (see page 185).

Dementia most simply means an impairment of mental ability (from the Latin *de* [down from] + *mens* [mind]) caused by brain dysfunction, implying that a decline has occurred from a previously stable level. More specific medical definitions, however, have been advanced. The influential psychiatric *Diagnostic and Statistical Manual of Mental Disorders,* now in its fourth revised edition (DSM-IV), requires the development of multiple cognitive deficits sufficient to interfere with normal social or occupational functioning (American Psychiatric Association, 1994). The DSM-IV criteria have been influenced by behavioral neurologists who have emphasized identification of key areas of impairment and, by implication, the neuroanatomic basis of these deficits. *Dementia* has thus been formally defined as an acquired and persistent impairment in intellectual ability that affects at least three of the following five domains: memory, language, visuospatial skills, complex cognition, and emotion or personality (Cummings and Benson, 1992). It will be recalled that these five realms are assessed in the mental status examination (Chapter 2), and, like the other syndromes in this book, deficits can be confidently elicited by comprehensive neurobehavioral evaluation.

Dementia has traditionally been assumed to result from damage to the cerebral cortex, and the term "higher cortical function" has often been invoked to describe the cognitive and emotional functions that are compromised in dementia and other neurobehavioral syndromes. Whereas it is certainly true that many of the neural operations that account for human behavior take place in the cortex, it is equally apparent that regions in the subcortex such as the thalamus, basal ganglia, and cerebral white matter participate in these activities as well. This chapter will review dementia as a syndrome of widespread brain involvement that includes but is not confined to cortical gray matter. Because the brain acts as an integrated whole to produce the totality of human behavior, dementia can result from afflictions of either cortical or subcortical structures or from a combination of regional pathologies. The description of these disorders will highlight a theme frequently elaborated heretofore regarding the importance of distributed neurobehavioral networks throughout the brain that mediate specific functions. Dementia illustrates how disruption of these widespread circuits at many points can cause identifiable syndromes that coalesce into one multifaceted clinical entity.

The list of conditions that result in dementia is a long one, and new entities, such as the AIDS dementia complex, are frequently added as they are discovered. A classification of the dementias that has particular relevance to this book, presented in Table 12.1, is based on the primary regions of neuropathologic involvement. Recent information has underlined the importance of subcortical gray matter diseases in the causation of dementia (Cummings and Benson, 1984), and cerebral white matter disorders have also been recognized as being commonly associated with the syndrome (Filley et al., 1988). Still another group of disorders leads to dementia because of diverse neuropathological lesions that affect various combinations of brain regions. This classification will form the basis for considering brain-behavior relationships in dementia; other clinical and basic aspects of dementia are reviewed in detail elsewhere (Cummings and Benson, 1992).

The classification given in Table 12.1 is useful but not without controversy. The idea of subcortical dementia (see page 183), popularized as a conceptual scheme to characterize the dementing illness seen in progressive supranuclear palsy (Albert et al., 1974) and Huntington's Disease (McHugh and Folstein, 1975) some 20 years ago, has met with significant criticism because of difficulties securely delineating "subcortical" features of dementia and the fact that both cortical and subcortical diseases often have pathology far removed from the primary site(s) of involvement (Whitehouse, 1986). Nevertheless, dementing disease and injury do affect the brain in quite distinct ways, and clinical experience suggests that viewing dementia as solely due to cortical deterioration is inaccurate. As would be expected in the area of brain-behavior relationships, different sites of pathologic damage appear to manifest themselves in distinct dementia syndromes. This chapter will endeavor to illustrate the general profiles of impairment that result from cortical, subcortical, and white matter dementias, using specific diseases and injuries as examples. The dementias are providing ample demonstration that the term

Table 12.1 Major causes of dementia and their neuropathologic basis

---

Cortical
    Alzheimer's Disease
    Pick's Disease

Subcortical
    Progressive supranuclear palsy
    Huntington's Disease
    Parkinson's Disease
    Wilson's Disease
    Hallervorden-Spatz Disease
    Friedreich's ataxia
    Olivopontocerebellar degeneration
    Chronic toxic and metabolic disorders
    Depression

White Matter
    Multiple sclerosis
    Toluene abuse
    Binswanger's Disease
    Normal pressure hydrocephalus
    Metachromatic leukodystrophy
    Cobalamin deficiency
    Traumatic brain injury
    AIDS dementia complex
    Alcohol abuse

Mixed
    Multi-infarct dementia
    Creutzfeldt-Jakob Disease
    Diffuse Lewy Body Disease
    General paresis
    Subdural hematoma
    Neoplasms
    Anoxia

"higher cortical function" is too limiting, and that the term *higher cerebral function* may be preferable.

Cortical Dementias

The most important dementia on any list is *Alzheimer's Disease* (AD). First described nearly a century ago by Alois Alzheimer in a 55-year-old woman who had a progressive four-year course of amnesia, aphasia, and personality change, the disease has been known since then as a cortical degenerative process featuring neuritic plaques and neurofibrillary tangles in addition to widespread neuronal cell loss (Alzheimer, 1907). Since Alzheimer's description, AD has evolved from an obscure clinicopathologic entity to one of the major medical problems of the developed world. By far the most common of the dementias, accounting for more than 50% of all cases, AD affects millions of Americans and is the primary reason for elderly persons to be institutionalized in nursing homes (Katzman, 1986).

The clinical course of AD is one of progressive decline, although periods of stabilization can be encountered. From the time of onset, the duration of the disease until death approximates 6 to 12 years, and no cases of remission have been reported (Cummings and Benson, 1992). Patients with extrapyramidal features appear to have a more rapid course (Mayeux et al., 1985), and it is also possible that those who develop the disease before age 65 decline at a more rapid rate (Seltzer and Sherwin, 1983). There is additional evidence that younger-onset patients have more language impairment than their older counterparts (Seltzer and Sherwin, 1983; Filley et al., 1986), suggesting that age may influence individual cognitive vulnerability in the disease. However, the neuropathologic process appears to be the same at all ages, and the former practice of dividing AD into "presenile" and "senile" categories is unjustified (Katzman, 1986).

The disease affects the hippocampus early in the course, as shown in Figure 12.1, accounting for the amnesia that nearly always heralds the onset. The parietal and temporal cortices (Figure 12.1) are also selectively damaged at an early stage (Katzman, 1986), leading to deficits in language, praxis, perception, visuospatial skills, and complex cognition (Cummings and Benson, 1992). Thus the classic cortical syndromes of aphasia (transcortical sensory or Wernicke's), apraxia (ideomotor or ideational), and agnosia (object agnosia or prosopagnosia) soon accompany the initial amnesia. The frontal association cortex is affected somewhat later, but primary sensory and motor cortices are preserved until very late in the disease. The severity of neuritic plaque and neurofibrillary tangle

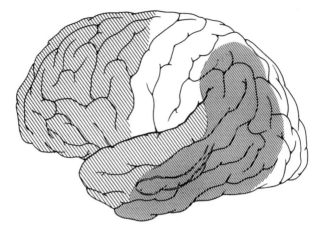

Figure 12.1 Cerebral areas selectively affected in early Alzheimer's Disease. Dark shading—severe involvement; light shading—moderate involvement. After Cummings and Benson, 1992.

formation parallels the degree of neuronal cell loss. It is the selective attack on hippocampal and association cortices that accounts for the specific neurobehavioral presentation of this disease.

As the disease advances, a rather predictable sequence of progressive clinical decline can be observed (Cummings and Benson, 1992). Amnesia remains a prominent feature, and its worsening leads to greater dependence on caregivers. Other cognitive deficits also become more evident, and problems with driving, financial competence, and home safety may appear. Personality change and paranoid delusions may appear transiently. Sphincteric incontinence eventually develops, and at this stage many patients require admission to nursing facilities. Finally, after many years of the illness, patients become bedridden, mute, and totally dependent; a persistent vegetative state ensues (Multi-Society Task Force on PVS, 1994), and death follows, often from a pulmonary or urinary tract infection.

The etiology of AD is unknown. Evidence has appeared in support of both genetic and environmental causes, but progress has been slow. Well-documented families with an autosomal dominant pattern of disease transmission and the strong association of Down's syndrome (trisomy 21) with AD have led to intensive work on the possibility of a causative gene on chromosome 21 (St. George-Hyslop et al., 1987). Other investigators have recently found evidence for AD loci on chromosome 14 (Schellenberg et al., 1992) and chromosome 19 (Corder et al., 1993). Intoxication with aluminum (Perl and Brody, 1980) and infection with a virus or viruslike agent (Prusiner, 1993) have also been proposed as etiologies. However, a genetic cause, probably involving a variety of nuclear genes (Clark and Goate, 1993) or even the mitochondrial genome (Parker et al., 1994), seems most likely, possibly in combination with environmental factors (Blass, 1993).

Efforts to treat the disease pharmacologically have centered mostly on the well accepted cholinergic cell loss in a region within the basal forebrain known as the nucleus basalis of Meynert (Whitehouse et al., 1982; Chapter 4). Effective therapy has been discouragingly elusive (Mayeux, 1990), but the recently approved drug tacrine (Knapp et al., 1994) may be of some palliative value in AD. Irreversibility, however, does not imply untreatability, and much can be done for patients and their families with informed and sympathetic counseling that can significantly lighten the burden of this dreaded illness. Effective medical therapy of AD must unfortunately await a better understanding of its cause.

The cognitive decline in AD offers a useful perspective on the mediation of intellectual function by the cortex. For many years it was thought that the major correlate of intellectual loss in AD was the presence of neuritic plaques (Blessed et al., 1968), but recent studies indicate that cortical synapse loss is more strongly correlated with measures of dementia severity (Terry et al., 1991). Thus the neuropathologic "tombstones" that define AD (Khachaturian, 1985) may not be central to the pathogenesis of the disease; multiple factors, genetic and environmental, all contribute to the loss of synapses that is the final common cause of clinical signs and symptoms (Blass, 1993). If this is true, then intellectual capacity depends critically on the number of cortical synapses, and efforts to maintain and even increase these numbers are reasonable. In this regard, there is intriguing evidence that higher educational and occupational levels may be a protective factor against the development of AD, implying that exposure to intellectual challenges—or "mental exercise"—can increase synaptic density and forestall the appearance of dementia (Mortimer and Graves, 1993). Animal studies showing that complex environments favor dendritic growth and increased brain weight (Greenough and Bailey, 1988) add further support to this idea. In contrast, once the disease is established, the decline in function may be

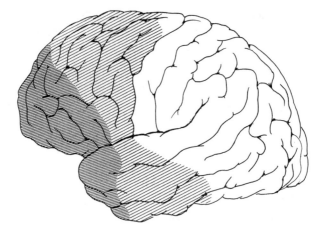

Figure 12.2 Cerebral areas selectively affected in early Pick's Disease. Dark shading—severe involvement; light shading—moderate involvement. After Cummings and Benson, 1992.

unaffected by premorbid educational achievement (Filley et al., 1985). There is, in summary, mounting evidence that microscopic intracortical events underlie the cognitive changes in AD, and a kind of behavioral neurology at the neuronal level in AD is emerging that promises to reveal insights into brain-behavior relationships of value equivalent to the classic work of Broca, Wernicke, and others of the nineteenth century who explored the effects of focal neurologic lesions.

Pick's Disease, often called lobar atrophy, is the other and much less common entry in the cortical dementia category (Pick, 1892). This disease shows a different pattern of cortical degeneration that produces a correspondingly distinct neurobehavioral profile reflecting frontal and temporal involvement. In contrast to AD, the hippocampus is spared initially, whereas the frontal and/or anterior temporal cortices are heavily damaged (Figure 12.2). Argyrophilic intracytoplasmic Pick bodies and "inflated" neurons called Pick cells are seen in some cases, but many cases show only neuronal dropout, and the status of those cases of lobar atrophy without Pick bodies or Pick cells is unresolved (Constantinidis et al., 1974). There may be a variety of frontotemporal degenerations, of which one has the classic histologic features of Pick's Disease and others do not (Filley et al., 1994).

Regardless of histology, however, the regional predilection of Pick's Disease and other frontotemporal degenerations usually distinguishes them from AD. A key clinical point is that manifestations of frontal and temporal lobe dysfunction predominate early in the course while memory is still unaffected (Filley et al., 1994). In contrast to the early amnesia, fluent aphasia, and relatively preserved personality of patients with AD, there is early disinhibition or nonfluent aphasia without initial memory loss in Pick's Disease. Here is a noteworthy example of a dementing illness in which memory dysfunction is *not* a presenting problem, and it illustrates the point that dementias each have a clinical "signature" when subjected to careful analysis. Diagnosis can be challenging, but detailed neurobehavioral evaluation in concert with neuropsychological testing and neuroimaging techniques can be quite revealing, particularly early in the disease course (Filley and Cullum, 1993). Later, when the degeneration is more advanced, the neurobehavioral distinction between AD and Pick's Disease is more difficult. Like AD, this disease has no known cause, although familial cases are described (Morris et al., 1984), and no medical therapy to reverse the disease is available.

Subcortical Dementias

The controversy surrounding the entity of *subcortical dementia* has not completely subsided, but the idea does offer some utility as a clinical and anatomic concept. The approach here will be to regard this category as a general heading under which a number of diverse conditions can be included by virtue of their clinical and pathologic similarities. Further study will undoubtedly refine this concept, but there is ample reason to pursue the notion that dementias present differing patterns of behavioral alteration because of the varying distribution of affected cortical and subcortical regions.

When the topic became current two decades ago, the first diseases listed as subcortical dementias were *progressive supranuclear palsy* (PSP), *Huntington's Disease* (HD), *Parkinson's Disease* (PD), and *Wilson's Disease* (WD). Standard textbooks address the neurology of these conditions (e.g., Adams and Victor, 1993), but, in brief, they all share dementia in association with some variety of movement disorder, and all are due mainly to pathology in the basal ganglia and related subcortical structures (Figure 12.3). HD, for example, regularly shows atrophy of the caudate

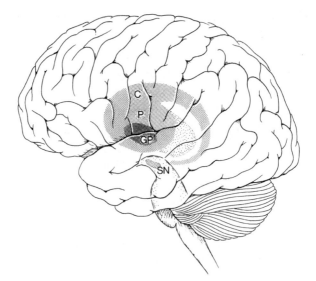

Figure 12.3 Basal ganglia primarily affected in subcortical dementias. C—caudate; P—putamen; GP—globus pallidus; SN—substantia nigra.

and putamen, and PD is strongly associated with loss of pigmented dopaminergic neurons in the substantia nigra. Although motor abnormalities are readily recognized and remain clinical hallmarks of these diseases, dementia has been appreciated as a cause of significant morbidity and has been subjected to considerable analysis. Rare neurologic conditions including *Hallervorden-Spatz Disease, Friedreich's ataxia,* and *olivopontocerebellar degeneration* have also been added to the list. On somewhat less secure grounds, *chronic toxic and metabolic disorders* cause neurobehavioral impairment that can be viewed as subcortical dementia (Cummings and Benson, 1992); this notion suggests that the acute confusional state (Chapter 3) can become chronic if the insult is persistent and that this "chronic confusional state" has clinical and pathological similarities to subcortical dementia. Finally, the *dementia syndrome of depression*—contentious both because many prefer to separate depression from dementia altogether and because its pathologic anatomy is still mysterious—has been included in this group (King and Caine, 1990).

Clinical research on the original four diseases has been actively pursued. The first modern formulation of subcortical dementia described four cardinal features of patients with PSP: slowness of thought processes, forgetfulness, personality changes including apathy and depression, and impaired ability to manipulate acquired knowledge (Albert et al., 1974). A similar clinical profile was noted a year later in patients with HD (McHugh and Folstein, 1975). Neuropsychological studies of patients with PD (Cummings, 1988) and WD (Medalia et al., 1988) also found deficits of this nature. These impairments, primarily indicating problems in the timing and activation of cortical processes rather than disruption of the cortex itself, have been interpreted as representing *fundamental* deficits in the areas of arousal, attention, mood, and motivation (Albert, 1978). In contrast, the *instrumental* functions of memory, language, praxis, and perception have been regarded as intact in subcortical dementias but not in cortical dementias, in which amnesia, aphasia, apraxia, and agnosia are common (Albert, 1978). Despite the seeming vagueness of the clinical features of subcortical dementia and the presence of pathology that can extend, as in PD, into the cortex, several studies have documented measurable neuropsychological differences between various cortical and subcortical dementias (Huber et al., 1986; Pillon et al., 1986; Brandt et al., 1988). Precise distinction of these syndromes can still be problematic for the clinician, but the concept of relatively specific neurobehavioral deficits generated by subcortical pathology appears to be gaining credibility (Drebing et al., 1994).

Most controversial is the dementia syndrome of depression, although there is no doubt that depression is a common disorder that often enters into the differential diagnosis of amnesia or dementia. The term "pseudodementia" has been applied to this condition (Wells, 1979). Without question, dementia as defined earlier can occur in severe depression (Caine, 1981), and the common assumption that depression is a "functional" illness as opposed to the "organic" syndrome of dementia is outmoded and of no clinical utility. It is undeniable that multiple cognitive deficits diagnostic of dementia can develop in the context of depression, and these are quite conceivably due to structural or neurochemical pathology in ascending subcortical systems concerned with the regulation of mood (King and Caine, 1990). Patients with depression are often cognitively slow, inattentive, forgetful, unmotivated, and hypoactive—a profile sometimes referred to as *psychomotor retardation*—and their predictably poor performance on mental status examination justifies the term "dementia" as surely as in a patient with AD. Dementia, as emphasized earlier, does not imply untreatability, and the recognition of the reversible dementia syndrome of depression is one of the most important tasks the behavioral neurologist is called upon to perform.

Before leaving the topic of depression, a brief review of the possible cerebral basis of *mood disorders* is in order. A summary statement at this point can only conclude that no secure neuropathology and hence neuroanatomy of these disorders is available. In part because of the generally efficacious neuropharmacologic treatment of depression and bipolar disorder, theories of pathogenesis have centered on disturbances of neurotransmitter systems, and studies on structural brain changes have been inconclusive. What few investigations there are on the mood disorders suggest findings similar to those of schizophrenia—ventriculomegaly, sulcal widening, and hypofrontality on functional imaging studies (Jeste et al., 1988)—but these are of course nonspecific. Studies of secondary mood disorders—those due to neurologic conditions such as traumatic brain injury, stroke, brain tumor, epilepsy, multiple sclerosis, and degenerative disease—have implicated the frontal lobes, temporal lobes, and basal ganglia (Guze and Gitlin, 1994). It will be recalled that these regions represent a considerable overlap with areas implicated in schizophrenia (Chapter 9). The suggestion has been made, in fact, that psychosis considered as a whole constitutes a continuum of disease on which both mood disorders and schizophrenia may be found (Crow, 1990). If this idea proves to be correct, then the cerebral basis of these conditions may be very similar indeed.

From a clinical point of view, a useful broad generalization is that psychiatric disorders are more likely to occur with dysfunction of subcortical than cortical structures (Salloway and Cummings, 1994). The fundamental functions of arousal, attention, mood, and motivation are organized primarily by brain stem, diencephalic, and limbic regions, and damage to these subcortical areas is associated with a wide variety of behavioral alterations such as depression and psychosis that are traditionally viewed as psychiatric in nature. Such a view implies that the understanding of psychiatric illness in general may be found in the study of subcortical systems, and perhaps the term "neuropsychiatric" is a better descriptor of the effects of subcortical disease (Salloway and Cummings, 1994). Regardless of terminology, however, the unifying principle linking psychiatric disorder and subcortical dysfunction does offer an interesting insight into brain-behavior relationships and helps chart a research agenda that can improve our knowledge of many of the most disabling human afflictions.

White Matter Dementias

The cerebral white matter occupies approximately half the volume of the adult cerebrum (Miller et al., 1980). White matter functions to connect cortical and subcortical areas within and between the hemispheres, facilitating rapid and efficient interregional communication by the substantial increase in conduction velocity conferred by the myelin investing most cerebral axons. Although behavioral neurologists have theorized about white matter tracts and their significance (Wernicke, 1874; Geschwind, 1965), this large anatomic component of the brain has been relatively neglected in comparison to the scrutiny given to cortical and subcortical gray matter. With the advent of magnetic resonance imaging (MRI), a technique providing detailed differentiation of gray and white matter areas, elegant in vivo imaging is helping to expand our knowledge of brain diseases that alter behavior by virtue of their assault on the brain's white matter. In turn, a greater understanding of the role of white matter in higher function is also developing.

There are three major constituents of the cerebral white matter: projection fibers, commissural fibers, and association fibers. Projection fibers are involved with elemental motor and sensory systems and have little to do with the representation of higher functions. The fibers of main interest for our purposes are the commissural and association fibers, which are depicted in Figure 12.4. The major commissural system, of course, is the corpus callosum, a huge tract connecting all cerebral areas, but connections between the hemispheres are also made by the anterior commissure, the hippocampal commissure, and, in some brains, the thalamic massa intermedia. The intrahemispheric association fibers are still more complex. First, there are short association fibers, also known as arcuate or U fibers, which connect adjacent cortical gyri. In addition, there are five long association fiber bundles, each of which connects the frontal lobe with one or more of the other cerebral lobes. These are the arcuate (superior longitudinal) fasciculus, the superior occipitofrontal fasciculus, the inferior occipitofrontal fasciculus, the uncinate fasciculus, and the cingulum.

The importance of white matter in elemental motor and sensory capacities is indisputable, but it has been less clear how or even if white matter contributes to higher function. It is true, unquestionably, that complex synaptic events such as long-term potentiation (LTP) (Chapter 4) take place in the cortex. Nevertheless, clinical evidence as well as theoretical

---

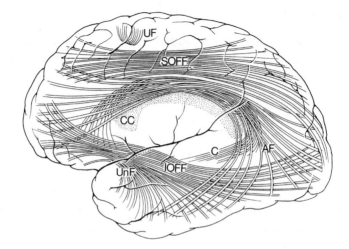

Figure 12.4 Cerebral white matter tracts primarily affected in white matter dementias. UF—U fibers; CC—corpus callosum; SOFF—superior occipitofrontal fasciculus; IOFF—inferior occipitofrontal fasciculus; AF—arcuate fasciculus; UnF—uncinate fasciculus; C—cingulum.

considerations compel the view that behavioral neurology risks a perilous omission if the white matter is disregarded. One familiar area, for example, is the investigation of hemispheric disconnection by sectioning of the corpus callosum, usually performed for the relief of intractable epilepsy; a generation of study has demonstrated that interhemispheric cognitive integration is indeed mediated by the corpus callosum (Seymour et al., 1994). Outside of this setting, however, clinical instances of callosal syndromes such as pure alexia (Chapter 5) and callosal apraxia (Chapter 6) are uncommon. In contrast, primary diffuse involvement of the cerebral white matter does occur in a substantial number of diseases and with traumatic brain injury. Without exception, these disorders have all been reported to result in some form of neurobehavioral impairment (Filley, in press). Dementia is the most common of the cerebral white matter syndromes recognized to date, and will be reviewed in some detail.

Multiple sclerosis (MS) provides the prototype example of white matter dementia. Although early descriptions of cognitive and emotional dysfunction in MS were made over a century ago by Jean Marie Charcot (1877), the many neurobehavioral manifestations of the disease have received little attention until recently. The availability of MRI has been a major development in this area, because the presence, distribution, size,

Neurobehavioral Anatomy

and configuration of white matter lesions is now readily accessible through noninvasive means (Goodkin et al., 1994), and meaningful correlations between neurobehavioral dysfunction and lesion characteristics can be made. Dementia has been the syndrome most often described, although depression, psychosis, and syndromes related to focal cerebral demyelination are also encountered. Careful neuropsychological studies have found that a majority of MS patients have significant cognitive impairment, especially if the disease is of the chronic-progressive type (Heaton et al., 1985). An important clinical point is that brief cognitive tests such as the Mini Mental State Examination (MMSE) (Folstein et al., 1975; Chapter 2) are quite insensitive to dementia in MS (Franklin et al., 1989). This phenomenon undoubtedly relates to the distinct verbal emphasis of the MMSE, which minimizes nonlinguistic impairments; in contrast to AD, for example, attention is more impaired in MS than is language (Filley et al., 1989a). Findings from MRI studies of MS patients indicate that the severity of dementia is related to the lesion area of white matter disease (Franklin et al., 1988; Rao et al., 1989), strongly implying that normal white matter is required for normal mentation. Moreover, MS patients with predominantly frontal white matter plaques have deficits on tests sensitive to frontal lobe function, suggesting that focal white matter lesions can result in isolated impairments (Arnett et al., 1994). Typically, however, MS is a diffuse disease, and dementia is more likely than focal syndromes. Because of the prominent attentional deficit, absence of aphasia, and other features, MS dementia has been described as a subcortical (Rao, 1986) or white matter dementia (Filley et al., 1988). Both designations are accurate and conceptually useful, but MS and the entities that follow in this section will be regarded as white matter dementias because behavioral neurology is based on careful scrutiny of demonstrable and specific pathologic abnormalities that permit meaningful clinical correlations to be made.

Another convincing example of white matter dementia can be seen as a sequel of chronic *toluene abuse*. This unfortunate recreational practice has recently been securely identified as a cause of dementia by virtue of widespread injury to cerebral white matter (Rosenberg et al., 1988). In addition, a variety of corticospinal and cerebellar signs have been documented (Hormes et al., 1986). Toluene, an inexpensive and readily available euphoriant found in spray paints and solvents, is often inhaled in large quantities for protracted periods that may extend for years. By virtue of its lipophilicity, toluene has a high affinity for the brain (Hormes et al., 1986), and white matter is selectively affected, whereas gray matter in the cortex and the subcortical nuclei is spared (Rosenberg et al., 1988). The dementia syndrome has a typical subcortical pattern, with inattention, apathy, and forgetfulness but preservation of language function (Hormes et al., 1986). MRI is sensitive to the white matter changes, showing loss of differentiation between gray and white matter and increased periventricular white matter signal intensity (Filley et al., 1990). The association of these abnormalities with dementia is bolstered by their significant correlation with the severity of dementia as determined by neuropsychological testing (Filley et al., 1990).

Binswanger's Disease (BD) is an old entity (Binswanger, 1894) that has recently come to life again because of the sensitivity of MRI to presumably ischemic white matter changes in the elderly brain (Filley et al., 1989b). BD is traditionally regarded as a dementia in hypertensive patients who have ischemic demyelination of the hemispheres, frequently accompanied by lacunar infarctions (Babikian and Ropper, 1987). It is possible that these often-seen white matter changes, which have been given the name "leukoaraiosis" (Hachinski et al., 1987), represent an incipient form of BD (Filley et al., 1989b). It has been found that white matter lesions are associated with hypertension, as is BD (van Swieten et al., 1991), and many studies have indicated that in both demented persons (Almkvist et al., 1992) and normal elderly persons (Junque et al., 1990; Ylikoski et al., 1993; Schmidt et al., 1993), white matter changes adversely affect attention and speed of information processing. Another study has suggested that these deficits only occur when a certain threshold area of white matter involvement has been exceeded (Boone et al., 1992). Thus, the evidence seems to suggest that white matter changes on MRI represent a pathologic change in many cases that may lead to BD, but the details of the progression from asymptomatic leukoaraiosis to the dementia of BD are lacking. What is clear is that attentional deficits associated with leukoaraiosis are quite reminiscent of findings in other disorders of cerebral white matter. Multi-infarct dementia, a more common form of vascular dementia, is considered in the next section.

Normal pressure hydrocephalus (NPH) is a condition of dementia, gait disturbance, and incontinence that can occasionally be traced to a previous history of traumatic brain injury, meningitis, or subarachnoid hemorrhage but is usually idiopathic. This disorder is commonly held to be a reversible dementia, as it can sometimes be effectively treated with ventricular shunting precedures (Adams et al., 1965). Pathologic studies have revealed that the periventricular white matter bears the brunt of the damage (Del Bigio et al., 1993), and ventricular dilation without cortical involvement is evident neuroradiologically. Clinical recovery from NPH is presumably due to reduction of periventricular white matter compression after shunting, although the potential for recovery diminishes as the duration of hydrocephalus increases (Del Bigio, 1993).

The genetic disease of myelin known as *metachromatic leukodystrophy* (MLD) typically presents in early childhood, but cases beginning in adolescence or adulthood have been described. Dementia is typically the most prominent feature of these cases (Shapiro et al., 1994). MLD is an autosomal recessive disease of myelin formation due to a deficiency of the enzyme aryl sulfatase A (Austin et al., 1968). MRI scanning reveals extensive cerebral dysmyelination in advanced cases of MLD (Filley and Gross, 1992). In addition to dementia, psychosis is strongly associated with late-onset MLD, perhaps because of involvement of frontal and limbic system white matter (Filley and Gross, 1992; Hyde et al., 1992).

Cobalamin (vitamin B_{12}) *deficiency* is a known cause of cerebral white matter damage (Adams and Kubik, 1944), in addition to its well-known effects on the spinal cord, optic nerves, and peripheral nervous system. Focal demyelinative lesions in the brain are similar to those in the dorsal and lateral columns of the spinal cord that cause subacute combined degeneration. The most common cause of cobalamin deficiency is pernicious anemia with failure of intrinsic factor production. Involvement of the nervous system can occur, however, even before the onset of hematologic abnormalities. Dementia has been described as one of many neurologic and psychiatric manifestations of cobalamin deficiency (Lindenbaum et al., 1988), and prominent features include mental slowing, memory impairment, and depression (Cummings and Benson, 1992). Lesions of the cerebral white matter are presumably responsible for the dementia, and treatment with parenteral vitamin B_{12} may be beneficial if the deficiency has not been prolonged.

Traumatic brain injury (TBI) has many effects on the brain, as reviewed in Chapter 11, and inclusion of TBI within the category of white matter dementia is not meant to ignore the other pathologies that occur. However, the most common and consistent pathological finding in TBI is damage to cerebral and upper brain stem white matter in the form of diffuse axonal injury (DAI) (Adams et al., 1982). Although DAI clearly involves axonal damage, there is also significant disruption of myelin; cell bodies in the gray matter are largely spared. Thus it is not inappropriate to consider the injury of DAI as falling most heavily on white matter regions of the brain. This kind of injury very likely accounts for the persistent inattention and difficult emotional alterations that characterize posttraumatic dementia (Filley et al., 1986). Moreover, it is likely that DAI is the most important cause of an entire spectrum of posttraumatic neurobehavioral syndromes, ranging from the persistent vegetative state (Jennett and Plum, 1972) to the postconcussion syndrome (Oppenheimer, 1968).

The acquired immunodeficiency syndrome (AIDS) has been recognized to be frequently associated with dementia, a syndrome dubbed the *AIDS dementia complex* (ADC) (Navia et al., 1986a). More recently, the terminology "HIV–1-associated dementia complex" has been put forth (American Academy of Neurology AIDS Task Force, 1991). Pallor in the subcortical white matter is common (Navia et al., 1986b) and the term "HIV leukoencephalopathy" is appropriate for many cases of AIDS with dementia (Budka, 1991). The pathologic basis of the dementia is uncertain; however, loss of cortical neurons has not been consistently found (Seilhean et al., 1993), and it seems likely that damage to cerebral white matter plays a prominent role in the clinical presentation (Price et al., 1988). A superimposed viral infection, progressive multifocal leukoencephalopathy, also attacks the white matter in many AIDS patients (Krupp et al., 1985), adding to the neurobehavioral severity in these cases.

Alcohol abuse is associated with a plethora of effects on the nervous system, many of which are due to thiamine deficiency, coexistent systemic illness, and secondary traumatic brain injury. The existence of alcoholic dementia has been debated, some maintaining that only amnesia related to the Wernicke-Korsakoff syndrome (Chapter 4) has been documented (Victor et al., 1989), and others concluding that dementia unrelated to thiamine deficiency does indeed exist (Lishman, 1981; Cummings and Benson, 1992). Despite this controversy, there exists a substantial body of recent evidence implicating selective loss of cerebral white matter both in laboratory animals exposed to alcohol (Hansen et al., 1991) and in humans with alcoholism (de la Monte, 1988; Jensen and Pakkenberg, 1993). The reversal of cerebral atrophy as measured by computerized tomography (CT) scans in chronic alcoholics also argues for a role of white matter damage in producing alcoholic dementia (Carlen and Wilkinson, 1987).

Table 12.2 Clinical differentiation of dementia syndromes

Neurobehavioral domain	Cortical	Subcortical	White matter
Attention	Normal	Inattention	Inattention
Memory	Amnesia	Retrieval deficit	Retrieval deficit
Language and speech	Aphasia	Palilalia, hypophonia	Dysarthria
Visuospatial function	Constructional apraxia	Motoric impairment	Motoric impairment
Complex cognition	Failed performance	Slowed performance	Slowed performance
Emotion and personality	Personality change	Depression, psychosis	Depression, psychosis
Motor function	Apraxia	Extrapyramidal signs	Corticospinal and cerebellar signs
Sensory function	Agnosia	Normal	Visual defect, hearing loss, hypesthesia

The diversity of conditions characterized by significant damage to cerebral white matter might imply that their neurobehavioral features are equally variable. There are, however, recurrent patterns that appear in the group as a whole (Filley et al., 1988). As a general rule, the white matter dementias have been shown to resemble the subcortical dementias in most respects (Table 12.2). An important point is that attentional dysfunction appears to be more prominent in both groups than in the cortical dementias. In the realm of memory, a retrieval deficit characterizes the memory loss of both groups, in contrast to the learning deficit (amnesia) seen in cortical dementia. Language is usually preserved in dementias that spare the cortex, but speech is not; *palilalia*, the involuntary repetition of words and phrases, and *hypophonia*, a decrease in the volume of voice, are often seen in subcortical gray matter dementias, and dysarthria is common in white matter dementias. Visuospatial skills are impaired in all dementias, but cortical disease causes a conceptual deficit best termed "constructional apraxia," whereas subcortical gray and white matter diseases produce impairment based on motor aspects of performance. Complex cognition is also impaired universally, but in contrast to the failure of performance in cortical disorders, the subcortical and white matter dementias result in a pronounced slowing of cognition. Emotion and personality differ in that the cortical dementias tend to have milder manifestations such as personality change, whereas the other categories frequently display severe depression or frank psychosis. Finally, abnormalities of motor and sensory function are distinguishable. Cortical dementia often shows apraxia, in contrast to extrapyramidal or corticospinal and cerebellar signs. Similarly, cortical dementia often shows agnosia, as opposed to normal sensory function or primary impairment in vision (visual field defects or blindness), audition (hearing loss or deafness), and tactile sensation (hypesthesia or anesthesia).

Mixed Dementias

Few systems of classification are flawless, and there are, in the case of dementia, several disorders for which another category must be created. Some conditions do not exclusively or even primarily affect cortical gray, subcortical gray, or cerebral white matter, and their pathology is diverse enough to produce quite variable clinical manifestations.

One well-recognized member of this group is *multi-infarct dementia* (MID), a type of vascular dementia in which cerebral infarction may damage any of the zones listed above and result in a wide variety of deficits that defies inclusion in a single dementia category (Roman et al., 1993). MID classically presents with a stepwise progression of acute cerebral insults, the cumulative effect of which is advancing dementia, and is regarded by many as the second most common cause of dementia after AD (Cummings and Benson, 1992). The neurobehavioral features of MID are predictably variable, depending on the brain areas involved. Another form of vascular dementia involving multiple infarcts is the *lacunar state,* in which multiple small subfrontal gray and white matter ischemic lesions known as lacunes produce a dementia syndrome with prominent frontal lobe features (Ishii et al., 1986). The lacunar state shares much in common with BD (discussed earlier), a dementing illness due to subcortical white matter ischemia.

Creutzfeldt-Jakob Disease (CJD) is a rapidly progressive transmissible dementia with prominent myoclonus and a characteristic electroencephalographic pattern of periodic high-amplitude discharges. A novel infectious agent consisting of protein and no nucleic acid ("prion") is responsible in most cases, but 10 to 15 percent of patients inherit the disease as a result of a germline mutation in the prion protein gene (Prusiner, 1993). The disease involves spongiform degeneration and neuronal loss in the cortex, basal ganglia, thalamus, and brain stem, and occasionally axonal damage and demyelination in the cerebral white matter as well (Cummings and Benson, 1992). No treatment to reverse or stabilize CJD is available, and the disease is uniformly fatal within one to two years of onset in most cases (Masters and Richardson, 1978).

Diffuse Lewy Body Disease (DLBD) is a degenerative disorder related to PD but characterized by Lewy bodies distributed throughout cortical and subcortical regions (Burkhardt et al., 1988). As a result, DLBD manifests dementia in addition to parkinsonism due to the greater burden of Lewy bodies. Other prominent features of DLBD are the frequent occurrence of psychiatric features, most notably delusions, and the appearance of myoclonus in some patients, which raises the possibility of CJD (Burkhardt et al., 1988). A fluctuating confusional state has been observed in many patients (Byrne et al., 1989). A relatively new addition to the list of dementias, DLBD has been found by some to be more common than MID and exceeded in prevalence only by AD (Crystal et al., 1990).

General paresis is uncommonly seen in the present era but was formerly one of the most prevalent causes of dementia. Prior to the introduction of penicillin, this form of neurosyphilis accounted for up to 30% of admissions to mental hospitals, and many patients exhibited grandiose delusions and expansive mania (Cummings and Benson, 1992). The causative spirochete *Treponema pallidum* shows a predilection for the frontal cortex, and this feature may account for the psychiatric presentation of some untreated cases. However, many other patients have a "simple" dementia without prominent psychosis, presumably due to general paresis involving other cerebral areas and the frequent coexistence of syphilitic meningitis, meningovascular syphilis, and syphilitic gummas (Cummings and Benson, 1992). The current AIDS epidemic may potentiate the severity of general paresis and other forms of neurosyphilis in AIDS patients, but treponemal infection is a continuing problem even in otherwise healthy individuals (Simon, 1985).

Mass lesions including *subdural hematoma* (Perlmutter, 1961), which are often unassociated with significant head trauma in the elderly, and brain *neoplasms* (Hunter et al., 1968) affect the cerebrum diffusely, especially if there is an associated increase in intracranial pressure. The dementia syndrome resulting from these lesions can include many diverse neurologic signs and neurobehavioral alterations, depending on the areas primarily and secondarily involved. Other clinical features, such as headache and seizures, are common as well. Subdural hematomas and neoplasms, especially benign tumors such as meningioma, represent potentially reversible causes of dementia.

Cerebral *anoxia* can result from inadequate blood oxygenation, insufficient cerebral perfusion, or anemia with poor oxygen-carrying capacity (Cummings and Benson, 1992). Although chronic pulmonary and cardiac disease can each cause a dementia syndrome due to anoxia, more common and dramatic is the acute onset of anoxic brain injury following cardiopulmonary arrest, carbon monoxide poisoning, strangulation, or anesthetic accidents (Cummings and Benson, 1992). Profound anoxia can of course lead to brain death or the persistent vegetative state (Multi-Society Task Force on PVS, 1994), but lesser degrees of oxygen deprivation can result in severe dementia (Richardson et al., 1959). Diffuse laminar cortical necrosis, usually also involving the hippocampus, is the typical pathology due to anoxia (Dougherty, et al. 1981), but delayed cerebral demyelination developing 10 to 14 days after the anoxic insult is occasionally seen (Plum et al., 1962).

References

Adams, J.H., Graham, D.I., Murray, L.S., and Scott, G. 1982. Diffuse axonal injury due to nonmissile head injury: an analysis of 45 cases. *Ann Neurol;* 12: 557–563.

Adams, R.D., and Kubik, C.S. 1944. Subacute degeneration of the brain in pernicious anemia. *N Engl J Med;* 231: 1–9.

Adams, R.D., and Victor, M. 1993. *Principles of Neurology.* 5th ed. New York, McGraw-Hill.

Adams, R.D., Fisher, C.M., Hakim, S., et al. 1965. Symptomatic occult hydrocephalus with "normal" cerebrospinal fluid pressure: a treatable syndrome. *N Engl J Med;* 273: 117–126.

Albert, M.L. 1978. Subcortical dementia. In: Katzman, R., Terry, R.D., and Bick, K.L. (eds.). *Alzheimer's Disease: Senile Dementia and Related Disorders* New York, Raven, pp. 173–180.

Albert, M.L., Feldman, R.G., and Willis, A.L. 1974. The "subcortical dementia" of progressive supranuclear palsy. *J Neurol Neurosurg Psychiatry;* 37: 121–130.

Almkvist, O., Wahlund, L.-O., Andersson-Lundman, G., et al. 1992. White-matter hyperintensity and neuropsychological functions in dementia and healthy aging. *Arch Neurol;* 49: 626–632.

Alzheimer, A. 1907. Über eine eigenartige Erkrankung der Hirnrinde. *Allg Z für Psychiatr;* 64: 146–148.

American Academy of Neurology AIDS Task Force. 1991. Nomenclature and research case definitions for neurologic manifestations of human immunodeficiency virus—type 1 (HIV–1) infection. *Neurology;* 41: 778–785.

American Psychiatric Association. 1994. *Diagnostic and Statistical Manual of Mental Disorders.* 4th ed. Washington, D.C., American Psychiatric Association.

Arnett, P.A., Rao, S.M., Bernardin, L., et al. 1994. Relationship between frontal lobe lesions and Wisconsin Card Sorting Test performance in patients with multiple sclerosis. *Neurology;* 44: 420–425.

Austin, J., Armstrong, D., Fouch, S., et al. 1968. Metachromatic leukodystrophy (MLD). VIII. MLD in adults: diagnosis and pathogenesis. *Arch Neurol;* 18: 225–240.

Babikian, V., and Ropper, A.H. 1987. Binswanger's disease: a review. *Stroke;* 18: 2–12.

Binswanger, O. 1894. Die Abgrenzung der allgemeinen progressiven Paralyse. *Berl Klin Wochenschr;* 31: 1102–1105, 1137–1139, 1180–1186.

Blass, J.P. 1993. Pathophysiology of the Alzheimer's syndrome. *Neurology;* 43 (suppl 4): S25–S38.

Blessed, G., Tomlinson, B.E., and Roth M. 1968. The association between quantitative measures of dementia and of senile change in the cerebral grey matter of elderly subjects. *Br J Psychiatry;* 114: 797–811.

Boone, K., Miller, B.L., Lesser, I.M., et al. 1992. Neuropsychological correlates of white-matter lesions in healthy elderly subjects. A threshold effect. *Arch Neurol;* 49: 549–554.

Brandt, J., Folstein, S.E., and Folstein, M.F. 1988. Differential cognitive impairment in Alzheimer's disease and Huntington's disease. *Ann Neurol;* 23: 555–561.

Budka, H. 1991. Neuropathology of human immunodeficiency virus infection. *Brain Pathol;* 1: 163–175.

Burkhardt, C.R., Filley, C.M., Kleinschmidt-DeMasters, B.K., et al. 1988. Diffuse Lewy Body Disease and progressive dementia. *Neurology;* 38: 1520–1528.

Byrne, E.J., Lennox, G., Lowe, J., and Godwin-Austen, R.B. 1989. Diffuse Lewy body disease: clinical features in 15 cases. *J Neurol Neurosurg Psychiatry;* 52: 709–717.

Caine, E.D. 1981. Pseudodementia: current concepts and future directions. *Arch Gen Psychiatry;* 38: 1359–1364.

Carlen, P.L., and Wilkinson, D.A. 1987. Reversibility of alcohol-related brain damage: clinical and experimental observations. *Acta Med Scand Suppl;* 717: 19–26.

Charcot, J.M. 1877. *Lectures on the Diseases of the Nervous System Delivered at La Salpetriere.* London, New Sydenham Society.

Clark, R.F., and Goate, A.M. 1993. Molecular genetics of Alzheimer's Disease. *Arch Neurol;* 50: 1164–1172.

Constantinidis, J., Richard, J., and Tissot, R. 1974. Pick's disease: histological and clinical correlations. *Eur Neurol;* 11: 208–217.

Corder, E.H., Saunders, A.M., Strittmatter, W.J., et al. 1993. Gene dose of apolipoprotein E type 4 allele and the risk of Alzheimer's disease in late onset families. *Science;* 261: 921–923.

Crook, T., Bartus, R.T., Ferris, S.H., et al. 1986. Age-associated memory impairment. Proposed diagnostic criteria and measures of clinical change: report of a National Institute of Mental Health work group. *Dev Neuropsychol;* 2: 261–276.

Crow, T.J. 1990. The continuum of psychosis and its genetic origins. *Br J Psychiatry;* 156: 788–797.

Crystal, H.A., Dickson, D.W., Lizardi, J.E., et al. 1990. Antemortem diagnosis of diffuse Lewy body disease. *Neurology;* 40: 1523–1528.

Cullum, C.M., Butters, N., Troster, A.I., and Salmon, D.P. 1990. Normal aging and forgetting rates on the Wechsler Memory Scale-Revised. *Arch Clin Neuropsychol;* 5: 23–30.

Cummings, J.L. 1988. Intellectual impairment in Parkinson's Disease: clinical, pathologic, and biochemical correlates. *J Geriatr Psychiatry Neurol;* 1: 24–36.

Cummings, J.L., and Benson, D.F. 1984. Subcortical dementia. Review of an emerging concept. *Arch Neurol;* 41: 874–879.

Cummings, J.L., and Benson, D.F. 1992. *Dementia. A Clinical Approach.* 2nd ed. Boston, Butterworth-Heinemann.

de la Monte, S. 1988. Disproportionate atrophy of cerebral white matter in chronic alcoholics. *Arch Neurol;* 45: 990–992.

Del Bigio, M.R. 1993. Neuropathological changes caused by hydrocephalus. *Acta Neuropathol;* 85: 573–585.

Dougherty, J.H., Rawlinson, D.G., Levy, D.E., and Plum, F. 1981. Hypoxic-ischemic brain injury and the vegetative state: clinical and neuropathologic correlations. *Neurology;* 31: 991–997.

Drebing, C.E., Moore, L.H., Cummings, J.L., et al. 1994. Patterns of neuropsychological performance among forms of subcortical dementia. *Neuropsychiatry Neuropsychol Behav Neurol;* 7: 57–66.

Filley, C.M. In press. Neurobehavioral aspects of cerebral white matter disorders. In: Fogel, B.S., Schiffer, R.B., and Rao, S.M. (eds.). *Comprehensive Neuropsychiatry.* Baltimore, Williams and Wilkins (in press).

Filley, C.M., and Cullum, C.M. 1993. Early detection of frontal-temporal degeneration by clinical evaluation. *Arch Clin Neuropsychol;* 8: 359–367.

Filley, C.M., and Gross, K.F. 1992. Psychosis with cerebral white matter disease. *Neuropsychiatry Neuropsychol Behav Neurol;* 5: 119–125.

Filley, C.M., Brownell, H.H., and Albert, M.L. 1985. Education provides no protection against Alzheimer's Disease. *Neurology;* 35: 1781–1784.

Filley, C.M., Heaton, R.K. and Rosenberg, N.L. 1990. White matter dementia in chronic toluene abuse. *Neurology;* 40: 532–534.

Filley, C.M., Kelly, J., and Heaton, R.K. 1986. Neuropsychologic features of early- and late-onset Alzheimer's Disease. *Arch Neurol;* 43: 574–576.

Filley, C.M., Kleinschmidt-DeMasters, B.K., and Gross, K.F. 1994. Non-Alzheimer fronto-temporal degenerative dementia. A neurobehavioral and pathologic study. *Clin Neuropathol;* 13: 109–116.

Filley, C.M., Franklin, G.M., Heaton, R.K., and Rosenberg, N.L. 1988. White matter dementia: clinical disorders and implications. *Neuropsychiatry Neuropsychol Behav Neurol;* 1: 239–254.

Filley, C.M., Davis, K.A., Schmitz, S.P., et al. 1989b. Neuropsychological performance and magnetic resonance imaging in Alzheimer's disease and normal aging. *Neuropsychiatry Neuropsychol Behav Neurol;* 2: 81–91.

Filley, C.M., Heaton, R.K., Nelson, L.M., et al. 1989a. A comparison of dementia in Alzheimer's Disease and multiple sclerosis. *Arch Neurol;* 46: 157–161.

Folstein, M.F., Folstein, S.E., and McHugh, P.R. 1975. "Mini–mental state." A practical method for grading the cognitive state of patients for the clinician. *J Psychiat Res;* 12: 189–198.

Franklin, G.M., Heaton, R.K., Nelson, L.M., Filley, C.M., and Seibert, C. 1988. Correlation of neuropsychological and magnetic resonance imaging findings in chronic/progressive multiple sclerosis. *Neurology;* 38: 1826–1829.

Geschwind, N. 1965. Disconnexion syndromes in animals and man. *Brain;* 88: 237–294, 585–644.

Goodkin, D.E., Rudick, R.A., and Ross, J.S. 1994. The use of brain magnetic resonance imaging in multiple sclerosis. *Arch Neurol;* 51: 505–516.

Greenough, W.T., and Bailey, C.H. 1988. The anatomy of memory: convergence of results across a diversity of tests. *Trends Neurosci;* 11: 142–146.

Guze, B.H., and Gitlin, M. 1994. The neuropathologic basis of major affective disorders. *J Neuropsychiatry;* 6: 114–121.

Hachinski, V.C., Potter, P., and Merskey, H. 1987. Leuko-araiosis. *Arch Neurol;* 44: 21–23.

Hansen, L.A., Natelson, B.H., Lemere, C., et al. 1991. Alcohol-induced brain changes in dogs. *Arch Neurol;* 48: 939–942.

Heaton, R.K., Nelson, L.M., Thompson, D.S., et al. 1985. Neuropsychological findings in relapsing-remitting and chronic-progressive multiple sclerosis. *J Cons Clin Psychol;* 53: 103–110.

Hormes, J.T., Filley, C.M., and Rosenberg, N.L. 1986. Neurologic sequelae of chronic solvent vapor abuse. *Neurology;* 36: 698–672.

Huber, S.J., Shuttleworth, E.C., Paulson, G.W. et al., 1986. Cortical vs subcortical dementia: neuropsychological differences. *Arch Neurol;* 43: 392–394.

Hunter, R., Blackwood, W., and Bull, J. 1968. Three cases of frontal meningiomas presenting psychiatrically. *Br Med J;* 3: 9–16.

Hyde, T.M., Ziegler, J.C., and Weinberger, D.R. 1992. Psychiatric disturbances in meta-chromatic leukodystrophy. Insights into the neurobiology of psychosis. *Arch Neurol;* 49: 401–406.

Ishii, N., Nishahara, Y., and Imamura, T. 1986. Why do frontal lobe symptoms predomi-nate in vascular dementia with lacunes? *Neurology;* 36: 340–345.

Jennett, B., and Plum, F. 1972. The persistent vegetative state after brain damage: a syn-drome in search of a name. *Lancet;* 1: 734–737.

Jensen, G.B., and Pakkenberg, B. 1993. Do alcoholics drink their neurons away? *Lancet;* 342: 1201–1204.

Jeste, D.V., Lohr, J.B., and Goodwin, F.K. 1988. Neuroanatomical studies of major affective disorders. A review and suggestions for further research. *Br J Psychiatry;* 153: 444–459.

Junque, C., Pujol, J., Vendrell, P., et al. 1990. Leuko-araiosis on magnetic resonance imag-ing and speed of mental processing. *Arch Neurol;* 47: 151–156.

Katzman, R. 1976. The prevalence and malignancy of Alzheimer disease. *Arch Neurol;* 33: 217–218.

Katzman, R. 1986. Alzheimer's Disease. *N Engl J Med;* 314: 964–973.

Khachaturian, Z.S. 1985. Diagnosis of Alzheimer's disease. *Arch Neurol;* 42: 1097–1105.

King, D.A., and Caine, E.D. 1990. Depression. In: Cummings, J.L. (ed.). *Subcortical De-mentia.* New York, Oxford, pp. 218–230.

Knapp, M.J., Knopman, D.S., Solomon, P.R., et al. 1994. A 30-week randomized con-trolled trial of high-dose tacrine in patients with Alzheimer's Disease. *J Am Med Assoc;* 271: 985–991.

Kral, V.A. 1962. Senescent forgetfulness: benign and malignant. *Can Med Assoc J:* 86: 257–260.

Krupp, L.B., Lipton, R.B., Swerdlow, M.L., et al. 1985. Progressive multifocal leukoen-cephalopathy: clinical and radiographic features. *Ann Neurol;* 17: 344–349.

Lindenbaum, J., Healton, E.B., Savage, D.G., et al. 1988. Neuropsychiatric disorders caused by cobalamin deficiency in the absence of anemia or macrocytosis. *N Engl J Med;* 318: 1720–1728.

Lishman, W.A. 1981. Cerebral disorder in alcoholism. *Brain;* 104: 1–20.

Masters, C.L., and Richardson, E.P. 1978. Subacute spongiform encephalopathy (Creutzfeldt-Jakob disease). *Brain;* 101: 333–344.

Mayeux, R. 1990. Therapeutic strategies in Alzheimer's disease. *Neurology;* 40: 175–180.

Mayeux, R., Stern, Y., and Spanton, S. 1985. Heterogeneity in dementia of the Alzheimer type: evidence of subgroups. *Neurology;* 35: 453–461.

McHugh, P.R., and Folstein, M.E. 1975. Psychiatric syndromes of Huntington's chorea: a clinical and phenomenologic study. In: Benson, D.F., and Blumer, D. (eds.). *Psychiatric Aspects of Neurologic Disease,* Vol. 1. New York, Grune and Stratton, pp. 267–285.

Medalia, A., Isaacs-Glaberman, K., and Scheinberg, I.H. 1988. Neuropsychological impair-ment in Wilson's Disease. *Arch Neurol;* 45: 502–504.

Miller, A.K.H., Alston, R.L., and Corsellis, J.A.N. 1980. Variation with age in the volumes of grey and white matter in the cerebral hemispheres of man: measurements with an image analyzer. *Neuropathol Appl Neurobiol;* 6: 119–132.

Morris, J.C., Cole, M., Banker, B.Q., and Wright , D. 1984. Hereditary dysphasic dementia and the Pick-Alzheimer spectrum. *Ann Neurol;* 16: 455–466.

Mortimer, J.A., and Graves, A.B. 1993. Education and other socioeconomic determinants of dementia and Alzheimer's disease. *Neurology;* 43 (suppl 4): S39-S44.

Multi-Society Task Force on PVS. 1994. Medical aspects of the persistent vegetative state. *N Engl J Med;* 330: 1499–1508, 1572–1579.

Navia, B.A., Jordan, B.D., and Price, R.W. 1986a. The AIDS dementia complex: I. Clinical features. *Ann Neurol;* 19: 517–524.

Navia, B.A., Cho, E.-S., Petito, C.K., and Price, R.W. 1986b. The AIDS dementia complex: II. Neuropathology. *Ann Neurol;* 19: 525–535.

Oppenheimer, D.R. 1968. Microscopic lesions in the brain following head injury. *J Neurol Neurosurg Psychiatry;* 31: 299–306.

Parker, W.D., Parks, J., Filley, C.M., and Kleinschmidt-DeMasters, B.K. 1994. Electron transport chain defects in Alzheimer's disease brain. *Neurology;* 44: 1090–1096.

Perl, D.P., and Brody, A.R. 1980. Alzheimer's disease: x-ray spectrometric evidence of aluminum bearing accumulation in neurofibrillary tangle bearing neurons. *Science;* 208: 297–299.

Perlmutter, I. 1961. Subdural hematoma in older patients. *J Am Med Assoc;* 176: 212–214.

Pick, A. 1892. Über die Beziehungen der Senilin Hirnatrophie zur Aphasie. *Prager Med Wochenschr;* 17: 165–167.

Pillon, B., Dubois, B., Lhermitte, F., and Agid, Y. 1986. Heterogeneity of cognitive impairment in progressive supranuclear palsy, Parkinson's disease, and Alzheimer's disease. *Neurology;* 36: 1179–1185.

Plum, F., Posner, J.B., and Hain, R.F. 1962. Delayed neurological deterioration after anoxia. *Arch Int Med;* 110: 18–25.

Price, R.W., Brew, B., Sidtis, J., et al. 1988. The brain in AIDS: central nervous system HIV–1 infection and AIDS dementia complex. *Science;* 239: 586–592.

Prusiner, S.B. 1993. Genetic and infectious prion diseases. *Arch Neurol;* 50: 1129–1153.

Rao, S.M. 1986. Neuropsychology of multiple sclerosis. A critical review. *J Clin Exp Neuropsychol;* 8: 503–542.

Rao, S.M., Leo, G.J., Haughton, V.M., et al. 1989. Correlation of magnetic resonance imaging with neuropsychological testing in multiple sclerosis. *Neurology;* 39: 161–166.

Richardson, J.C., Chambers, R.A., and Heywood, P.M. 1959. Encephalopathies of anoxia and hypoglycemia. *Arch Neurol;* 1: 178–190.

Roman, G.C., Tatemichi, T.K., Erkinjuntti, T., et al. 1993. Vascular dementia: diagnostic criteria for research studies. *Neurology;* 43: 250–260.

Rosenberg, N.L., Kleinschmidt-DeMasters, B.K., Davis, K.A., et al. 1988. Toluene abuse causes diffuse central nervous system white matter changes. *Ann Neurol;* 23: 611–614.

Salloway, S., and Cummings, J. 1994. Subcortical disease and neuropsychiatric illness. *J Neuropsychiatry;* 6: 93–99.

Schellenberg, G.H., Bird, T.D., Wijsman, E.M., et al. 1992. Genetic linkage evidence for a familial Alzheimer's disease locus on chromosome 14. *Science;* 258: 668–671.

Schmidt, R., Fazekas, F., Offenbacher, H., et al. 1993. Neuropsychologic correlates of MRI white matter hyperintensities: a study of 150 normal volunteers. *Neurology;* 43: 2490–2494.

Seilhean, D., Duyckaerts, C., Vazeax, R., et al. 1993. HIV–1-associated cognitive/motor complex: absence of neuronal loss in the cerebral neocortex. *Neurology;* 43: 1492–1499.

Seltzer, B., and Sherwin, I. 1983. A comparison of clinical features in early- and late-onset primary degenerative dementia: one entity or two? *Arch Neurol;* 40: 143–146.

Seymour, S.E., Reuter-Lorenz, P.A., and Gazzaniga, M.S. 1994. The disconnection syndrome. Basic findings reaffirmed. *Brain;* 117: 105–115.

Shapiro, E.G., Lockman, L.A., Knopman, D., and Krivit, W. 1994. Characteristics of the dementia in late-onset metachromatic leukodystrophy. *Neurology;* 44: 662–665.

Simon, R.P. 1985. Neurosyphilis. *Arch Neurol;* 42: 606–613.

St. George-Hyslop, P.H., Tanzi, R.E., Polinsky, R.J., et al. 1987. The genetic defect causing familial Alzheimer's disease maps on chromosome 21. *Science;* 235: 885–890.

Terry, R.D., Masliah, E., Salmon, D.P., et al. 1991. Physical basis of cognitive alterations in Alzheimer's Disease: synapse loss is the major correlate of cognitive impairment. *Ann Neurol;* 30: 572–580.

van Swieten, J.C., Geyskes, G.G., Derix, M.M.A., et al. 1991. Hypertension in the elderly is associated with white matter lesions and cognitive decline. *Ann Neurol;* 30: 825–830.

Victor, M., Adams, R.D., and Collins, G.H. 1989. *The Wernicke-Korsakoff Syndrome and Related Neurologic Disorders due to Alcoholism and Malnutrition.* 2nd ed. Philadelphia, F.A. Davis.

Wells, C.E. 1979. Pseudodementia. *Am J Psychiatry;* 136: 895–900.

Wernicke, C. 1874. *Der Aphasische Symptomencomplex.* Breslau, Cohn and Weigert.

Whitehouse, P.J. 1986. The concept of subcortical and cortical dementia: another look. *Ann Neurol;* 19: 1–6.

Whitehouse, P.J., Price, D.L., Struble, R.G., et al. 1982. Alzheimer's disease and senile dementia: loss of neurons in the basal forebrain. *Science;* 215: 1237–1239.

Ylikoski, R., Ylikoski, A., Erkinjuntti, T., et al. 1993. White matter changes in healthy elderly persons correlate with attention and speed of mental processing. *Arch Neurol;* 50: 818–824.

Epilogue

The neurology clinic, with its abundance of unfortunate but instructive lesions of the brain, serves as a continuously operating laboratory for the exploration of human behavior. The physician's first responsibility is the care of patients, but this imperative is rendered more attainable and more intelligent by attention to the ceaselessly fascinating relationships between brain and behavior. That is, the welfare of patients in need and the understanding of the brain are both well served by the study of neurobehavioral syndromes consequent to brain disease or injury.

The intent of this book has been to describe the anatomy of higher brain function through an analysis of neurologically induced behavioral dysfunction. The syndromes of behavioral neurology have therefore formed the basis of the approach. It is clear that this method is constrained by the necessarily limited number and variety of patients who come to medical attention, but for the truly human capacities that characterize our species, there is no satisfactory animal substitute. Many aspects of brain-behavior interactions can be fruitfully illuminated by other methods, but for the direct analysis of human behavior there is no alternative to the careful and systematic study of brain-damaged individuals.

Yet the identification of regions of the brain concerned with various behaviors is only a beginning. Despite the elegance of remarkable neuroimaging techniques that provide increasingly detailed views of relevant areas, many other levels of analysis will be necessary as the understanding of brain-behavior relationships becomes more sophisticated. The field of neuropharmacology, for example, which this book has barely considered, will clearly need to be more closely integrated with the neurobehavioral architecture of the brain now emerging. Neurophysiology, to which occasional reference has been made in these pages, has an indispensable role as well, elucidating precisely *how* the brain operates once it has been determined *where* its operations are localized. At still more basic levels, biochemistry, molecular biology, and genetics will provide fundamental data on the origin, development, and plasticity of the brain. Complementary to these approaches will surely be the rapidly developing fields of neuropsychology and cognitive science. In contrast to the basic neurosciences, these disciplines consider the broader aspects of behavior, gathering and synthesizing data from many sources to elucidate the function of the brain as a whole. More than philosophy could ever do alone, these diverse lines of inquiry will continue to shed light on the ancient questions of brain and mind that can now be illuminated by empirical data.

It is perhaps not too fanciful to presume that even the intractable problem of consciousness may begin to yield to the combined efforts of investigators addressing the relationship of brain and behavior. The assumption that consciousness is equivalent to self-awareness may be a useful first step, but its assignment to any single neuron, nucleus, tract, gyrus, or lobe of the brain seems misguided. Can consciousness therefore be explained as an emergent property of the brain's component parts working in synchrony, much as the music of an orchestra arises from the concerted actions of its musicians? Although such an appealing image must for now remain metaphorical, the nature of consciousness cannot even be approached without the systematic accumulation of neuroscientific information that provides a framework for its consideration.

To conclude this survey of brain and behavior, then, it is indisputable that what has been learned offers a provocative vista of what lies ahead. The prospects for understanding ourselves have never been brighter, and the opportunities to improve the human condition never more promising. Perhaps the sufferings of the patients who provide the basis for so much of what we know can best be made meaningful through the knowledge gained from their misfortune.

Glossary of Neurobehavioral Terms

Abulia—Severe apathy or loss of motivation, commonly seen with bilateral medial frontal lesions. See *Apathy.*

Acalculia—An acquired disorder of calculation that may follow damage to the left or, less often, the right cerebral hemisphere. See *Anarithmetria.*

Acquired sociopathy—A syndrome of disinhibition and antisocial behavior resulting from bilateral orbitofrontal damage.

Acute confusional state—A rapidly evolving disorder of attention. See *Delirium.*

Agnosia—A failure of recognition through one sensory modality; visual, auditory, and tactile agnosias have been described.

Agraphia—An acquired disorder of writing, often seen with aphasia and other neurobehavioral syndromes.

Akinetic mutism—A disorder of profound abulia usually due to extensive medial bifrontal destruction. See *Abulia.*

Alcoholic hallucinosis—A transient (hours to days) or prolonged (weeks to months) syndrome of auditory hallucinations, often persecutory, in the setting of alcohol withdrawal.

Alexia—An acquired disorder of reading; alexia with agraphia and alexia without agraphia (pure alexia) are classic syndromes.

Alexia with agraphia—An acquired reading and writing disturbance due to a left angular gyrus lesion.

Alexia without agraphia—An acquired reading disturbance with normal writing due to lesions in the left occipital lobe and the splenium of the corpus callosum (also called pure alexia).

Amnesia—An acquired disorder of memory, implying an impairment of new learning, caused by lesions in the medial temporal lobe, diencephalon, or basal forebrain.

Amusia—An acquired loss of musical skill due to focal or diffuse brain lesions, often in the right hemisphere.

Anarthria—Inability to speak resulting from damage to the motor systems subserving speech. See *Dysarthria.*

Anarithmetria—An isolated deficit in calculation ability, seen occasionally with left parietal lesions. See *Acalculia.*

Angular gyrus syndrome—Gerstmann's syndrome, anomic aphasia, and alexia with agraphia, all seen in association with left angular gyrus lesions.

Anomia—Impaired ability to identify objects by name, characteristic of aphasia; a synonym is dysnomia.

Anomic aphasia—A fluent aphasia in which the major deficit is in naming, typically due to a lesion in the left angular gyrus.

Anosodiaphoria—Awareness of but unconcern about disability, usually seen with right hemisphere lesions. See *Anosognosia* and *Denial.*

Anosognosia—Unawareness of disability, usually seen with right hemisphere lesions. See *Denial* and *Anosodiaphoria.*

Anterograde amnesia—Inability to learn new information in patients with amnesic syndromes.

Anton's syndrome—A form of anosognosia in which there is unawareness of cortical blindness.

Apathy—An impairment of motivation, seen with bilateral medial frontal lesions and in depression.

Aphasia—An acquired disorder of language, typically due to focal left hemisphere lesions; a synonym is dysphasia.

Aphemia—A nonaphasic syndrome of mutism or severe dysarthria resulting from a small lesion of the lower portion of the left precentral gyrus.

Aphonia—Inability to speak resulting from damage to the vocal apparatus. See *Dysphonia.*

Apperceptive visual agnosia—Failure to recognize a visual stimulus because of impaired visual perception; seen with bilateral occipital lesions.

Apraxia—An impairment of learned motor activity, commonly seen with aphasia-producing lesions; classic forms are limb-kinetic, ideomotor, and ideational; a synonym is dyspraxia.

Aprosody—A disorder of the emotional or affective components of language, associated with focal right hemisphere lesions; a synonym is aprosodia.

Associative visual agnosia—Failure to recognize a visual stimulus because of inability to derive its meaning even though it is adequately perceived; seen with bilateral occipitotemporal lesions.

Attention-deficit/hyperactivity disorder—A syndrome of inattention and/or hyperactivity beginning in childhood and persisting in some cases into adulthood; possibly associated with right frontal dysfunction.

Auditory agnosia—A failure of recognition through the auditory modality; pure word deafness and auditory sound agnosia have been described.

Auditory sound agnosia—Impaired recognition of nonverbal sounds, due either to bitemporal or unilateral right temporal lesions.

Balint's syndrome—Simultanagnosia, ocular apraxia (oculomotor apraxia or psychic paralysis of gaze), and optic ataxia; seen with bilateral occipitoparietal lesions.

Benign senescent forgetfulness—Mild memory retrieval impairment in elderly persons that does not cause the functional disability of amnesia or dementia.

Broca's aphasia—Nonfluent language production with relatively preserved auditory comprehension, typically due to a large lesion in the left inferior frontal lobe.

Callosal apraxia—Ideomotor apraxia in only the left hand of a patient with a lesion of the anterior corpus callosum.

Capgras syndrome—A delusional misidentification in which a patient believes a familiar person has been replaced by an impostor; seen with bifrontal and right hemisphere lesions.

Catastrophic reaction—Severe depression, agitation, and hostility in some patients with severe aphasia from left hemisphere lesions.

Central achromatopsia—Inability to perceive colors due to occipitotemporal lesions.

Charles Bonnet syndrome—Formed visual hallucinations associated with encroaching blindness due to ocular pathology.

Color anomia—Inability to name colors due to disconnection of visual from verbal areas; typically seen with pure alexia.

Coma—A disorder of arousal characterized by unarousable unresponsiveness due to focal upper brain stem or extensive bihemispheric dysfunction. See *Stupor.*

Concussion—A traumatically induced alteration in mental status.

Conduction aphasia—Impaired repetition with intact language fluency and auditory comprehension due to damage to the left arcuate fasciculus.

Confabulation—The recitation of fictitious experiences in response to direct questioning; sometimes but not always seen in amnesia.

Confusion—The inability to maintain a coherent line of thought despite adequate arousal and language function. See *Acute confusional state.*

Constructional apraxia—A term used to refer to visuospatial impairment; a synonym is apractagnosia.

Contrecoup lesion—A type of contusion involving the cerebrum directly opposite the site of impact in traumatic brain injury.

Contusion—A traumatically induced bruise of the cortex and underlying white matter, typically seen in frontal polar and anterior temporal regions.

Cortical blindness—Blindness due to bilateral damage to the primary visual cortices or their underlying white matter. See *Anton's syndrome.*

Cortical deafness—Deafness due to bilateral damage to the primary auditory cortices or their underlying white matter.

Coup lesion—A type of contusion involving the cerebrum directly underlying the site of impact in traumatic brain injury.

Crossed aphasia—Aphasia in a right-handed patient with a right hemisphere lesion.

Deep dyslexia—A syndrome of impaired reading characterized mainly by reading errors called semantic paralexias, due to left perisylvian lesions.

Delirium—An agitated acute confusional state featuring delusions, hallucinations, and autonomic overactivity (tachycardia, hypertension, fever, diaphoresis, tremor).

Delirium tremens—The classic delirium, associated with alcohol withdrawal.

Delusion—A fixed false belief; common in psychiatric illness and also a feature of neurologic disorders affecting the temporal lobes.

Dementia—An acquired, persistent impairment in intellectual function, with deficits in at least three of the following: memory, language, visuospatial function, complex cognition, and emotion or personality.

Dementia pugilistica—A syndrome of dementia, ataxia, and parkinsonism in boxers as a result of repeated blows to the head.

Denial—Explicit refusal to acknowledge disability, usually seen with right hemisphere lesions. See *Anosognosia* and *Anosodiaphoria*.

Developmental dyslexia—Difficulty in learning to read despite adequate schooling and general intelligence. See *Alexia*.

Diffuse axonal injury—Widespread shearing injury to white matter and axons in the brain stem, hemispheres, and corpus callosum; seen in all forms of traumatic brain injury.

Disconnection syndrome—A neurobehavioral syndrome due to interruption of cerebral gray or white matter structures linking cortical areas; callosal and intrahemispheric syndromes are recognized.

Disinhibition—Diminished control over inappropriate social and sexual impulses, often seen with bilateral orbitofrontal lesions.

Disorientation—Inability to recall one's name, the place, and the date; the latter two are reliable standard indicators of recent memory function.

Distractibility—Susceptibility to distraction by inessential elements of experience; often seen with bilateral orbitofrontal lesions.

Dorsolateral syndrome—A form of frontal lobe dysfunction characterized by executive function deficits, due to bilateral involvement of dorsolateral areas.

Dressing apraxia—Acquired difficulty with dressing due to confusion in the orientation of clothing; usually seen with right parietal lesions.

Dysarthria—An acquired disorder of speech representing damage to the motor system subserving articulation. See *Anarthria*.

Dysphonia—An acquired disorder of voice reflecting damage to the vocal apparatus. See *Aphonia.*

Echolalia—The repetition of words or phrases without the direction to do so; can be seen in mixed transcortical aphasia, but also in Alzheimer's Disease and schizophrenia.

Echopraxia—The imitation of gestures without the direction to do so; associated with dorsolateral frontal lesions.

Environmental agnosia—Inability to recognize familiar surroundings, due to a lesion in the right temporooccipital region.

Epilepsy—A condition characterized by recurrent unprovoked seizures due to an abnormal electrical excitability of the cortex; a synonym is seizure disorder. See *Seizure.*

Executive function deficits—Difficulty with planning, sustaining, and monitoring behavior, seen with bilateral dorsolateral frontal damage.

Expressive amusia—Impairment in the execution of music, typically due to right hemisphere lesions.

Extinction—Failure to report a stimulus on the side of the body opposite to a hemispheric lesion when simultaneous stimuli are presented to both sides; can be elicited in visual, auditory, and tactile modalities. See *Hemineglect.*

Formication—A tactile hallucination characterized by the sensation of insects crawling on the skin.

Frontal alexia—A syndrome of literal alexia (letter reading better than word reading) associated with left inferior frontal lesions; also known as anterior alexia or the third alexia.

Frontal lobe incontinence—Loss of bladder or bowel control about which the patient is unconcerned, due to bilateral medial frontal lesion.

Gait apraxia—A disorder of gait not due to primary motor or sensory disturbance; often seen with frontal lobe dysfunction due to bifrontal lesions or hydrocephalus.

Gerstmann's syndrome—Agraphia, acalculia, right-left disorientation, and finger agnosia; classically associated with left angular gyrus lesions. See *Angular gyrus syndrome.*

Geschwind syndrome—The interictal personality syndrome of some patients with temporolimbic epilepsy.

Global aphasia—Nonfluent language production with poor auditory comprehension, typically due to large left perisylvian lesions.

Global aphasia without hemiparesis—Global aphasia due to separate left hemisphere lesions in Broca's and Wernicke's areas that spare the precentral gyrus and, therefore, do not cause right hemiparesis.

Hallucination—A sensory experience without an external stimulus; seen in a wide range of neurologic conditions as well as in psychiatric disorders.

Hemineglect—Neglect for sensory stimuli contralateral to the side of a cerebral lesion; more common with right than left hemisphere lesions. See *Neglect*.

Hypergraphia—A tendency to produce excessive amounts of written material in the form of journals, diaries, poetry, and the like; seen in some patients with temporolimbic epilepsy.

Hypophonia—An abnormally low volume of voice, seen in Parkinson's Disease and other subcortical gray matter diseases.

Hypoxic-ischemic injury—Brain damage resulting from hypoxia and/or ischemia due to systemic trauma associated with traumatic brain injury.

Ideational apraxia—Difficulty executing a series of motor acts even though the individual acts can be performed in isolation; seen with left parietal or diffuse involvement.

Ideomotor apraxia—Difficulty executing learned motor movements to verbal command; usually seen with left perisylvian lesions. See *Callosal apraxia.*

Illusion—A misperception of a sensory stimulus; seen in the same clinical context as hallucinations.

Inattention—Deficient ability to respond to external stimuli, either bilateral (as in confusional states) or unilateral (as in focal, usually right hemisphere lesions).

Jargon aphasia—Severe Wernicke's aphasia with rapid paraphasic speech and abundant neologisms.

Klüver-Bucy syndrome—The combination of hypersexuality, placidity, hyperorality, "psychic blindness," and hypermetamorphosis; seen after bilateral anterior temporal lobe damage in higher primates and humans.

Korsakoff's psychosis—A chronic amnesia that follows many cases of untreated Wernicke's encephalopathy in alcoholics with thiamine deficiency; a more accurate term would be "Korsakoff's amnesia."

Lacunar state—A form of vascular dementia due to multiple, small, subfrontal strokes (lacunes) in the basal ganglia and deep hemispheric white matter.

Limb-kinetic apraxia—Impairment of delicate motor acts in a limb contralateral to a premotor lesion.

Locked-in syndrome—A state of quadriplegia with spared vertical eye movements and eye blinking, and normal mental status; seen with large pontine lesions (also called the de-efferented state).

Macropsia—A visual illusion in which the image appears to be increased in size.

Medial frontal syndrome—A form of frontal lobe dysfunction characterized by prominent apathy, due to bilateral involvement of medial frontal areas.

Metamorphopsia—A visual illusion in which the image appears to be distorted in shape.

Micrographia—A tendency to produce very small handwriting seen in Parkinson's Disease.

Micropsia—A visual illusion in which the image appears to be decreased in size.

Mixed transcortical aphasia—An aphasia syndrome resembling global aphasia, but with spared repetition, typically due to large extrasylvian lesions of the left hemisphere; also known as isolation of the speech area.

Moria—An inappropriately excited and childish affect seen in patients with bilateral orbitofrontal lesions. See *Witzelsucht*.

Motor impersistence—Inability to persist at a willed motor act; seen with right hemisphere lesions, particularly in the right frontal lobe.

Mutism—Failure to speak, seen in severe aphasia, acute aphemia, advanced dementia, akinetic mutism, anarthria, aphonia, and a variety of psychiatric disorders.

Neglect—Failure to report, respond to, or orient to sensory stimuli that is not due to primary sensory dysfunction. See *Hemineglect*.

Neologism—A type of paraphasic error in which a new and meaningless word is produced; seen in aphasia, particularly fluent aphasia, and schizophrenia.

Nonaphasic misnaming—A naming deficit in patients with acute confusional state characterized by selective impairment in naming related to a highly personalized system of reference (e.g., "ship" for "bed" and "captain" for "doctor").

Nonfluency—A feature of spontaneous speech in aphasia characterized by reduced phrase length (five words or less), agrammatism, impaired linguistic prosody, and dysarthria; typical of Broca's aphasia and other nonfluent aphasias.

Object agnosia—A form of visual agnosia characterized by the inability to recognize familiar objects; seen with left side or bilateral occipitotemporal lesions.

Ocular apraxia—Inability to direct voluntary gaze to a target visual stimulus, also called "oculomotor apraxia" or "psychic paralysis of gaze"; a component of Balint's syndrome.

Optic aphasia—Inability to name visually presented objects but with preserved recognition, associated with left posterior subcortical lesions; a mild form of object agnosia.

Optic ataxia—Impairment of visually guided limb movements; a component of Balint's syndrome.

Orbitofrontal syndrome—A form of frontal lobe dysfunction characterized by prominent disinhibition, due to bilateral involvement of orbitofrontal areas; also known as "acquired sociopathy."

Palilalia—Involuntary repetition of words or phrases, seen in Parkinson's Disease and other subcortical gray matter diseases.

Palinacousis—Recurrence of an auditory experience after removal of the auditory stimulus; usually seen with temporal lobe lesions.

Palinopsia—Recurrence of a visual image after removal of the visual stimulus; usually seen with right occipitoparietal lesions.

Paraphasia—An abnormality of aphasic speech characterized by letter or word substitutions; a paraphasic error can be literal (or phonemic), verbal (or semantic), or neologistic.

Peduncular hallucinosis—Formed visual hallucinations of a benign or entertaining nature associated with midbrain lesions.

Perisylvian aphasias—The aphasias resulting from damage around the Sylvian fissure and characterized by impaired repetition: Broca's aphasia, Wernicke's aphasia, conduction aphasia, and global aphasia.

Perseveration—Continuation or recurrence of an activity without an appropriate stimulus; frequently seen with dorsolateral frontal lesions, but can also occur with lesions in other areas.

Persistent vegetative state—A condition of preserved arousal but absent cognition and emotion due to extensive bihemispheric destruction.

Postconcussion syndrome—Headache, dizziness, insomnia, inattention, memory disturbance, and depression following concussive traumatic brain injury, related to diffuse axonal injury.

Posttraumatic amnesia—An impairment of new learning following the recovery of consciousness after traumatic brain injury.

Primary progressive aphasia—Nonfluent aphasia resulting from idiopathic degeneration of the left perisylvian region.

Prosopagnosia—A form of visual agnosia characterized by inability to recognize familiar faces; seen with right side or bilateral occipitotemporal lesions.

Pseudobulbar affect—Involuntary weeping or laughter in patients with disinhibition of facial musculature due to bilateral corticobulbar involvement.

Psychomotor retardation—Slowing of mental and motor activity, commonly seen in depression but also a feature of bilateral medial frontal lesions (see *Apathy* and *Abulia*) and diseases of the basal ganglia.

Pure word deafness—Impaired recognition of speech sounds, due either to bitemporal or unilateral left temporal lesions.

Receptive amusia—Impairment in the perception of music, often associated with right hemisphere lesions.

Reduplicative paramnesia—A delusional belief that a familiar place has been relocated to another site; seen with bifrontal and right hemisphere lesions.

Retrograde amnesia—Inability to remember information acquired before the onset of a brain disorder.

Schizophreniform psychosis—A psychotic illness resembling schizophrenia but presumably related to pre-existing temporolimbic epilepsy.

Seizure—An involuntary clinical event caused by a paroxysmal and excessive electrical discharge of cortical neurons; a common type of seizure is complex partial seizure disorder. See *Temporolimbic epilepsy.*

Simultanagnosia—Inability to recognize all elements of a visual scene simultaneously; a component of Balint's syndrome.

Stimulus-bound behavior—Inappropriate activity based on excessive attention to insignificant or irrelevant stimuli; often encountered with dorsolateral frontal lesions.

Stroke—An acute interruption of the cerebral circulation causing focal destruction of brain tissue; a less preferred synonym is cerebrovascular accident (CVA).

Stupor—A disorder of arousal characterized by unresponsiveness that can only be overcome by vigorous and repeated stimuli. See *Coma.*

Subcortical aphasia—Aphasia due to deep lesions of the left hemisphere involving the thalamus, basal ganglia, or subcortical white matter.

Subcortical dementia—Dementia due to involvement of the basal ganglia and related subcortical gray matter structures.

Sympathetic apraxia—Ideomotor apraxia in the left hand of a patient with right hemiparesis from a left hemisphere lesion.

Tactile agnosia—Impaired recognition of tactile stimuli, due to lesions of the contralateral parietal lobe.

Temporolimbic epilepsy—a type of seizure disorder in which the irritable focus lies in the temporal lobe; the same disorder as temporal lobe epilepsy, and closely related to complex partial seizure disorder and psychomotor seizure disorder. See *Seizure.*

Toxic-metabolic encephalopathy—An acute confusional state due to systemic intoxication or metabolic disturbance. See *Delirium.*

Transcortical aphasias—The aphasias resulting from damage outside the perisylvian region and characterized by preserved repetition: transcortical motor aphasia, transcortical sensory aphasia, and mixed transcortical aphasia.

Transcortical motor aphasia—A nonfluent aphasia resembling Broca's aphasia but with spared repetition, typically due to a lesion in the left frontal lobe that is medial, anterior, or superior to Broca's area.

Transcortical sensory aphasia—A fluent aphasia resembling Wernicke's aphasia but with spared repetition, typically due to a lesion in the left parietotemporal region posterior or inferior to Wernicke's area.

Verbal apraxia—A term used by speech pathologists to imply nonfluent speech with dysarthria.

Viscosity—A tendency in some patients with temporolimbic epilepsy to be verbose, repetitious, and detailed; also known as "stickiness."

Visual agnosia—A failure of recognition through the visual modality; apperceptive and associative visual agnosias have been described.

Wernicke's aphasia—Fluent language production with poor auditory comprehension, typically due to a lesion in the posterior portion of the left superior temporal gyrus.

Wernicke's encephalopathy—A disorder seen most often in alcoholics with thiamine deficiency, consisting of a triad of acute confusional state, ophthalmoplegia, and gait ataxia.

Wernicke-Korsakoff syndrome—The combination of Wernicke's encephalopathy and Korsakoff's psychosis.

White matter dementia—Dementia due to involvement of white matter pathways in the brain stem and cerebral hemispheres.

Witzelsucht—Inappropriate jocularity seen in patients with bilateral orbitofrontal lesions. See *Moria.*

Index

Callosal apraxia, 188, 207
Callosal disconnection, 110
Capgras syndrome, 24, 118, 207
Catastrophic reaction, 125, 126, 207
Central achromatopsia, 106, 207
   vs. color anomia, 106
Cerebellum, 5, 8
Cerebral cortex, 9–12
   allocortex, 11
   Brodmann areas of, 9, 10*f*
   gray matter, 9–12
   neocortex, 11
Cerebral dominance, 73–76
   handedness and, 73–76
   for language, 74–76
Cerebral hemispheres, 5–7
   four lobes of, 5–7
   gyri/sulci of, 5
Cerebral white matter, 55–56, 167–170, 177–178, 187
   association fibers, 187
   attention disorders and, 55–56
   commissural fibers, 187
   DAI and, 167–170
   dementias, 177–178
   projection fibers, 187
Cerebrospinal fluid (CSF), 8
Cerebrovascular disease, 96
   ideomotor apraxia and, 96
Cerebrum, 5–8, 76–77
   Broca's area, 76*f*, 77
   Brodmann areas, 77
   diencephalon, 5–8*f*
   hemispheres, 5–7
Charcot, Jean Marie, 188
Charles Bonnet syndrome, 24, 207
Churchland, Patricia, 3
Clinical-anatomic correlation method, 73
Closed head injury, 163–164
Cobalamin deficiency, 191
Cognition/thought, 15, 72, 131, 156
   disorder, 156
   emotion and, 131

Cognition/thought, (*Continued*)
   language and, 72
   See also Complex cognition
Cognitive science, 18
Color anomia, 106, 207
Coma, 46, 169, 172, 207
   posttraumatic, 167–168
Complex cognition, 33–35
   alternating sequence tasks and, 34
   dementias and, 194
   frontal lobes and, 33
   interpretation of idioms and, 34
   multistep arithmetic problems, 24
   recognition of similarities and, 34
   word list generation and, 34
Computer(s), 12–13
   brain and, 12–13
   as serial processors, 12
Computerized tomography (CT), 17, 171
Concussion, 169–170, 207
   post-, syndrome, 169–170
   TBI and, 169–170
Conduction aphasia, 78, 207
Confabulation, 61, 207
Confusion, 46, 50, 207
   definition of, 50
Consciousness, 2–3, 27–28, 46, 49, 169
   content of, 27, 46, 49
   dysfunction, 46
   level of, 28, 46
   TBI and loss of, 169
Constructional apraxia, 91, 116–117, 194, 207
Contrecoup lesions, 164–165, 207
Contusion, 164–165, 207
   coup/contrecoup lesions, 164–165
Corpus callosum, 55, 187–188
Cortical blindness, 102, 207

Neurobehavioral Anatomy

Lacunar state, 210
Language, 30–32
 aphasia vs. dysarthrias/
  dyphonias, 30
 definition of, 71
 dementias and, 193
 naming and, 78–79
 neuroanatomy of, 72–86
 propositional, 119
 six aspects of, 30–31
 speech and, 71
 thought/cognition and, 72
 See also Language disorders;
  Language lateralization
Language disorders, 16, 71–86
 left perisylvian zone and, 16
Language lateralization, 73–76
 handedness and, 73–76
 early development and, 75–76
Learning, 62, 65–66, 96
 new, 62, 65–66
 skill, 62, 96
Liepmann, Hugo, 92, 94
Liepmann-Geschwind model of ideomotor apraxia, 94, 95*f*
Limbic system, 131–135
 amygdala and, 133
 cingulate gyrus, 133
 hippocampus, 133
 hypothalamus, 133
 major sensory systems and,
  133–135*f*
 septal region,133
Limb-kinetic apraxia, 92–93, 210
Locke, John, 3, 11
Locked-in syndrome, 49, 210
Long-term potentiation (LTP), 66–
  67, 187
 NMDA receptor and, 67
Luria-Nebraska Battery tests, 39

MacLean, Paul, 132–133
Macropsia, 25, 210

Magnetic resonance imaging (MRI),
  17, 188, 194
Magnetoencephalography (MEG),
  17–18
Mania, 52
Materialism, 3–4
 dualism and, 3
 "identity theory" and, 3
Medial frontal syndrome, 153, 156–
  157*t*, 210
 akinetic mutism, 156
 apathy, 156
 incontinence, 156–157
 transcortical motor aphasia, 156
Medulla, 8
Memory, 16, 29–30, 59, 61, 63–68,
  96, 133
 declarative, 61
 immediate, 29, 59
 implicit/explicit, 61
 learning vs., 59
 loss, 175
 neuroanatomy of, 61–65
 procedural, 61, 96
 recent, 29–30, 59, 63, 65
 remote/knowledge, 29, 30, 59,
  67–68
 synapses and, 66–67
 verbal/nonverbal, 63
 working, 60
 See also Memory disorders
Memory disorders, 16, 59–68, 175
 medial temporolimbic system
  and, 16
Mental status examination, 25–40*t*, 176
 arousal, attention, motivation
  and, 25–28
 brief screening examination, 36
 complex cognition and, 33–35
 language, 30–32
 memory and, 29–30
 mood/affect and, 35–36
 standardized testing, 37–40
 visuospatial function, 32–33

Neurobehavioral Anatomy

Nonaphasic misnaming, 51, 211
Nonfluency, 211
Normal pressure hydrocephalus
    (NPH), 190–191
Neuropsychological testing, 176

Object agnosia, 211
Occipital lobe, 5–6
Ocular apraxia, 91, 211
Olfactory hallucinations, 24, 25
Olivoponto cerebellar degeneration,
    184
Opercula, 9
Optic aphasia, 211
Optic ataxia, 211
Oral apraxia, 96
Oral tendencies, 143
Orbitofrontal syndrome, 153–155,
    211
    acquired sociopathy, 154–155
    disinhibition, 153
    distractibility, 153
    moria, 153
    witzelsucht, 153

Palilalia, 193, 211
Palinacousis, 24, 212
Palinopsia, 24, 212
Papez, James, 132
Papez circuit, 65, 132*f*
Parallel processing, 12–13
    vs. serial processing, 12–13
Paranoid delusions, 24
Paraphasia(s), 31,212
    verbal, 51
Parietal lobe, 5–6
Parkinson's Disease (PD), 183–185
Partial seizures, simple/complex, 136
Peduncular hallucinosis, 24, 212
Perisylvian region, 76*f,* 79, 95–96,
    212
    aphasias, 76, 212
    ideomotor apraxia and, 95–96
    language and, 79

Perseveration, 212
Persistent vegetative state (PVS), 48–
    49, 164, 166, 212
    AD and, 180
Phrenology, 13–14
    mind-brain dualism and, 13
Pia mater, 8
Pick's disease, 143, 150, 152, 182–183
    behavioral disturbances, 150,
    152
    lobar atrophy, 182
    memory dysfunction, 183
Pituitary gland, 8
Placidity, 143
Pons, 8
Popper, Karl, 3
Positron emission tomography (PET),
    17–18, 55
Postconcussion syndrome (PCS),
    169–170, 212
Posterior cerebral artery occlusion,
    166
Posttraumatic amnesia (PTA), 168, 212
Prefrontal cortex, 60
    attention and, 60
Primary progressive aphasia, 77, 212
Procedural memory, 96
    apraxia and, 96
Progressive supranuclear palsy (PSP),
    177, 183, 184
Prosody, 77, 119
    gesture and, 119
    propositional language and, 119
Prosopagnosia, 105, 107, 108, 212
Pseudobulbar affect, 36, 212
Psychiatric disorders, 186
    subcortical dysfunction and,
    186
Psychiatry, neurology and, 131
Psychology, 2. *See also*
    Neuropsychology
Psychomotor retardation, 212
Pure word deafness, 212
Reading (in aphasia testing), 31

224   Neurobehavioral Anatomy

Receptive amusia, 212
Reduplicative paramnesia, 24, 212
Regional cerebral blood flow (rCBF), 17
Remote memory, 29, 30, 59, 67–68
  AD and, 68
  as knowledge, 67
  localization, 68
  loss, 67–68
Repetition (in aphasia testing), 31
Retrograde amnesia, 60–61, 212
Right hemisphere syndromes, 113–127t
  constructional apraxia and, 116–117
  dressing apraxia and, 118–119
  emotional disorders and, 123–127
  humor and, 126–127
  neglect and, 114–116
  spatial disorientation and, 117–118
Russell, Bertrand, 3
Ryle, Gilbert, 3

Schizophrenia, 24, 52, 123, 138–140, 186
  auditory hallucinations in, 24
  brain weight and, 139
  emotional disorders in, 123
  hypofrontality and, 139–140
  left temporal dysfunction and, 139
  mood disorders in, 186
  neuropathology of, 139
  positive/negative features of, 140
  temporolimbic system and, 138
Schizophreniform psychosis, 138–140, 141, 143, 145, 213
  TLE and, 138–140, 145, 213
  as sensory-limbic misconnection, 138

Searle, John, 2–3
Seizure disorder, 136, 213
  generalized, 136
  partial, 136
  See also Epilepsy
Sensory-limbic connectivity, 138, 145
  temporal lobe syndromes and, 138, 145
Septal region (limbic system), 133
Simultanagnosia, 106, 108, 213
  optic ataxia and, 106
Single photon emission computed tomography (SPECT), 17
Skill learning, 96
Skinner, B.F., 3
Spatial disorientation, 117–118
  environmental agnosia, 118
  Capgras syndrome, 118
  reduplicative paramnesia, 118
Speech, 30, 71, 77, 193
  dementias and, 193
  language and, 71
  nonfluency, 77
  spontaneous, (in aphasia testing), 30
Spurzheim, Johann Kaspar, 13
Standardized mental status testing, 37–40
Stimulus-bound behavior, 155, 213
Stroke, 72, 213
  language disorders and, 72
Stupor, 213
Subarachnoid hemorrhage, 166
Subcortical aphasia, 81, 213
Subcortical dementia, 177–178t, 183–186, 213
  acute confusional state, 184
  depression syndrome, 184–186
  fundamental deficits, 185,186
  HD and, 177, 183, 185
  instrumental functions, 185
  PD and, 183–185
  PSP and, 183